THE DRUIDS

THE DRUIDS

Celtic Priests of Nature

JEAN MARKALE

Translated from the French by Jon Graham

Inner Traditions International
Rochester, Vermont

Inner Traditions International
One Park Street
Rochester, Vermont 05767
www.InnerTraditions.com

First U.S. edition published by Inner Traditions 1999

Originally published in French under the title *Le Druidisme, Traditions et dieux des Celtes*
by Éditions Payot 1985

Library of Congress Cataloging-in-Publication Data
Markale, Jean.
[Druidisme. English]
The Druids : Celtic priests of nature / Jean Markale.—1st U.S. ed.
p.   cm.
Includes bibliographical references (p.   ) and index.
ISBN 0-89281-703-8 (alk. paper)
1. Druids and Druidism.   I Title.
BL910.M3717   1999
299'.16—dc21   98-47665
CIP

Printed and bound in the United States

10 9 8 7 6 5 4 3 2 1

Text design and layout by Virginia Scott
This book was typeset in Minion with Goudy Text Lombardic Caps
as the display typeface

Inner Traditions wishes to express its appreciation for assistance given by the government
of France through the ministère de la Culture in the preparation of this translation.

Nous tenons à exprimer nos plus vifs remerciements au government de la France et le
ministère de la Culture pour leur aide dans le préparation de cette traduction.

CONTENTS

FOREWORD

Since 52 B.C. the inhabitants of France and western Europe have forgotten who they once were. They have even forgotten the site of their defeat at the hands of the rationalism of Julius Caesar, conqueror and secondhand proconsul, a man deeply convinced that he was a king before whom universal posterity would one day bow. Alésia[1] has been forgotten, yet this was the place from which point everything took a decisive turn. Through the tangents and chance events of conquest, a Mediterranean mentality, one built on a belief in universalism and the logic of an exclusive third party, slowly but surely replaced the barbarous state of mind that was nourished on sensibility, that rationalized dialectically, and that trusted in the activity of individuals in the midst of human communities. Though perhaps more unstable and more fragile, these communities were also more warmhearted. The inhabitants of western Europe forgot they were the children of the Celts, and when they realized that they had been swindled by Latin orators who were masters of the art of deception by virtue of impeccably devised sophisms, they rushed headlong toward Christianity, thinking to find in it the elements that would feed their inner fire, a fire that, in truth, had never been extinguished. Alas, this had no better outcome than their initial turn to Rome.[2] Not only did no one remember where the Alésia of Vercingetorix was located, but the remote paths of the authentic spiritual tradition that the Celts had nourished and exalted could no longer even be recognized.[3]

This oblivion, this "debraining" (to borrow the term dear to Alfred Jarry), has been deeply felt during the twentieth century by people of goodwill who, through the mutations of a society that has entered into the final stages of decomposition, have begun to ask whether the West may have taken a wrong turn in giving precedence to the material world over that of the spiritual one. The problem stated in this way is false, though, in that matter and spirit are only two faces of one reality. But the reality is that Westerners today, panicked by the conviction they have lost their spirit's deepest roots and have been deceived by a form of Christianity that no longer responds to their aspirations, have a tendency to seek refuge in the philosophies of nonbeing that play such a large role in Eastern religions. As honorable as it may be, this course will resolve nothing; the Orient has its own logic and system of values that are not necessarily the same as those of the West. On the contrary, it even seems that the Eastern mentality is in fundamental opposition with the Western state of mind. This statement is made with no value judgment implied. There is therefore a risk of incomprehension, artificial syncretism, and illusion, all leading to a very uncomfortable situation that in no way responds to the hope one has of finding the "true way." First of all we must accept the inescapable fact that there is no single true way, but that there are ways whose goal may be identical, yet whose formulations are quite different. Above all we should beware of a taste for the exotic. One always looks to find elsewhere what one cannot find at home, the world adorned with the thousand and one colors bestowed by a change of scenery. When Lanza del Vasto wrote his *Pilgrimage to the Sources* he had no idea that he was unleashing a vast emigration toward Oriental mirages. Voyages to Katmandu are not always constructive—not even those prompted by an inner light.

Why seek elsewhere for what exists at home? Pilgrims to Katmandu and others like them have the trump card of responding that there is no longer a Western tradition and the sole means of emerging from their dilemma is by entering the Eastern tradition. It should be said that no great efforts have been expended by these types of people to seek out such a Western tradition, a tradition, moreover, that great pains have been taken to mask and conceal for the sole benefit of Judeo-Roman Christianity. Yet this tradition exists within our reach and requires only a little effort to be rendered visible. The main requirement is to shed one's biases and the sterile attitude best expressed by the adage "it goes without saying." Although somewhat battered by centuries of rejection if not outright combat, this Western tradition exists and is perfectly youthful and ready to nourish those who are able to ask. True, this requires a certain amount of effort, a personal search, a *quest* even, at the end of which one has no certainty of discovering the mysterious entrance to the castle of the Grail. It is so much simpler to lean on a normalized, hierarchical institution that provides every guarantee, one that is very comforting because it is so well established. Benches are waiting at every stop. You even can remain there for hours watching the coming and going of the trains.

The discovery of the Western tradition is transmitted by the knowledge of our cultural past—our authentic cultural past and not what has been taught for centuries in schools of the Mediterranean hegemony. In the last analysis, this is only the past of Greco-Roman antiquity that has been more or less altered to the taste of the day. Before the Alésia disaster something else existed, another system of values, of apprehending the real, of thinking and feeling, another conception of the spirit. This did not all disappear from one day to the next. Remaining today are not only the classified remnants in museums and libraries, but living seeds that ask only to be sown.

These remnants are the seeds, and these seeds can produce fruits other than those known at the present time. And these fruits will necessarily differ from the fruits that existed before the period of the Roman conquest. The times are no longer the same and society has evolved in an irreversible fashion. It would be absurd to try and restore druidism, the religion of the Gauls and the majority of the Celtic peoples, by making it a contemporary religion. Druidism being both the archetype of Celtic society and its emanation, any attempt to reinstate it would run counter to the very principles of the druids and result in total mental confusion. Unfortunately this is precisely what is occurring: druidism has so inflamed people's imaginations that by virtue of the very fact that its tenets are poorly known, it has become a crystallization point for all the phantasms of a spirituality waiting in the wings. In truth, druids and druidism are known only through hearsay, which has allowed for the worst kind of mass-market writing on the subject. "The religion of the Gauls is both little and poorly known. It remains little known because the documents that concern it are far from being assembled and classified," said Henri Gaidoz, the founder of *La Revue Celtique,* in 1879. Today more documents have been discovered and they are better classified. But much more remains to be done before it is possible to understand just who the druids were and what druidism consisted of. Indeed Henri Gaidoz observed that thanks to the poor understanding of the Gallic religion there was too much of a tendency to consider it *only* as a philosophical system, thus eliminating all its ritual and even magical aspects. "This system and consequently the religion of the Gauls have been labeled with the name *druidism,* a word coined in this century from the word the Gauls gave to their priests, this word corresponds to no historic reality."[4]

Here it is necessary to slightly correct Gaidoz's judgment by specifying that the term *druidism* was already used by the medieval Irish to designate, in a very vague fashion, anything connected with the druids, and that this term, for our contemporaries, covers everything concerning the Celtic religious domain, intellectual speculations, cultural or magical practices, various beliefs, and the so-called profane sciences that have come down from the Celtic priesthood. But it is accurate to say that the word *druidism* remains very murky to the extent that it designates not only a religious system but a vast intellectual, technical, and spiritual tradition, common to all Celtic peoples and characteristic of Celtic societies, that was lost, not through the fault of Romanization—which Ireland never knew—but because of Christianity. In one sense druidism is the totality of religious, artistic, intellectual, social, and scientific conceptions of the Celts from the time before their conversion to the Christian religion.

Such a wide range has given to druidism its sheen of nobility. But as we are so ill informed as to the true content of this system, we must concede that all assumptions are possible. Since the end of the eighteenth century, where in Great Britain as in Brittany, some believed to find in the fantasies of some crackpots the "truth" about druidism, the imagination has been at work overtime speaking or writing the worst kinds of elucubrations on the religion of the Celts. Truth obliges us to say that, until the most recent times, druidism has been more often dreamt than rediscovered. It indeed seems that druidism is dead and gone, buried in the shadows, or melted into a very specific form of Christianity such as that found in Ireland or Brittany. However, in that religions never really disappear completely, something remains, and particularly in the manner in which Westerners, especially the rural populace, live their spirituality. As Gaidoz said in 1879, "Chased from the temples, the Gallic gods found refuge in our countryside." Today this affirmation still holds true.

This is why it is necessary to explore the somewhat murky universe of druidism. Something of it still remains, not only in the countryside, but in its irrefutable testimonies from authors of antiquity. It is still necessary that these remnants and testimonies be made known. Such is the goal of this book.

PART ONE

THE
DRUIDS

*W*hat is best known to us of druidism concerns the druids themselves. This is not the paradox it seems in that, as essential figures of the different Celtic societies that succeeded one another in western Europe, descriptions of druids have been provided by historians and chroniclers of classic antiquity as well as by the insular Celts themselves when they were compelled under Christianity's influence to use writing to preserve their ancestral traditions. Consequently, in regard to druids, we possess irrefutable documentation that often dates back to the time of the druids themselves. And there is a world of difference between these descriptions—that while fragmentary are nonetheless historically based—and the romantic imagery that has echoed so tenaciously into our own time that portrays the druid as an aged, balding and bearded man, haloed by a supernatural light as he majestically harvests mistletoe with his golden scythe, vaticinating in total abandonment during a storm or sacrifice of human victims on immense stone altars known as dolmens.

Any study of the druids must begin with a process of demystification, because the romantic image of the druids is largely the result of our ignorance. As a result of the lack of actual documentation, the imaginations of poets have created images of the druids that are emotionally moving and that satisfy the taste for the marvelous. It is the most inflexible prerogative of the poet to invent what doesn't exist, and no one faults Chateaubriand for the magnificent way he brought the character of the druidess Velléda to life. Unfortunately historians, sometimes duly licensed and often in complete good faith, have taken the delirious fantasies of the romantic age as a bonafide currency, especially the visions of those antiquarians now known as the "druidomaniacs," for whom everything Celtic was beautiful, grandiose, sublime, and universal. The romantic dream was transmitted by the rediscovery—real or imagined—of an autochthonous Celtic past, in which the druids held a choice place, supposedly in possession of the most audacious secrets of Celtic thought, thus placing great value on them and in the role they have been thought to play.

The most important of these is the belief that the druids were in actuality at the heart of Celtic society, a society that without their existence would remain incomprehensible, for they truly possessed the "Celtic secrets." It was on the druids that hinged the deeds and gestures of these people, who, for want of a better term, have been dubbed Celts. The term Celts refers to a conglomeration of peoples of various origins joined together by the framework of a unique civilization and from a territory that extended from Bohemia to the British Isles, from the plains of the Po River to the mouth of the Rhine, with extensions into Eastern Europe and Asia Minor. This Celtic civilization was moreover much more complex than has been previously imagined.

In fact it was unique but multiple, both in space and time. In Caesar's era, the first century B.C., the Galatians of Asia Minor, though constituting a homogenous group themselves, were integrated into the framework of Hellenistic life: the Gauls of the Cisalpine (the plain of the Po) became Roman citizens; those of the Narbonne (Southern Gaul) were viniculturalists, merchants, or Roman legionnaires; those of the Celtic region (between the Seine and the Garonne Rivers, and also including Switzerland) gradually became agriculturists but conserved more of their warrior past than the others. As for the Britains of British Isle, they were cattle breeders rather than farmers and maintained more of their ancient traditions, as well as their royal lineage. To the west, the Gaels of Ireland, who did not speak quite the same language as the others, were profoundly different. Never touched by Romanization, they evolved in isolation and remained deeply attached to a pastoral society they maintained through the period of Christianization into the twelfth century. What is more, the appearence of Celtic society is quite recognizable sometime around the fifth century B.C. On the continent it gradually disappeared, swallowed up in the Gallo-Roman synthesis after Caesar's conquest of Gaul, but on the isle of England it endured until sometime in the sixth century A.D. Repressed by the Angles and the Saxons, Celtic society has even managed to survive to the present day, to a degree, in the country of Wales and the Armorican area of Brittany. In Ireland, despite the vicissitudes of history, it has never ceased to exist—all of these considerations testify to the complexity of the Celtic phenomenon.

There are, however, common traits shared by all members of this ancient civilization that we rediscover in both time and space, traditions that have been passed from generation to generation—through oral means alone at the beginning since the Celts prohibited the use of writing. Being Celtic was a way of life, characterized by the practice of livestock breeding and accompanied by a very competitive system of agriculture, thanks to perfectly forged iron tools (the Celts were excellent metal workers). Celtic was also a language of Indo-European origin, a single tongue in the beginning that soon divided into two branches, Gaelic and Britannic (Gallic, Breton, Cornish, Welsh). And finally, before Christianization, Celtic was also a philosophical, judicial, metaphysical, and religious system common to all Celts, without exception. It is this system that today we call "druidism."

This expresses the importance of the druids in Celtic life. And let us add right off that their role was not solely religious. Caesar's testimony is essential in this regard:

> In all of Gaul, two classes of men are honored in particular, since the plebian is hardly better than a slave. Concerning these two classes one is that of the druids, the other is that of the *equites*. The first look after holy matters and concern themselves with sacrifices, both public and private. They regulate all matters concerning religion. A great number of young people come to them for instruction, and they are the beneficiaries of great respect. In fact it is they who judge all public and personal disputes, and when a crime has been committed or a murder occurs, or when an inheritance or land boundary is contested, it is they who decide and it is they who determine the damages and penalties. If an individual or a group does not accept their decision then they are forbidden all sacrifices, a punishment that seems to be the most serious among the Gauls.... All these druids are under the command of a single druid who exercises ultimate authority upon them. The druids do not customarily go to war or pay taxes as do the other Gauls. They are exempted from military service and all other obligations. (*De Bello Gallico*, VI, 13)

The assertions of the Roman proconsul can sometimes be subject to question, especially when they are political justifications or when they gloss over the proconsul's own failures. But in this instance Caesar's reports on Gallic customs appear to have come from the most reliable sources. He knew the Gauls, intentionally surrounded himself with their tribal chieftains, and chatted with anyone who could bring him information about this adversary. At the beginning of his expedition in Gaul, Caesar was assured of the collaboration of the Atrebate chieftain Commios, who he had imposed upon the Atrebates and the Morini as king; Caesar also knew the Aeduen druid Diviciacos quite well. He made Diviciacos his ally against the chieftain Dumnorix, Diviciacos's own brother. As little as one may desire to seriously consider the prerogatives and privileges attributed by Caesar to druids, the astonishing fact remains that it was the druids who held almost all spiritual and temporal power in Gallic society. Add to this the fact, indicated by numerous Irish epic texts, that the king did not have the right to speak prior to the druid in an assembly, and one gets an idea of druidic omnipotence.

That said, all the context is of an Indo-European structure. Without referring in any way to the idea of race, since it concerns social structures, the Gallic people entered well and truly into the tripartite system. Caesar is quite clear regarding this: there were three classes in Gallic society, of which one, the plebeian, was insignificant. The other two were the equites, who were the warriors, and the druids. The social division was a question of a class, not of caste, an important distinction.

Indeed, in the opinion of all religious historians the druids were the Celtic equivalent of the Indian Brahmans and the Roman Flamens, even if their name is entirely different (Brahmans and Flamens are linguistically related). It is known that the Brahmans are recruited exclusively by their birth in a certain caste that is the normal consequence of Hindu beliefs concerning the cycle of reincarnations, and the Roman Flamens made up a college to which entrance was only granted by co-optation. The druids, to the contrary, did not form a closed society. Anyone, no matter who they were—royal family member, warrior, artisan, shepherd, farmer, perhaps even a slave—could gain access (even if only to the lower ranks) on the condition of having pursued the necessary, long and arduous studies. In sum, a person became a druid both by vocation and probation. The Christian religion, heir to the druidic religion on more grounds than one, can be brought to mind in this regard concerning the recruitment of its priests.[1]

As was the case (at least in the beginning) for all the clergy of the

Indo-European structure, the druidic sacerdotal class had the task of organizing and administrating both divine and human affairs. The present-day Brahmans, because of their historical evolution and the vicissitudes of Indian society, have solely retained the spiritual aspect of this duty and have abandoned their political power to systems that have become increasingly secular. In regard to the Flamens and the minor role they were soon reduced to in the Roman republic, it is secularization that must again be discussed. Indeed, if at the time of Rome's monarchy the rex was the master of the sacred and the profane, it quickly came to pass that a division was made between temporal power and spiritual power. In fact secularism was invented by the Roman republic despite the paradoxical evolution of a purely formal, clearly nationalistic and civic religion into which all the major bodies of the state were integrated. In this light, given the fact that druids have disappeared, drowned in Romanization and Christianization, there is little that can be said about the hypothetical evolution of their status. But one thing is certain: never did there exist even the smallest nuance of difference between the sacred and the profane in Celtic society. The question never arose. The fact that from the time of Ireland's Christianization it was almost exclusively the kings and the *fili*—the heirs of the druids—who became bishops or abbots and who held temporal and spiritual powers concurrently is absolute proof of a monism that is sometimes hard for the contemporary mindset to comprehend.

The denomination *druids* was quite vast and included numerous specializations. It would be ridiculous to compare a Gallic druid with a twentieth-century Roman Catholic priest, especially in countries where the separation of church and state is a primary factor. It is possible to see a certain equivalence between the druid and a village priest of the nineteenth century, before the time when the laws of compulsory education came into effect and the secular teacher appeared. For if the druid was a priest, he was also certainly something more, and within the druid class itself many distinctions were made. Greek and Latin authors were fully aware of this. Though it may seem that they never quite understood the subtleties of these distinctions and the hierarchical system, in that they called the druids "philosophers," and sometimes "mages," which certainly are not the same thing. There was even mention of "singing poets" and "soothsayers." Diodorus Siculus specifies that no sacrifice could be performed without the aid of one of these "philosophers."

1

The Druids' Name

The authors of antiquity always spoke of the druids with a certain admiration. Never did the Greek and Latin historians confuse them for lowly magicians. The Aeduen Diviciacos, already mentioned by Caesar, was also mentioned by Cicero who prided himself on having known and spoken with him: "He claims to know the laws of nature that the Greeks call physiology, and he predicts the future, either by omens or conjectures" (*De Divinatione,* I, 40). Later authors went even further: Ammianus Marcellinus (XV, 9) links the druids to the disciples of Pythagoras. Hippolytus (*Philosophumena,* I, 25) asserts that they had assiduously studied the Pythagorean doctrine, whereas Clement of Alexandria (*Stromata,* I, XV, 71) reports a tradition according to which Pythagoras was both the student of the Brahmans and the Galatians—in other words the Galatian druids.

Any connection between the druids and Pythagoras seems highly unlikely, but traditional belief about the Celts testifies to a certain kinship between Pythagorism and druidism—at least in accordance with what the Greeks could comprehend of it, for their grasp of it was poor. The fact, however, remains that they did recognize druidism as possessing the value of a perfectly honorable philosophical system, and even though their understanding was incomplete and, in truth, erroneous (for its lack of precise information, different systems of logic, opposing mentalities, a commitment to syncretism), the Greeks were astonished that barbarians could possess a religious and philosophical tradition of such high intellectual and

7

even spiritual quality. This did not prevent them, or Latin authors, from displaying a very confused knowledge of the duties of druids and their denominations.

We have seen the offices of philosophers, mages, and singing poets (bards) attributed to the druids, but, as Cicero said, given the fact that they gave themselves over to the art of augury, they were also *vates,* and from this word contemporary neodruidism (of which we will speak more of later) has coined the word *ovate,* which simply signifies "soothsayer," and designates the lower ranks of participants at a druidic assembly *(gorsedd).* Caesar, still speaking of Diviciacos, used the term *sarcedos,* a word that defines the druid as an authentic "priest," not only in the Latin sense but in the universal sense attributed to this word. Otherwise it would have been a question of *aeditus,* the guardian priest who served at a temple dedicated to a particular deity, the equivalent of a present-day parish priest, or in Britain, a rector, who truly has canonical responsibility for the sanctuary. When the word *magus* is used by the Roman naturalist and scholar Pliny the Elder (A.D. 23–79) and others to translate the word *druid,* it is done so without any depreciative connotation. The mages of Assyria or the Near East were not only magicians, but also priests, astronomers (or astrologers, since scientific observation was commingled with astrological speculation), scholars, philosophers, and soothsayers, and for the majority of ancient authors the druids were also doctors and theologians who were seen as the equivalent of Greek or Oriental sages. They are at times referred to as *semnotheists* who have more of a kinship with the priests of the mysteries and religions that were beginning to invade the Greco-Roman world at that time than to the administrators of the state religion that was the doctrine of Rome. The term *eubages* or *euhages* also should be seen as as a name designating the druids-diviners category. This term is used in the work of Ammianus Marcellinus who translated the Greek historian Timagenes (first century B.C.) into Latin; in fact, *euhages* is a bad transcription of a Gallic *vates* (passed as such in Latin) by the intermediary of a Greek *uateis.*

There is, however, a druidic name that has provoked considerable debate for some time. It can be found in the eighth book of *Caesar's Commentaries,* written by Hirtius, but which was taken as a person's proper name: *gutuater.* Four Gallo-Roman inscriptions use this term, once as a proper name (in Puy-en-Velay) and three times as a common noun. The formulation *gutuater Martis* in one of these cases leaves no room for doubt: it concerns a priest dedicated to Mars, this deity replacing a Gallic war deity. *Gutuater* is therefore an indication of a sacerdotal function. There is nothing mysterious about this word, as the term *gutu,* literally meaning "voice," and the term *-ater* (or *tater,* related to the Indo-European root of the name of father) are both found there. He is the "Father of the Voice" or the "Father of Speech," a priest charged with preaching or charged with pronouncing the invocations, praises, or satires of a clearly religious nature. The meaning depicted in this last acceptance of the word has its Irish equivalent.

Thanks to precious medieval manuscripts that in large part have carried down to us the epic pagan tales of the Gaels, Ireland is a particularly rich source of material essential to completing what we know about the druids. What matters is not the age of the manuscripts themselves—their having been taken from the eleventh to the fifteenth centuries—for they are generally modernizations or new transcriptions of older manuscripts. In Ireland it was the druidic class that was Christianized first, so it would be suprising if the information furnished by the Christian monks was not drawn from the best sources, that being the oral pagan tradition still vital in the first centuries of Christianization. For however one may want to consider them as epic, marvelous, and mythological symbols, it is here that the druids appear in all their complexity, as well as in the totality of their functions, hence the numerous names they bear that are difficult to define with exactitude.

The generic term for the sacerdotal class is *drui,* a strict equivalent of the Gallic word transcribed by Caesar as *druis,* and transcribed by those who came after as *druida.* But it is quite evident that, as in Gaul, the Gaelic *drui* designates a person belonging to the upper ranks of this sacerdotal class. At the time in which Christianity made its appearance in Ireland the term *drui* seems to have lost its importance, no longer designating a person as anything other than an individual of an inferior class who is solely concerned with sorcery. It is the second category, that of the vates, that then appears to become the most prestigious. Indeed the Irish *file* (plural *fili* or *filid*) corresponds with the Gallic *vates,* but with all the noble duties of the ancient druid. This does not mean that before Christianization the fili had prevailed over the druids; it is only evidence of the actual situation in the fourth century at the time of Saint Patrick's preaching in

Ireland when numerous denominations appear within the fili category, corresponding to various specializations.

First there was the *sencha* (often used as a proper name like the Gallic *gutuater*) who is essentially a historian, an annalist charged with maintaining and spreading the philosophical or historical tradition, and even with delivering the funeral oration for a hero. There was also the *brithem* who had the duties of a judge, arbitrator, legislator, and ambassador. The *scelaige* specialized in epic or mythological tales, while the *cainte* was similar to a gutuater, a master of magical chants who is charged with the duty of pronouncing the community's invocations, execrations, benedictions, and curses. This individual plays an important role in numerous Irish epics and his powers are singled out as being formidable. Finally, there was the *liaig,* a kind of doctor who made use of plants, magic and surgery, the *cruitire,* a harpist whose music had a magical character (it was sometimes music that caused tears, laughter, sleep, or death), and the *deogbaire,* a cupbearer, who had the knowledge of substances that are not only intoxicating but also hallucinogenic.

The divinatory specialization is assumed by the *faith,* a word that is the exact equivalent of the Gallic *vatis,* but it is still uncertain whether the faith belonged to the fili category. It cannot be settled whether or not the faith was a file, and it is likely that there were changes due to Christianization. Prediction was ill regarded by the Christians, and it is possible that at the time of their conversion the fili abandoned their divinatory duties, which were then taken on by lower ranking figures who no longer had the benefit of sacerdotal status in the new society. This hypothesis is corroborated by the fact that the druids were held at arm's length of the saceradoce established by Saint Patrick and his successors at the time of Christianization. In the end, the fili, once baptized—and most often ordained as priests or consecrated as bishops—abandoned the druidic offices that were veiwed as suspect, if not contrary to the Christian spirit. For this reason, our information remains incomplete.

It also can be noted that the bards are absent from this nomenclature, even though the word *bard* exists in Gaelic and ultimately was employed to designate poets and popular singers. Did the Irish bard have a fixed status? Was he really part of the sacerdotal class? The answer to these questions is probably yes, if comparison is made with Gaul and Wales where the bardic tradition was maintained in the Christian context until the end of the Middle Ages. In fact, among the Welsh, and to a certain degree among the Armorican Bretons, the bard was the druid's heir, whereas in Ireland it was the file who filled this role.

The variety of names used to designate the various functional categories within the druidic class, however, shouldn't cause us to forget that the essential name remained the word *druid*.

This word has come under severe scrutiny. The modern forms—*druide* in French, *druid* in English, *derwydd* in Welsh, and *drouiz* in Armorican Breton—are all scholarly reconstructions that date back no further than the end of the eighteenth century. Today the popular word, resulting from the logical evolution of the language, is *draoi* in modern Gaelic, meaning "sorcerer," and *dryw*, meaning "kinglet," in contemporary Welsh; the word has become lost in the Armorican Breton vocabulary. These scholarly reconstructions are based on the most ancient of attested forms used by Caesar, and Latinized into *druis* (genitive *druidis*), to which the ancient Gaelic *drui* closely corresponds.

These observations are of great importance for they constitute proof that druidism, and consequently the druids, have vanished from popular memory as a religious institution and that this has been the case for centuries. Only Wales and Ireland have retained a vague remembrance, which is evidence in itself of a formal depreciation. It is significant that the semantic evolution of the old Irish *drui* has led to the meaning of "sorcerer." This change is linked to the dissatisfaction that arose in Ireland at the time of Christianization with the druids who were reduced to the rank of second-rate magicians to the benefit of the fili who found—or maintained—their position at the heart of Celto-Christian civilization. It is impossible, contrary to what some well-intentioned experts would have us believe, to discover any mention whatsoever of the druids in any tale or song from the popular tradition, notably in the Armorican area of Brittany.[1] Such attempts smack of the purest kind of druidomaniac delirium.

It is not forbidden to pose questions on the subject of the signification of the word *druid*. For several centuries the etymology provided by Pliny the Elder has been uncritically adopted from the famous passage (*Natural History*, XVI, 249) in which he speaks of the druids' veneration of mistletoe and the tree that bears it, the oak. And Pliny adds: "They will not perform any ritual without the presence of a branch from that tree so much so that it seems possible that the name of the druids is taken from the Greek." It has been concluded that the word *druid* comes from the Greek *drus,* "oak," and this explanation, which has had a hardy life, is still encountered in certain serious works of our own century.

This is a question of an analogical etymology, built on a simple resemblance and consolidated by the actual role of the oak in druidic religion. Greek and Latin authors made great use of this kind of etymology as did authors of the Middle Ages. As to the numerous popular etymologies, they are all of the same order and even, at times, create a subtle rapport that pure linguistic science tends to overlook. The phonetic Kabbala is real and it is necessary to be on your guard for what is hidden behind an apparently aberrant piece of reasoning. But in this instance the relationship between the word *druid* and the Greek *drus* is nonexistent.[2] Moreover, why would the name for Gallic druids have a Greek provenance? Logically it must be of Celtic origin. It so happens that the Gallic word for oak was *dervo* (this is one of the few Gallic words we know for certain), *daur* in Gaelic, *derw* in Welsh, and *derv* (collective noun, *dervenn* in the singular, *deru)* in Vannetais Breton. It is certainly difficult to hang the various forms of the word *druid* on to these words.

In addition Pliny's text is quite confused. The naturalist did not expressly state that the origin of *druids* was the Greek word *drus.* He said only that the druids got their name from the Greek. It was outside commentators who decided upon this particular etymology, and we will see that, contrary to what one might think, Pliny the Elder is not so far from the truth.

If one refers to the form of the word provided by Caesar, *druides,* which presupposes a singular *druis* in the nominative, and also to the Irish *druid,* the word can only be traced back to the ancient Celtic *druwides,* which can be easily parsed into *dru-,* an augmentative prefix in the superlative sense (which can be seen in the French adjective *dru*), and in *wid,* a term related to the Indo-European root of the Latin *videre,* "to see," and to the Greek *idein,* also "to see" or "to know." The meaning is therefore perfectly clear: the druids are the "all-seeing" or the "all-knowing," which appears to be in conformance with the various duties with which they were entrusted.

The famous scholia found in the Roman poet Lucan's (A.D. 39–65)

Pharsalia, which are invaluable for the facts they provide on the Gauls and their customs, furnish information concerning the etymological subject Pliny corroborates: the druids "are named after trees because they inhabit remote forests."[3] The passage from *Pharsalia* on which the scholiast exercised his talents concerns a large forest near Marseilles where the druids officiated in open-air sanctuaries called *nemeton.* It can also be observed that it isn't just oak trees but trees in general, that they take their name from. In the end, this is exactly what Pliny the Elder actually said.

This leads to a curious observation that there exists an undeniable connection in the Celtic languages between the word signifying *science* and that signifying *tree—vidu* in Gallic (the root of which provides *koed* in Welsh and Vannetais Breton, and *koad* in other dialects of Brittany). Is this a case of simple homonymy? Or is it again a question of the phonetic Kabbala? Celtifiers speak only of a homonymy. But how then does one explain this same ambiguity in other Indo-European traditions, particularly in regard to the Germanic Odin? The name Odin, which is also Wotan (Woden in Saxon), can be traced back to the ancient Wôthanz attested to by Tacitus in which Germanists see the root *wut* that signifies "sacred madness," therefore, "the complete science." This is certainly within the character given to Odin in the Nordic sagas where he blinds one of his eyes intentionally so that he can see magically, and who is the master of the "runes," those magical inscriptions carved seemingly haphazardly on pieces of wood much in the same manner as the Irish satirist druids carved incantations on hazel and yew branches. The root *wut* presents a strange kinship with the Germanic word recognizable in the English *wood,* meaning the same thing. Moreover, one of the poems of the Scandinavian *Edda* describes how Odin, while hanging from a tree (a shamanic ritual that also existed in pagan Ireland) freed himself with the strength of the runes he summoned up. Odin-Wotan is the god of learning, the preeminent magician-god, who is not without resemblance to Gwyddyon, son of the goddess Dôn and hero of the fourth branch of the Welsh *Mabinogion.*[4] The name of Gwyddyon, though it can refer to the root *gwid,* which means "science" (the Armorican Breton *gwiziek,* "scholar," "knowing"), can also quite possibly stem from the root of the Gallic *vidu,* in the sense of the tree (and become *coit* in Middle Gallic before taking the form *coed*). If Odin-Wotan and Gwyddyon, two individuals who are veritable druid-gods, are simultaneously linked to the idea of science and tree, is it not likely that the name druid possesses the same ambivalence? Nothing should astonish us about the relationship between science—especially religious science—and trees. The fundamental myth about the Tree of Knowledge imbues the traditions of every people. And if druids are the all-knowing, they are also the "men of the tree," those individuals who officiate and teach in the sacred clearings found in the middle of the forests.

2

THE DRUIDIC HIERARCHY

The Druidic sacerdotal class included specialized functions. The problem that arises for us now is trying to understand what governed the relationships between the various constituents of this class, and how best to define what might have been the cohesive factor holding together this seemingly large group.

By beginning with the historical elements that concern Ireland's Christianization (which started in the fifth century A.D.), it is possible to discern rivalries and opposing factions that existed within this druidic class. Indeed if one examines either the literal or legendary history of Saint Patrick, the evangelist of Ireland, one is led to believe that the Christian apostle ran directly into the hostility of the kings and druids, and that Saint Patrick converted the fili, making them the new religion's intellectual elite.[1] It is likely that Saint Patrick played off the rivalry between the druids and the fili, favoring the latter, and bestowing upon them the mission of pursuing his work while they simultaneously combated the magic practices attributed to the druids.

This statement is true as far as it goes, but attentive examination of the relations between the fili and the druids give it no further basis. First of all, in all the texts there is a tendency to confuse druids and fili, because many see the two classifications as simply a dispute of terminology. On the other hand, in the evolution of the Gaelic society of Ireland—evolution that is in no way comparable with what occurred in Gaul—we can maintain that there was a slippage of function between the druids and the fili, who, let us say again, are not terribly different from the druids in that they are members of the same class, and in Ireland the term *druid* essentially serves as a general designation of a member in the druidic class. All that can be assumed is that the term *druid* in Saint Patrick's time served for the most part to qualify someone as a magic worker, whereas the fili was more of an intellectual, a true druid as we understand the term. Irish hagiography could not have not taken this slippage into account, all the more because Saint Patrick himself was captured as an adolescent by Irish pirates (he was Breton) and spent several years as the slave of a druid, that is a magic worker. Thus Patrick knew what the truth of the matter was. Not only must Saint Patrick have learned certain techniques from this druid, but in giving the fili preference over the druids, he prepared the future cadres of Christianity, especially from the intellectual, philosophical, judicial, and political point of view.

The upshot of all this is that the distinction between druids and fili has nothing whatsoever to do with rivalry or opposition, but with function. Moreover, the rapid passage of Ireland from paganism to Christianity, for which it had become somewhat of a spearhead, definitively proves it was the entire druidic class that converted, leading all the other classes of Irish society with them. This gives an indication of the true power druids held in Celtic society. When a social class assumes such importance, it is because it constitutes a coherent and organized whole.

On this point—except for details of interpretation and nuances of vocabulary—the texts of ancient Greece and Rome and the Irish texts (both epic and hagiographic) are in perfect agreement. In all of them there is a druidic sacerdotal class, consisting of priests, diviners, and poet-philosophers, whose responsibilities include: practicing theology and metaphysical speculations, presiding over sacrifices, performing the daily worship and various rituals, transmitting the doctrine to disciples, and governing political life as an intermediary between the divine and human world.

It is conceivable that such an organization was not the result of chance but rather the result of a system that alloted tasks and responsibilities. The druidic sacerdotal class was firmly structured, even if its structures were not always visible in the foreground. A characteristic example can be taken from the Gallic War, most particularly the moment of Vercingetorix's attempt to liberate Gaul from the Romans. If only the telling of the events of the Gallic War are considered, it can be said with almost no exception that the druids are strangely and inexplicably absent. But when one is knowledgeable about the social organization of the Celts, one cannot doubt their presence for a moment, especially their decisive action in all the political and military events that occurred between 58 and 52 B.C. The revolt instigated by Vercingetorix in 52 B.C. wouldn't have had the least chance of taking shape without the patronage of the druidic class. In fact, this revolt started in the land of the Carnutes where the central sanctuary of Gaul was located, and then with surprising speed gained ground throughout the entire territory inhabited by the Gauls.[2] The rapid spread of this revolt is proof of the existence of an organization that had branches extending among all the different Gallic peoples (though they were rivals in other respects and often very different from one another) that was capable of mobilizing large numbers of people whose interests were too often divergent. The revolt of Genabum, and the beginning of Vercingetorix's endeavor at his Arverne base, can have no other explanation.

All of this assumes the existence of some sort of hierarchy among the druids. Caesar was the first person to have observed this and he affirmed it in completely unambiguous terms: "A sole chief commands all these druids and exercises supreme authority over them; when this chief dies, if one of the others is his equal in dignity he will succeed him, but if there are several who have the same status, then the dispute over the top spot will be settled by the suffrage of the druids or, at times, even by armed combat" (VI, 13). The selection, therefore, of what could be called the *archdruid* was fairly flexible and, when all was taken into account, fairly democratic. Authority was created by the value of the individual, and if there were several individuals of equal value, then one had recourse to an election. Certainly, as in all electoral opinion, passions could run high and partisan positions could harden, hence violence was a last resort. But there was no automatic or hereditary succession. This was in the spirit of druidism since it was not a question of a caste system like the Brahmans of India, nor of a college as for the Flamens, but of a class to which one accedes through one's capabilities and intellectual merits.

So there was one chief of all the druids. Caesar was speaking of Gaul, but it remains unclear what he considered the boundaries for Gaul at that time. In any event, this Gaul was a conglomeration of peoples, oftentimes with divergent interests and conflicting politics, peoples who jealously guarded their autonomy, if not their total independence. Caesar's testimony can be taken two ways: either each group of people in Gaul had its own druids who elected a single chief from within their own ranks, or the druids of each people chose a single chief for all of Gaul. This raises a question of fundamental importance: Is druidism a national, international, or supranational institution? In any case this question should be asked with caution, taking into account that the idea of nation and the concept of nationalism didn't have the same signification for the Gauls of the time of Vercingetorix, for the Britons during Arthur's reign, for the Irish during the Age of Saints, as it does for our contemporaries molded from infancy in the structures of a somewhat Hegelien nation-state.

The situation seems paradoxical. On one hand the druidic institution concerns all the Celts with no exception: Gaels and Britons from Ireland to others from the country of Galatia in Asia Minor—even if doubt exists as to the presence and effective role of this last group (there is no mention anywhere of Galatian druids, but this in no way proves their nonexistence). Furthermore, druidism, along with language, is one of the only known glues of Celtic unity. On the other hand, through their social role and the office they performed in regard to the king (or his equivalent), the druids seemed to have a national destiny limited to their native people. This is particularly thrown into relief by a passage from the great Irish epic, the *Tain Bô Cualngé,* concerning the famous druid of Ulster—Cathbad. In this passage, King Ailill of Connaught has just asked the Ulster exile, Fergus, the identity of the magnificent individual he sees in the army of his enemies. Fergus responds: "He is the foundation of the sciences, the master of the elements, the entrance to Heaven; he blinds the eyes, he seizes the strength of the foreigner through the intelligence of the druids, to wit Cathbad, the amicable druid, with the druids of Ulster around him."[3] This scene is not only a kind of summary of the druidic function, but also serves as the portrayal of a remarkable person surrounded by his subordinates: Cathbad, chief of the Ulster druids. In another Irish epic, *The Siege of Druim Damhgaire,* two druids oppose one another in magical combat, each aided by druids of lesser importance. And these two druids are in the service of two enemy kings, which would seem to show the fundamental link between the druid and the people to whom he belongs. Moreover, the historical druid Diviciacos, of whom Caesar and Cicero spoke, clearly appears to have been engaged in the political life of his people, the Aeduens, even when this political life went contrary to the interests of other Gallic peoples.

In addition, if—as according to Caesar—the druids were not subject to military service, nothing forbid them from making war, having only the condition that it was done of their own accord. The Aeduen druid Diviciacos, a solid partisan of alliance with Rome, did not hold back, and the epic druid of the Ulaid, Cathbad, father of the king Conchobar, is presented as both druid and warrior. He was also wed to a woman-warrior. As for the mythical druid Mog Ruith, the hero of *The Siege of Druim Damhgaire,* even if his combats were magical in nature, he nonetheless led a desperate war against the druids of his enemies. It was not a question of patriotism here—this concept being stripped of all significance in the context of ancient Celtic societies—but rather the devotion to a cause, as well as to that of one's people of origin instead of a king or a chosen people. In any event, this proves that the druid belonged in one way or another to a predetermined people whose destiny he shared. It would seem in this case that druidism was a national, or at the very least, a tribal phenomenon.

Yet the druidic institution extends beyond the narrow framework of the people or the tribe. Once again Caesar is an essential witness. In speaking about the druids who were to choose a single chief, he adds: "At a certain time of the year, they gathered together on consecrated ground in the land of the Carnutes, which is regarded as the center of all of Gaul. Converging on this spot are individuals who are involved in disputes that they give over to the druids for their advice and judgment" (VI, 13). There is nothing ambiguous about this: the druids of all Gallic peoples gathered together in one spot. Perhaps they used the occasion to elect a supreme leader, a sort of Gallic archdruid. But Caesar doesn't say. Yet the fact that any individual, no matter what group of people he belonged to, could come and present his case constitutes proof that druidism was an institution that extended beyond the framework of the people or the tribe, which is altogether supranational. This obviously assumes the existence of a feeling of Gallic community, which the adventure of Vercingetorix also serves to bring into light. In sum, the sanctuary of the land of the Carnutes where the druids gathered was an *omphallos,* a sacred and symbolic center. Was this Saint-Benoit-sur-Loire or Fleury-sur-Loire, as has often been suggested?[4] Or even Suêvres (Sodobria, the ancient Sodo-Brivum) in Loir-et-Cher?[5] It hardly matters. This same idea of a sacred center can be found in Ireland, a country that was divided into four kingdoms (these, further divided into numerous tribes). The prehistoric hill of Tara became the mythical center of the isle—the omphallos around which the great political and cultural gatherings were held, and the seat of a fifth, symbolic kingdom (Midhe, or the middle) over which the Ard Ri (the Supreme King) of Ireland theoretically ruled. It should be noted that the same custom existed in the Hellenic world, in that Delphi was a kind of neutral territory for the often rival and enemy Greek cities, who, under the protection of the Oracle of Delphi, deposited their treasure there around the stone omphallos that marked a symbolic center of the universe.

But this is not all. The question having been raised of a supranational druidic institution, one can go further still, thanks again to Caesar's testimony: "Their doctrine has been elaborated in Great Britain, and from there, it is thought, brought to Gaul; still in our days the majority of those who wish to deepen their knowledge of this doctrine go there for their studies" (VI, 13). Here we find ourselves again in Gaul, even though the insular Britons could have been of the same origin as the Gauls (especially after the Belgian migrations to Great Britain at the beginning of the first century B.C., and who may have spoken a British tongue almost identical to the Gallic language.[6,7] Curiously, Irish tradition has the druids coming from "the isles of the north of the world" and shows future druids and young people going to Scotland (or a completely different part of Great Britain) for their initiations. Indeed, Scotland is north of Ireland, a fact that is not without interest to our purpose.

There is no reason to doubt Caesar. An intimate of the druid Diviciacos, Caesar knew quite well—if only for reasons of politics and strategy—what threads tied Gaul to the isle of Britain. These threads were numerous. During the Veneti revolt in 56 B.C., Caesar had taken note of the fact that the Britons had sent aid to the Armoricans, and he deemed that any lasting conquest of Gaul would require the conquest of the British island. This conquest, as is known, was partial and incomplete, but it indicated the extent of the proconsul's defiance of the people who were rightly suspected of being the true masters of Celtic thought. A thought that, situated at the very antipodes of the Roman system, constituted a permanent danger.

Thus the existence of some sort of international center of druidism finds expression here. Was this a sanctuary? Without a doubt. But above all this was a school charged with the maintenance of a tradition and its spread to those with a claim upon it. It is remarkable nevertheless that the Irish texts all indicate the importance of the isle of Britain in the initiation of young people. And it is there that the hero Cuchulainn went to complete his education—and he was not alone. What isn't known is whether this druidic center was unique and, if it was, where it was located. Several hypotheses have been put forth, in particular that of Bangor in the north of Wales. The name Bangor signifies "college" or "assembly," and is also found in this same form in Ireland and in Belle-île en Mer, in Armorican Brittany, testifying perhaps to two branches of the Welsh Bangor. It is possible that this could be the Isle of Mona, the mysterious Môn of Welsh tradition that today is Anglesey. In A.D. 58 there was a huge establishment of druids there, according to the testimony of Tacitus (*Annals,* XIV, 29–30), an establishment that was ravaged and destroyed by the Roman army of Suetonius Paulinus at the time of the general uprising in Britain.

Whatever the case, all these observations reveal that the druidic institution was simultaneously powerfully structured within the framework of the tribe and people, within the framework of all of Gaul, and within the framework of the original Celtic community. This confirms our conviction that druidism was the religion of *all* the Celts and helps to clarify the idea that the druidic institution with its structures and hierarchy of a "federal" tendency, was absolutely inseparable from the Celtic society with which it formed a common body and of which it constituted the spiritual skeleton.

3

THE DRUIDS AND SOCIETY

From the beginning of the first century B.C. until the sixth century A.D., the druidic institution disappeared slowly, but not brutally, in Ireland, Britain, and Gaul. There has been much inquiry as to the causes of this disappearance, and numerous answers have been supplied. The most common being that of druidism's interdiction by Roman authorities. But this is an error. In regard to religion the Romans were—undoubtedly because they were fundamentally agnostic—the most tolerant people who ever lived. They accepted an extremely wide assortment of types of worship in Rome, watching only to ensure that none would disturb public order. And if they did persecute the Christians, it was for political reasons, because the Christians refused to sacrifice to the gods of the state and because they acted seditiously toward the state. That is all. There was never the slightest spiritual or metaphysical motivation behind the Roman attitude toward the Christians. It was the same for druidism. The Romans never forbade the worship itself; they forbade the teaching of the druids because they deemed it a threat to the social order the Romans sought to impose.[1] But it is quite obvious that by preventing the druids from sharing their teachings and by replacing the druidic schools with Roman schools (such as the one in Autun), a mortal blow was delivered to the religion itself.

A second reason often put forward to explain the disappearance of the druidic institution is the triumph of Christianity. The argument has much more merit, but it needs to be integrated into a complex group of factors and forms only a partial response to the question of this disappearance.[2]

The same holds true for the disappearance of the Gallic language—a disappearance due in large part to the fact that it was the Latin of Christianity that got the better of Gallic, the language of the unconverted *pagani,* the "pagans," and not the Latin of the Roman conquerors. At any rate, Ireland, which never experienced Roman occupation, kept its Celtic language while painlessly converting to Christianity. All this underscores that the problem is not so simple to resolve.

In reality the disappearance of the institution of druidism coincided exactly with the disappearance of the Celtic societies. Once Gaul began to follow the Roman model, and once the Gallic people were caught in the gears of Roman laws and prudently authorized to become Roman citizens, the institution of druidism no longer had any reason to exist.[3] On the isle of Britain, Romanization was superficial, and from the days of the end of the empire—and often even before—the Celtic society for a time came back to the forefront before finally succumbing to the assault of the Saxons. But this society, as in Ireland, was already Christian and was maintained only because the Christian priests, monks, abbots, and bishops strictly played the same social role as that previously performed by the ancient druids.[4] The Celtic structure of Ireland endured until the twelfth century, until the coming of the Cistercians and the takeover by Henry II Plantagenet, but only because of the particular nature of Irish Christianity. In Gaul, as in Armorican Brittany, druidism died as a result of the death of Celtic society.

This is not to say that *all* druidism disappeared. Religions never collapse from one blow. What died was the institution of druidism itself—its organization, hierarchical system, teachings, and the influence it had on social and political life. It is infinitely possible that once their teachings were banned, certain druids retired to remote regions where they secretly continued to spread their doctrine to those who wished to hear it. But how many of those there may have been is hard to know. The number may have been small. If the druid schools were still maintained clandestinely for a while after the conquest, it was probably under a form that altered more and more with each generation. Testimonies from the third and fourth centuries indicate the existence of druids and druidesses who were still active—but in what a state! They were no more than fortune-tellers and prophets of the lowest quality—hedge wizards. That these persons might have picked up some or all of the heritage of the ancient druids is possible, but it must be noted that they hardly turned it to a profit, nor did they leave an indelible sign of their presence in history.

Next, it is important to emphasize another observation. If druidism had left traces, it only would have been in the consciousness of people, in people's minds. The subsequent history of Roman Gaul, rather than Frankish Gaul, deserves study in terms of this postulate, as well does the fashion in which the first Gallic Christians lived. And then, in that all nonofficial traditions were repressed, it can be rediscovered in what is called "popular wisdom." The treasury of tales, folk songs, customs, superstitions, and religious rituals in the territory of ancient Gaul can become a gold mine of information for those who patiently and objectively search for possible survivals of druidism. It is the same in Great Britain where, under the Saxon-Christian veneer, many strange substrata exist. It was in Scotland, a Celtic country, that Freemasonry was born in the eighteenth century. In the country of Wales, a region that remained very Celtic despite the weight of the Methodist religion, a neodruidic movement appeared at the end of the nineteenth century that subsequently spread nearly everywhere. Even though this neodruidism was the result of a bizarre intellectual syncretism in which the imagination played an almost exclusive role, it was certainly not without good reason.

The resurgence of a druidic spirit, even one invented from whole cloth, corresponds to a profound need in the unconscious desire. This druidic spirit is surely not dead, but it still needs to be defined. And it still needs to be supported by adequate social structures that will truly allow it to manifest. This is not the case.

Let me repeat, druidism (with all the reservations that can be taken with this recent term) has no value, nor even any existence outside of the Celtic society that gave it birth. In some way druidism was the essential cause of Celtic society, and was also its consequence, hence the importance of the druid within that society.

A famous Irish epic, *The Drunkenness of the Ulaid,* presents the situation like this: "One of the prohibitions of the Ulaid [the people of Ulster] was that of speaking before the king spoke, and it was one of the king's prohibitions to speak before his druids spoke."[5] With regard to the king, the role of the druid cannot be better, or more succinctly, described than that. A good parallel can be made with what Saint John Chrysostom said regarding the priests of these ancient peoples when he said: "The Celts had people called druids for their priests who were experts in divination and in all other sciences; the kings were forbidden to act or make any decision without them to such extent that in actuality it was the druids who commanded, the kings were no more than the servants and administrators of their intentions."[6] In light of other anecdotal evidence, the commentary of Saint John Chrysostom appears somewhat exaggerated. There is no direct hierarchical connection between the king and the druid, and the latter is not a superking. The druid *counsels* and the king *acts*. But the counsels of the druids were not permitted to be ignored or refused, especially in a society that refused to make a distinction between the sacred and the profane. At the festivals, the druid's place was to the right of the king, and even as the king appeared as the pivot of society, the druid was in some manner society's "conscience." Without the druid the king is nothing. At the time of the war with the Gauls, Cotus was the supreme magistrate (a substitute for king) of the Aeduens. For political reasons, Caesar—by skillfully manipulating Gallic laws—"obliged Cotus to renounce his power and transfer his authority to the hands of Convictolitavis who, according to the custom of the city, had been named by the priests to the vacant magistrate's seat."[7] There are many such examples, all equally explicit.

This conception appears perfectly logical, and its archaic character, contrary to what happened in other Indo-European societies, accentuates it while also justifying it. We are indeed in a purely Indo-European framework, which is a society whose structures are strictly regulated on the primitive Indo-European model that Georges Dumézil succeeded in clearly defining. The king was the leader of the second class, the warriors, but the druid belonged to the first class, the sacerdotal class. The theoretical—and in some ways theological—hierarchy thus assumed that the druid had primacy over the king, even if the king was the one who governed, and was the one who symbolized and embodied the unity of a given social group. It was a kingdom of the sacred type to the extent that the king—who was absolutely not an incarnation of a god, nor a divinized sovereign—was powerless unless his actions in the human world were applications of the plans of the world of the god to this world.[8] This was unequivocally not an absolute monarchy. Quite the contrary, the sovereign was more of a moral pivot around which the society was constructed. It was not a monarchy of divine right, either, as the term was understood in the Capetian era, the

25

Celtic king was not placed above the laws but strictly subject to them under conditions that defy even the imagination.[9] This was not a theocracy, since the king was *not* a priest. To an extent this practice—taken up again during the time of Charlemagne and the Holy Roman Empire, with its well-known and disappointing results—is an Indo-European archaism that had no other historical examples than that of the Celts. Among the Romans it already was considered little more than a mythological souvenir; among the Greeks and the Germans it was also a memory; among the Indo-Iranians, unverifiable.[10] All that remain are divine depictions in tales that date back very far in time indeed.

Since all that is above is as below, and vice versa, as is said in the famous *Emerald Table* of the Hermetists—interestingly the social structure of the Celts was built on this affirmation—the druid-king pair meet again in the mythological domain. Among the gods mentioned in the Celtic epics who are known collectively as the famous Tuatha de Danann, several seemed to form the same kind of coupling. The gods Ogma and Nuada are paired this way, especially in the tale of *The Battle of Mag-Tured,* Nuada being the king whose amputated arm was replaced with a silver limb, Ogma being the magician, the poet, the god of eloquence, he who charmed. It could also be argued that this role was held by the Dagda of the "inexhaustible cauldron" (one of the four major symbols of Irish myth that is similar in idea to the horn of plenty) and the club that killed when it strikes with one end and that resuscitated with a blow from its other end. Whether or not this was the case is unclear, all the more so in that the Dagda of the countless names appears to be the Great God of Ireland, following Lugh, who by his multiple duties and functions was in a class by himself.

This couple is perfectly recognizable in Germanic mythology with Odin-Wotan and Tyr. Odin is one-eyed because he is a seer; Tyr is one-armed because he gave his arm in exchange for a false oath that was profitable to the community of the gods. Odin is the master of science, runes, and magic, and on the whole represents sacerdotal power, while Tyr is the heroic warrior, the god of contracts, the stabilizing force. This couple can be recognized in the strongly historicized Roman tradition set down by Titus Livy. It is the one-eyed Horatius Cocles who draws the enemy away from the Sublicius Bridge with the power of his gaze, and it is the one-armed Mucius Scaevola who also loses his arm for a heroic false oath. And if one analyzes the tale of the founding of Rome, one cannot fail to draw a parallel between Romulus the warrior king and Numa Pompilius, the legislator king, inspired by the goddess Egeria.

This couple also has its equivalent in Vedic India, as shown by Georges Dumézil who sees the couple as a "bipartition of sovereignty," which "makes up part of the idea capital on which Indo-Europeans live."[11] Here we are dealing with Mitra, the sovereign jurist god, and Varuna, the sovereign magician god. Mitra is of "this world" and Varuna comes from the "other world." This couple forms a coherent whole that, under its apparent dual nature, remains an implacable monism. "To be complimentary in their services, Varuna and Mitra are antithetical, each feature of one creating a contrary feature in the other."[12] This alliance between druid and king in the Celtic domain, an alliance without which neither of them would have a true existence, indicates the strength of this monism.[13]

It is in the Arthurian legend—the Celtic tradition's last burst of energy as seen through the dubious Cistercian recuperations of the twelfth and thirteenth centuries—that the most striking example of this bifunctional druid-king couple has manifested, first with Merlin and Uther Pendragon, then with Merlin and Arthur. Merlin the Magician is indeed a complex individual of multiple origins, but it is certain that he embodies the druid to the extent that tradition was still capable of depicting one.[14] This is particularly true in his social duties.

If Merlin's story is followed, such as it was set down on the original outline of Robert de Boron who drew from Welsh tradition, the young prophet Merlin was first seen eliminating King Vortigern, a usurper in favor of the enthronement of Uther Pendragon. The king therefore could not be recognized as such without the consent of the druid. Consequently Merlin *counseled* Uther, but took pains to avoid direct intervention into the affairs of the kingdom. More than ever, he was the conscience of the king who was the true decision maker—but a decision maker who could not refuse his druid anything.

It is in profiting by Uther's violent passion for Ygerne of Cornwall that Merlin prepared for the coming of the predestined king, Arthur. Merlin encouraged and instigated the copulation of Uther and Ygerne, a coupling that was illegitimate in the light of social and religious morality, but necessary for the realization of the kingdom. It was Merlin, again who, through an intermediary, undertook the education of young Arthur, and it was he who established the trials by which Arthur would be recognized as a sacred monarch (the episode of the sword in the stone is the equivalent of the magic rituals that preceded the election of the king among the ancient Irish). It was Merlin who advised Arthur on all his actions, who made him undertake his expeditions, and who had him establish the Round Table and its company of knights. It was finally he who unveiled the great lineages of the Grail legend and instigated the famous Grail Quest. And the kingdom began to be in jeopardy on the day Merlin disappeared. Arthur-Mitra could not rightfully reign without Merlin-Varuna.

The king therefore depended upon the druid. It was not the druid that had chosen him, for the king was a warrior elected by his peers. But his election would have been invalid if it had not been ratified by the druid, or if there had been no ritual ceremony intended to recognize the man who would be king. The king could not act against the druid or scorn his advice and counsel. But each time the king asked something of him, the druid had to do it unless it was an impious act, for the druid was equally dependent upon the king. This original situation is only warrantable within the framework of a society where every political action is simultaneously a sacred action. In Celtic society there was no distinction between the sacred and the profane. Like the druid and the king, they were two faces of one reality.

This speaks to the eminent role of the druid in the political and social life of the people, tribe, or kingdom in which he finds himself. Whatever his actual specialization may be, he therefore found himself induced to have been political counselor, supreme judge, legislator, and ambassador, according to the need of the occasion. We have a Latin text *(Constantine's Panegyric)* that describes the arrival of the Aeduen druid, Diviciacos, who had come to speak before the Roman Senate to ask for assistance against the Sequani people: "When he was invited to be seated, he refused the offer that had been extended to him and he spoke, leaning on his shield." Diviciacos thus asserted himself as an ambassador and not as a druid. Numerous Irish texts speak of druids sent on missions to a foreign king. And there were also druids who went to their enemies' borders to make ritual incantations that were equivalent to a declaration of war.

To be fair, it must be said that druids were often peacemakers. A well-known episode from the Irish tale *The Drunkenness of the Ulaid* presents us with the Ulaid after a banquet at which spirits flowed freely, and quarreling came to blows, resulting in casualties and deaths. But it was enough for Sencha the druid to raise his "branch of peace" amid the combatants for the drunken Ulaid, who were running amok, to cause them to stand as quiet as little boys being reprimanded and threatened with the punishment of wearing a dunce's cap. This corroborates exactly with what Diodorous Siculus said: "Often on the battlefields, at the very moment when the armies approach each other with swords raised and lances thrust forward, these bards will advance into the midst of their adversaries and tame them, as though having cast a spell over wild beasts" (Diodorus, V, 31). It even happened that a druid could reduce a pitched battle to a combat of words—an oratorical jousting match—as is the case in another Irish epic, *The Banquet of Bricriu*. And as the Ulaid—it is always the Ulaid—became more heated during the course of this oratorical joust and threatened to pick up their weapons again, the druid Sencha intervened again to restore peace.

This peacemaker role in no way prevented the druid from participating in combat if there was a need, not even from being a military leader, a strategist. Even in Ireland during the early Christian period, the custom of monks going off to war continued. The example of Saint Colum-Cill is often cited, an ancient file turned abbot of a monastery, who didn't hesitate to massacre the troops of a king who didn't appreciate his behavior (and highly questionable behavior, it was).[15] Then there is the mythical druid Mog Ruith who is described as going into combat "with his shield of many colors and stars in a circle of white silver, a highly valued hero's sword at his left side, and two poisoned enemy spears in his hands."[16] Statements that the combat he would wage was essentially magical in nature had been in vain. Mog Ruith's armaments were, frankly, dreadful. And his enemies, who were druids like himself, were equally ferocious and well-armed warriors. Certainly we are dealing with a mythological narrative here, but Caesar said almost the same thing in regard to the druid Diviciacos when he exhorted "and demonstrated to him what great interest it would be to their common good to prevent the joining of the enemy troops so as to avoid having to fight such a great force at one time; this could be done if the Aeduens would have their troops enter Bellovaci territory and start to ravage their lands; having charged him with this mission he sent him to it."[17] On this occasion, following Caesar's orders, the Aeduen druid had to act as a killer rather than as a peacemaker.

All of this might seem quite odd to an observer of Indo-European customs. The Brahmans and the Flamens certainly didn't wage war and were even subject to taboos that went so far as prohibiting even looking at an armed troop. One can rest assured that in the Germano-Scandinavian domain, the warrior's position and the sacerdotal position were not contradictory; as the personage of Odin-Wotan, both warrior-god (but in magical war) and priest-god, seems to supply ample testimony. And if one leaves the Indo-European realm, there are many examples of warrior-priests among the Hebrews, as well as among Christians of every nationality. So the question is raised: Was the warlike character of the druid—even when temporary and nonobligatory—an Indo-European trait or the legacy of an autochthonous people that the Indo-European Celts subjugated upon their arrival in Western Europe, and with whom they formed the community that is called Celtic? More precisely, was druidism Celtic, or only half-Celtic? At this point no answer can be given on the strength of this lone observation. We will see later what more should be thought of it.

There is a counterpart to the theme of the druid-warrior. According to John Keating's *The History of Ireland,* which dates from the twelfth century but is a precious abridgment of the ancient tradition, a person could not be accepted amid the Fiana—that famous half-historical, half-mythological militia whose chief was Finn Mac Cumail, the father of Ossian—without being a poet (a member of the sacerdotal class). There is much that can be said about these Fiana of Ireland and this itinerant and fraternal community of warriors whose origins are obscure but who incontestably were the prototypes for the Knights of the Round Table.[18] Among them were precisely such figures as Tristan, Lancelot, and Gawain, men who merged the heroism of the warrior with the refinement of the courtier in a single individual: they were also poets and musicians, thus belonging to a certain extent to the class of "clerics," (again, the sacerdotal class).

Druids possessed yet another important social function. They were doctors. As Ammianus Marcellinus said, quoting Timagenes (XV, 9), and as Cicero said (*De Divinatione,* I, 40) in regard to the druid Diviciacos, their knowledge of "nature's highest secrets," and of the "natural laws called physiology by the Greeks" obviously made them quite capable of healing sickness and wounds. It is likely that the most important part of their therapeutic method was plant medicine. The famous passage in which Pliny the Elder describes the harvesting of mistletoe is quite explicit on this subject: "They believe that mistletoe taken as a drink gives fecundity to sterile animals and constitutes a remedy against all poisons" (*Natural History*, XVI, 249). Mistletoe was valued as a universal panacea, a veritable magic potion. But Pliny informs us of other plants—sage and vervain in particular—that, harvested in certain specific conditions, played an important role in medical treatments. Moreover, the Irish story of *The Battle of Mag Tured* demonstrates how Diancecht, the god of medicine, manufactured a fountain of health by throwing all the plants that grew in Ireland into a spring. Other epic tales insist that certain druids had the ability to perform surgical operations such as limb grafts. Are these fantastic tales or a reflection of a certain reality? It is difficult to say. Whatever the case, plant medicine and surgery did not occur without magical incantations. The old notion that every ailment of the body is also a spiritual ailment was an integral part of Celtic belief—as it was a belief of many other peoples who didn't wait for the advent of modern psychology and medical advances to discern the existence of psychosomatic disorders.

By this reckoning the druid was a medicine man like a shaman. With his magic incantations, the druid was not so different from the shaman who carries out his ecstatic journey to seek the souls of the ill, dying, or even dead individuals in the border regions of the Otherworld, and then restores them to the patients' bodies. This is not the sole occasion on which we will encounter points of similarity between druidism and shamanism, even if to do so means going beyond certain post-Dumézilian positions that, in the case of druidism, refuse to accept sources outside of the Indo-European world. It is important, however, not to neglect any source of information, especially when one considers the importance of shamanism in the plains of central Asia and in central Europe from where the Celts came. Why consider Odin-Wotan as the shaman-god par excellence, while refusing to entertain the idea of a druid-shaman? Keep in mind, of course, all the additional factors that are imperative by virtue of his appurtenance to another social group. By the same token, it is not forbidden to think that if druidism didn't vanish overnight, and maintained itself in altered and very fragmentary forms in Western folk tradition—the bone-setters, healers, hypnotists, and village magicians that abound in our time—that those who are truly medicine men are the remote descendants of the Gallic, Breton, and Irish druids. After all, the Gaelic word *draoi* has certainly taken on the meaning of "sorcerers." At the moment of the great combat of the two opposing heroes Cuchulainn and Ferdead in *The Cattle Raid of Cualngé,* the anonymous author of this Irish tale tells us of the arrival of the "warriors" and the "doctors"—members of the druid class—at the sides of two exhausted, wounded figures: "They examined herbs and medicinal plants and spoke a healing incantation over their wounds." And on the following day they brought them "magical drinks, incantations, and spells for alleviating their bloody wounds, their loss of blood and their mortal pains." This treatment, according to the following section of the tale, was successful enough to allow the two heroes to get up and start to try to kill one another again.

Above all else druids were "men of learning," which is the meaning behind their name. Their knowledge of tradition encompassed every domain—that of law, philosophy, and medicine, as well as theology, music, and poetry. Since the druids refused to use writing (save in the case of certain magical incantations), this knowledge was handed down orally, and it was only following the Christianization of Ireland that the fili, who had converted and become monks, were freed of the (magical) ban on writing and entrusted what remained of the tradition to precious manuscript form. But during the druidic era the transmission of knowledge could only be done orally, whether by the poets and storytellers who addressed the general public or by professors who spread a much more difficult, if not more esoteric, teaching to a small group of disciples—young people who desired to acquire an education or who wished to become either bards or druids. In any case the existence of druid schools is not a hypothetical fact. They did exist.

Again the supporting text comes from Caesar: "Many come, in their own right, to entrust their education in their [the druids] hands, but many are sent by their parents and relatives; it is said that they learn a very great number of verses there by heart; thus some remain in school for as long as twenty years" (Caesar, VI, 14). Another confirming text comes from Pomponius Mela (first century A.D.).... "They have ... masters of wisdom that they call druids.... They teach many things to the nobility of Gaul in secret, for twenty years, whether in caves or remote forests" (*De Choregraphia,* III, 2, 18). The "caves" and "remote forests" of which Mela writes are perhaps an allusion to the underground activity in which the druids sought refuge, but it must be noted that the druidic sanctuaries—and therefore their schools—were clearly far removed from daily life, often in the center of the forests. As to the teaching consisting of a great number of verses, this seems substantianted by the internal structure of Irish tales and, to a lesser extent, certain Welsh stories. These, especially the oldest, were full with strophes in verse, often of archaic language that was difficult to comprehend, and that certainly seems to have been the mnemotechnical structure around which the storyteller constructed his tale. This assumes that the druids taught their doctrine under a versified and most likely epic form, but that the language used was not accessible to everyone. One version of *Tain Bô Cualngé* is very revealing: "Cathbad the druid gave out the teaching to his students to the northeast of Emain, and eight among them were capable of the druidic science."[19] In other words, many were called but few were chosen. Another version of epic presents Cathbad in school: "One hundred scatterbrains were at his establishment, learning druidism."[20] One is tempted to consider druidic teaching as particularly difficult, not to mention esoteric, and therefore reserved for those whom, by possessing a certain kind of mind or having been initiated, would be capable of understanding what was taught and of passing it on in their turn. This legitimizes Caesar's claim that the druids forbade the use of writing "because they didn't wish their doctrine to be spread among the people."[21]

The druidic tradition is most often presented in the guise of tales where everything is knowingly blended—history, theology, philosophy, mythology, law, custom, and vaticination. Grammar, geography, and especially etymology, were also present, but what is most striking in this tradition—which we know essentially from Irish manuscripts, and to a lesser degree from Welsh manuscripts—is the tradition's refusal to disassociate myth from history. Contrary to the Romans, the Celts had thought of their history mythically, and, of course, at times had historicized their myths. Hence the ambivalence of Celtic tales, Irish in particular, (the famous *scela*) that are simultaneously heroic epics, historical chronicles, and mythological stories. From this combination also comes the difficulty, for all observers of good faith, but foreign to (and for good reason) the mental structures of Celtic society, to get their bearings there and make allowance for things that are cultural assumptions on the part of the audience. It is not so much for their esoterism that the meaning of the Celtic tales have remained obscure, but rather because of the historical displacement and the fundamental conceptual difference that has flowed out of that displacement. Having said that, it is possible that the druids intentionally wished to make their stories obscure, first, so as only to be understood by those with the ability to comprehend them, and second, for effectuating a better selection among those aspiring to be druids. There are many anecdotes in Irish stories concerning druids (or fili), who forced their disciples into aberrant activities, set traps for them, or sent them out on false scents. One cannot help but think of the Merlin of the Arthurian romances, who, each time he was asked a question responded with laughter or avoided answering the question all together. The same observation can be made regarding Perceval (or Peredur, or Parzival): he began by blindly following his mother's counsels literally, without having truly understood them, a cause of action that put him in all sorts of problematic situations. It is the same in Wolfram von Eschenbach's text when the hermit Trevrizent falsely recounts the history of the Holy Grail to Parzival. The majority of Celtic tales are ambiguous by nature, which hardly facilitates their translation and interpretation. But as much can be said of certain texts from the Scandinavian *Edda* and the sacred texts of Vedic India. After reading these it is hard to become astonished when reading the treatises on alchemy from the Middle Ages.

The Welsh or Irish example, which we know thanks to the later transcription by Christian monks, should not be considered only representative of the insular Celtic tradition. It can easily be projected upon continental Gaul. Caesar was explicit when he spoke of a tradtion that was transmitted orally by the druids by means of verse. And when Titus Livy, a Gaul from the Cisalpine, took the trouble to write a history of the founding of Rome, not only did he make copious use of Roman legends, but shamelessly made use of Gallic tales that must have still been known at his time, tales that are quite easily identified by textual analysis.[22] He is not, by the way, the only author of classical antiquity to draw material from Celtic sources. Echoes of it can even be found in Aristotle.[23] But as a general rule, the Greeks and Latins contented themselves with fragmentary accounts, as they had experienced great difficulties, it seems, in understanding the exact significance of these legends. Again, this was because of their different logic, and the absence of any dichotomy between myth and history among the Celts.[24]

However, those Greeks and Latins who had frequented the Gauls, who had listened to the Gallic druids and deemed them men with remarkable minds and men of a high level of thought, were aware that these druids didn't speak exactly as they did. It was Diodorus Siculus who declared:

"They say little in their conversations, expressing themselves in enigmas, and affecting a language that relies mainly on conjecture. They employ hyperbole a great deal, either to praise themselves or to humble others. In their speech they are threatening, haughty, and given to tragedy. They are intelligent however and capable of improving themselves" (Diodorus, V, 31). This is an excellent bit of testimony as it confirms that among the Gauls there were known heroic oral tales whose meaning—as a consequence of the accumulation of hyperbole and enigmas—was at times quite difficult to grasp. And it confirms that the characteristics of the Irish or Welsh epic itself was formed in the same mold as the Gallic epic of which we know relatively nothing, save for a few fragments retrieved by the authors of classical antiquity.

The druids, therefore, are shown to have been the trustees of a complex tradition, encompassing all the realms of the spirit for which they were the only ones capable of validly interpreting the profound meaning. Counselor to the king, the druid was also the counselor to the entire kingdom. Hence the judicial office was inherent within the sacerdotal class, even if the execution of its judgments engaged the responsibility of the king, or the secular arm as it was called in the Middle Ages. "It is indeed the druids that judge disputes, both public and private, and if a crime has been committed, if a murder has occurred, if a dispute has arisen over an inheiritance or a boundary line, then it is they who decide and evaluate damages and sanctions" (Caesar, VI, 13). The judicial function of the druids was universal. In Celtic society, where the distinction between public and private law did not exist, and where there was no public or private business, the laws—or the customs—could not be valid without reference to the higher plane of religion. In fact, judgments, decisions, and contracts were under the auspices of the gods, the sole trustees of law and justice. And it was the druids, the necessary intermediaries between the gods and men and priveleged interlocutors for the gods, who were charged with the application of divine law to particular cases. The judgment of a druid was beyond dispute. If a druid delivered a faulty judgment, it was he who would be punished by the gods. Examples on this subject abound in Irish literature. If through misfortune a druid rendered a flawed judgment he became ill, or disfigured, or the land of the tribe or kingdom turned barren. It was thus in the druid's interest to not make mistakes. Under this form of justice, which borrows its points of justification from the realm of the imaginary, if not truly the fantastic, the pains taken by Celtic societies to raise themselves to perfection is recognizable, and in any case the extreme concern for rigor they manifested in regard to the druids. For if the king was subject to an incalculable number of prohibitions, the druid did not suffer under any, save one: never make a mistake.

On the other hand ordinary mortals, kings included, were not permitted to ignore the druids' judgments. "If a particular individual or a people do not accept the druid's decisions, they are forbidden to perform sacrifices; this penalty is the most serious among them" (Caesar, VI, 13). This strangely prefigures the excommunication and interdictment often pronounced on a kingdom (coercive procedures of which the Christian Church of the Middle Ages made great use). As they also were considered "magicians," druids could cast "satires" against recalcitrant individuals. This method, which brings to mind the anathema of the Christians, was of a religious nature that places the culpable individual under the vengeful strikes of the deity. It was also of a social nature that cast shame and disgrace on the person concerned, and, of course, if we are to believe certain texts it was also of a magical nature that brought into play the underlying mysterious and "demonic" forces animating the world. The most characteristic example of this is the druid-satirist Athirne, who figures in two Irish stories, *The Wooing of Luaine* and *Siege of Dun Etair*. He is an Ulaid, but his compatriots are fairly scared of him and have given him the nickname of the *Troublemaker of Ulster*. It is true that he is an overbearing character; he made use of his position as druid and its powers to satisfy all his desires. And the claims he makes are exorbitant. He demands, under penalty of his invoking serious curses, the eye of a one-eyed king, the wife of another king, and the most beautiful jewels owned by certain families.[25] It is interesting to note that the Ulaid used him as a provocateur against other peoples—but that's another story. It is obvious that there is epic exaggeration in this case, but at the very least it shows that the powers of the druid, the master of incantatory magic, were quite formidable.

If the druid could not be mistaken, and if he was the master of incantatory magic, this also explains his role as soothsayer. Privileged interlocuter of the godhead, he is more than ever the "all-seeing one," he who knows how to read the great book of destinies. The Celts, like all other peoples of antiquity, possessed great confidence in omens and undertook no enterprise without first consulting the oracles. They were not the only ones to practice prophetic arts, but evidence shows that such arts were of considerable importance among them. "They avail themselves of soothsayers to whom they grant a great authority; it is through the flight of birds and the sacrifice of victims that these soothsayers predict the future, and how the entire people are kept in a state of dependency upon them" (Diodorus Siculus, V, 31). "The soothsayers have endeavored through their research to accede to the highest occurrences and secrets of Nature" (Timagenes, quoted by Ammianus Marcellinus, XV, 9). Irish tales abound with anecdotes in which soothsayers are seen predicting future events, for individuals as well as for society. And this is where one can first see the appearance of the *prophetesses*, such as the famous Fedelm of Connaught. The Gallicenes of the Isle of Sein, of whom Pomponius Mela spoke, should be mentioned here as well. They predicted the future, calmed storms, and could change their appearance. Recognizable in this figure as well is the prototype of Morgan, the fairy of the Arthurian romances, and her nine sisters, the mistresses of the mythical Isle of Avalon. In any case, the appearance of the prophetess is a clear indication that women could belong to the druidic class: if there is no reference to the rank of *druidess*, and if it holds likely that women didn't occupy the top seats of the druidic hierarchy, there is still the certainty of the fact that they could be prophetesses or poets. By this reckoning, the mythological figure of the triple Brigit (who became Saint Bridget of Kildare) goddess of poetry, science, and crafts, is very revealing. The same holds true for the goddess Morrigan who was also capable of metamorphosizing into a crow, a woman-warrior, or a prophetess. And what can be said about those female warriors, who are portrayed more or less as magicians and witches, traces of whom we find in both Irish epics and Welsh tales? The fairies of folktales and the mysterious maidens that Arthur's knights encountered (said maidens often being those who indicated which road to follow), from all evidence are to be ranked in the same category, keeping in mind that one is dealing with a very altered tradition that has been subject to numerous and diverse influences over both time and distance. After all, the image of the Three Fates, or the Three *Moerae* in Greece, is not so far from the prophetess figure, nor is that of the Sybil of Cumae, and the Pythia of Delphi. The latter was certainly a member of the sacerdotal class, even if her role was only that of a passive performer, as the priests were charged with the official interpretation of her vaticinations.

This said, it shouldn't be forgotten that the druids, making no distinction between their various categories, were *priests* above all. According to Caesar, druids "looked after sacred things, occupied themselves with public and private sacrifices, and governed all religious affairs" (Caesar, VI, 13). The custom among the Celts was that "no one makes a sacrifice without the presence of a philosopher (druid), as they believe they must go through the intermediaries of these men who know the nature of the gods and can, so to speak, converse in their language to make sacrifices of thanksgiving and to beseech their aid" (Diodorus Siculus, V, 31). Among all ancient peoples, sacrifices were considered the most important and significant manifestations of religion. Whether for the Celts they consisted of human or animal sacrifice, symbolic sacrifical rituals, or plant offerings is of no matter here. Whatever form they took, the druids presided over these sacrifices just as they performed other ceremonies (of which we have little information), in sacred clearings deep in the forests. Religion being inseparable from civil and military life by virtue of the principle of nondichotomy between the sacred and the profane, this purely sacerdotal aspect of the druids only can add to their actual power at the interior of Celtic society. Again it should be noted that without the druids there would have been no Celtic society and, conversely, without a society of Celtic structures, there could have been no druids.

PART TWO

THE BEGINNING TIMES

*I*n every tradition, doctrine, and institution of a religious nature there are explicit references to an *illo tempore*. These "times then" or "times of in the beginning" concern the appearence of the world, of gods, and of men, as well as the moment when a privileged or exceptional individual, a prophet or god-incarnate, has come to spread the "good news," the moment of the Revelation. It must be accepted that this *illud tempus* is an absolute necessity without which no belief or rite could be justified. Let us take this moment to address the absurdity of the quarrel between revealed religions and nonrevealed religions; it is a false quarrel due to the imperialism of the Roman Catholic Church and Islam, the most sectarian religions ever known because of their claims that their doctrines hold a unique and definitive truth. All religions have been established starting from a revelation, whatever it may have been and whatever subsequent judgment may have been delivered upon it. Every religion is revealed. Or else, none are.

For the least that can be said is that the circumstances surrounding the revelation are unclear. With all due deference to the thurifers of Christianity, the historical existence of Christ has never been proven, and the official texts concerning it—within the Church—have been so truncated, rearranged, or badly translated, that it is impossible outside the domain of faith to know the truth. Moreover, the true founder of Christianity is Saint Paul, and his meeting with Jesus on the road to Damascus is only an individual mystic experience that cannot, under pain of improper inference, be the same for every Christian. The same is true for Muhammed. His visions, whatever they may have been, were unverifiable subjective phenomena. As for the prophet's preaching, because it was set down in writing later by his disciples, the Koran does not allow us to actually know what Muhammed really said. Jesus and Muhammed wrote nothing themselves and undoubtedly would be surprised at the manner in which their words have been collected. It is true that while Jesus made reference to Moses, and Muhammed to Abraham, both of them were also taking refuge behind an *illud tempus*. But Abraham appears to have been a symbolic, if not a mythological figure, and Moses is a half-historical, half-legendary figure. Furthermore, the revelation Moses experienced on Mount Sinai is yet another example of an individual phenomenon. But this did not prevent Saint Augustine and the Fathers of the Church from mocking the mythological legends of the pagans, which they considered to be the most feeble fables—in the perjorative sense of the word—or as inventions of the devil by which to deceive a helpless world, an opinion that, without doubt, smacks of the purest mythology.

It is necessary to repeat that without faith (individual experience), the *illud tempus* of so-called revealed religions has no more standing than the multiple mythological stories issued from the so-called pagan or nonrevealed religions. The latter include no greater quantity of absurdities than the former. But the foundational tales of Christianity and Islam are no more credible than those of Hinduism, the religion of ancient Greeks, or druidism. Affirming this evidence is not to supply proof of agnosticism, it is simply to claim that no one has the right to claim to be the sole and unique depositary of the truth.

The Celtic texts have been reproached for being of later provenance, of having been gathered after Christianization, and thus of being truncated, rearranged, and badly translated. How is this different from the Christian texts that were written in Aramaic after the death of Christ, translated into Greek, then retranslated into Latin using the Greek text as a base? Where then is the Aramaic text of the Gospels? Moreover, the first Christian text (in reality Judeo-Christian) is the Apocalypse of Saint John, which was followed by the Epistles of Paul. As for the Gospels, they were set down later as an illustration of the Epistles. Christians convinced of the authenticity of their texts would be ill advised to refuse to consider the Celtic Irish and Welsh texts as having the same value as they recognize (without discussion) in their own, for this would be intellectual dishonesty. But over the course of the centuries the socioeconomic stakes have been such that choices have had to have been made by ducking the issue.[1]

This doesn't mean to imply that druidism is the "true" religion. It soley signifies that druidism, and all the texts belonging to it, are worthy of interest for the same reasons as are the great texts of Christianity or any

other religion. One will discover within them, through their specific beliefs and particular rituals, an original conception of the world and especially of the "Otherworld," and the same spiritual quest of human beings
facing their destinies. And it is not without reason that the Celts, principally the Irish, moved smoothly and without great problems from druidism to Christianity.[2]

4

ᚹHERE DID DRUIDISM COME FROM?

Until the end of the nineteenth century—and still in our time in certain milieus where the ravages of "esoteric" syncretism have gone unchecked—people have believed and continue to believe that druidism is connected with the megalithic monuments. Tourist guidebooks have long provided lists and descriptions of "druidic monuments," that is to say dolmens, menhirs, cromlechs, and barrow mounds. Out of these inaccurate appropriations arises the apocryphal imagery of the bearded druid, sacrificing his victims on a dolmen being used as a sacrificial table. After all, Obelix of Gaul, if we are to believe the authors of a famous comic strip, was the carver of the menhirs.[1] This belief casually ignores the fact that the megalithic monuments in the West can be dated from the fourth to second millennium B.C., whereas the Celts didn't appear until the end of the Bronze Age (900–700 B.C.), and that their existence is only historically verified from around the year 500 B.C. The megalithic monuments, which, incidentally, denote an evolved religion of a spiritualist nature, were constructed by peoples of whom we know almost nothing other than the fact that they had very little in common with the Celts.

These strange monuments have excited the imagination, partly for the reason that very few genuine Celtic monuments have been discovered. But this is because before coming under Greek or Roman influence the Celts never built temples. As the megaliths represent the remnants of a civilization preceding the Romans, in the past there has been a huge temptation to consider them as druidic monuments, all the more so because a means of accurately dating them was not available. The problem arises from persisting with this misperception now that we possess incontestable methods of archaeological reference.

However, when we lean out over the past—and even more so the remote past—nothing is either totally true or totally false. If folk tradition has linked druidism to the megaliths, it is perhaps because there is a certain rapport between them, even if vague or secondary in nature. After all, the Irish mythological texts make the megalithic mounds into the dwellings of the ancient gods; this placement cannot be due to chance, and assuredly poses a problem that cannot be avoided by seeking refuge behind archaeological convictions. In truth, certain Roman sanctuaries have become Christian churches, and the majority of Christian chapels are located on sites where older religious worship—Greco-Roman as well as Celtic or prehistoric—was celebrated. There are also many examples in the past of the re-use and reutilization of certain monuments. Furthermore, religions never completely die. There always remain certain elements of beliefs or rituals of the old religion within the new one taking its place. Thus there is nothing astonishing in the fact that druidism inheirited a certain legacy from previous populations the Celts found established on the lands that they came to occupy and with whom—for good or ill—they formed new communities. What remains to be determined is the exact portion of that heritage that came from each side.

This does not resolve the problem of druidism's origin. Was it a religion imported by the Indo-European Celts? If so, from where did they bring it? Or was it an autochthonous religion that was completely reformed, rethought, and restructured by the conquering Celts? The structure of druidism appears to be very clearly Indo-European. But what about the other elements of druidism? What about the beliefs, rituals, and certain manners of thinking and reasoning about the Beyond?

I have said that until the beginning of this century, it was believed that everything from before the Romans belonged to the Gauls, which is to say belonged to the Celts. It is in this sense that folk tradition made druid monuments out of the dolmens and menhirs. It so happens that with the end of the eighteenth century came a great rise in the number of strange theories on the origin of druidism.

It must be said that this era manifested an interest in the druids and everything concerning the Celts that bordered on a sudden and rash passion. The Scotsman Mac Pherson "discovered" the oldest Erse (Gaelic) poetry, thanks to which he composed his Ossianic songs, a bestseller that influenced the entire romantic generation, even when it was proved beyond doubt as a forgery. Then there was Welshman Iolo Morganwg who "revealed" a bardic tradition forgotten for centuries, reconstituting a druidic ritual that was truthfully speaking more cultural and intellectual than a form of worship, and truly founded neodruidism. It too was proved a forgery, yet one with considerable influence. The Breton authors La Tour d'Auvergne (a first grenadier of the Empire) and Le Brigant considered the Celtic language as the mother tongue of the entire human race and in all seriousness declared that Adam and Eve had spoken Breton in Eden. The funniest thing about this is that their readers didn't laugh at this notion either. This opened the door through which Hersart de la Villemarqué would "miraculously" rediscover druidic chants in the Armorican folklore of his time. In this context, which stressed the Occidental contribution to civilization as opposed to that of the Orient, which people had always believed to have been the absolute source of all human adventure, it was normal that people interested themselves in druidism and gave it a Western origin.

This is what Fabre d'Olivet did. An astounding character, heir of the Encyclopedists, concomitantly philosopher, mythographer—and mythomaniac—historian, and moralist, he claimed to have discovered documents (which he never revealed, like Mac Pherson, Morganwg, and Villemarqué) that proved druidism had emanated from the oldest of Western religions.[2] He went even further, coolly recounting the contentions—some four thousand years before Christ—between a young druid by the name of Ram and some heretical sects, namely some savage and bloodthirsty druidesses. According to Fabre d'Olivet, Ram preferred to go into exile rather than fight with his brothers and sisters, so accompanied by some faithful followers he emigrated to the East and soon found himself in India where he established himself and preached his religion, which endures to this day. I'm sure his identity has become clear by now: Ram is none other than the Indian Rama, and Hinduism is what remains of a pure and austere druidism. Why didn't anyone think of that sooner?

Fabre d'Olivet never cited his sources. He hid behind the secret traditions to which he had access, playing on the mystery, as would have any good, self-respecting Hermetist—everyone knows there are secrets that should not be revealed imprudently. Underneath it all, Fabre d'Olivet knew perfectly well the deontological code of any professional journalist worthy of the name. It would be good to reread here what Fustel de Coulanges wrote in 1879 in regard to Iolo Morganwg whose *Mystery of the Bards* had just been translated into French (a very rough translation, incidentally). "When a man comes to us and says: here is a series of sentences; it is I who present them to you first, but they are not mine, they are twenty-centuries-old, and they constitute an ancient religious doctrine; it is true that I cannot show you anyone in history who has professed this religion for fifteen centuries, nor a single line in a book that contains the slightest indication of this doctrine; but it doesn't matter; it is very old and I have it from the druids through an uninterrupted tradition. If someone tells us this, are we supposed to believe it?"[3] Fustel de Coulanges has always sinned by an excess of rationalism, but there are cases where rationalism is simply synonymous with good sense.

This would not be such a serious thing, and Fabre d'Olivet would have been considered one of those original minds that abound in history if he did not have such a dubious posterity. His story of Ram is an excellent scenario for an epic or high budget film and could have been the inspiration for a masterpiece. Unfortunately, his declaration that the good Western druid Ram was the Indian Rama, founder of the Eastern Aryan religion, poisoned the minds of a good many generations of Westerners since, especially as this false myth was picked up anew by Édouard Schuré in his book *Les Grands Initiés* (The Great Initiates) that appeared in 1895.[4] This book is a sort of bible for those who claim to be Hermetists or esotericists, as well as for those who honestly seek to inform themselves on matters left too long in the shadows. It is precisely in the name of honesty that it becomes necessary to denounce the dangerous fraud of this author who passes for a sage and an initiate (we are never told, incidentally, just what he is an initiate of).[5]

Édouard Schuré brought nothing new to the story of Ram, but was content to follow blindly in the footsteps of Fabre d'Olivet, who he took at his word, not feeling even the slightest urge to verify the tale. This failure is quite serious, especially if one considers that the chapter devoted to Rama in *Les Grands Initiés* is that which opens the book and is presented as a kind of fundamental postulate that ultimately leads to Jesus, the last of the lineage started by Ram. But there is something else here that is much more disturbing. The writing of Schuré is imbued with that of Gobineau, and his discourse concerning the difficulties encountered by the druid Ram is not innocent, for it reveals a virulent racism, an obvious, albeit sneaky anti-Semitism, and a delirious enthusiasm for the Nordic white race.[6,7,8] It is hardly necessary to insist on the utilization of such writings between the two world wars, or on the influence they could exert at the present time within certain intellectual or spiritual groups who dare not speak their names aloud.

The important thing to keep in mind is that the history of Ram is due to the imagination of Fabre d'Olivet. There is nothing—no text, no tradition—that allows us to declare that druidism is of Western origin and that it subsequently emigrated to India where it transformed into Hinduism. If there are comparisons to be made—and there are more than one—between druidism and Hinduism, they are totally normal comparisons that can be explained by traditional community of origin between the Celts and the Indians of the Ganges plains. To say that Hinduism came from the West, or that druidism came from the East, would be not only untrue but absurd.

It is necessary to clear this terrain left fallow for too long so that we may see more accurately. Because of a lack of ancient documents and precise references, we are obliged to examine the origin of druidism within its natural context—the place where it knew its fullest development: Europe, and more particularly, Western Europe.

But there are still snares to be avoided there, one being the correlation established by certain parties between Pythagorism and druidism. The origin of this alleged correlation is from a bad interpretation of certain texts from classic antiquity. Thus, Ammianus Marcellinus, citing Timagenes, reported that next to the fortune-tellers and bards, "the druids preponderate because of their genius, as well that determined by the authority of Pythagoras" (Ammianus Marcellinus, XV, 9). This phrase in no way establishes a relationship between the science of the druids and that of Pythagoras, but merely implies that the druids possessed a science that was in conformance with the definition given by Pythagoras. Because of this faulty correlation of Pythagoras and druidism, other later authors—both Greek and Roman—embellished on the similarities between the two doctrines. Clement of Alexandria went so far as to claim that Pythagoras himself "listened to the Galatians and Brahmans" (*Stromata*, I, XV), which amounts to saying he was a student of the druids.[9] On the other hand, other writers whose testimonies are never very convincing, such as the Greek Hippolytus, portrayed druids the heirs of Pythagoras, whose knowledge they would have obtained thanks to "Zalmoxis, Thracian-born slave of Pythagoras, who lived in those lands following the death of his master and provided them [Celts] the opportunity to study his philosophical system" (*Philosphumena*, I, 25). Let us note in passing that the historical existence of Pythagoras, like Homer, is quite problematic. What is known of him is that there was a philosophical system and an astral religion placed under the name of Pythagoras—and that is all. Outside of the immortality of the soul, anyone very familiar with the Pythagorean doctrine can attest that it is impossible to find any commonalty of thought there with that of druidism. This is what is declared as well by two generally well-informed classical authors, Valery Maximus ("They are convinced that the souls of men are immortal: I would say that they were foolish if the ideas of these barbarians clad in breeches weren't the same as those of Pythagoras clad in pallium," II, 6, 60) and Diodorus Siculus ("The Pythagorean doctrine prevails among them, teaching that the souls of men are immortal," V, 28). Apparently the sole point of concordance was the belief in immortality that the materialistic Greeks and Romans found so shocking.

Druidism did not originate in the Mediterranean region. If it had, the Greeks and Romans would not have failed to say so. It is true that they generally revealed themselves as stupefied to observe the grandeur and eminence of a doctrine that did not belong to their world, and which, therefore, they classified, for lack of a better word, as "barbarian." This term essentially designated the inhabitants of Europe who had not yet been ranked under Roman domination and who had not been touched by Greek civilization. One is forced to recognize a certain Nordic character of this population (or group of populations), who were feared by the Greeks, but who also fired their imaginations. Is this a memory of the era during which the Indo-European Dorians, who came from the north, encountered the Acheans of the Hellenic peninsula and the Cretans of the Aegean Sea? The traditions concerning the cult of Delphi always made reference to an Hyperborean Apollo; Cicero even goes so far as to see four different Apollos, of whom the third "came from the regions that were hyperborean to Delphi" (*De natura Deorum*, III, 23). All this evidence is an allusion to the mythological tale concerning Apollo's arrival in Delphi, his combat with the serpent Python, and his ultimate victory. In historical terms, this tale concerns the abrupt arrival of the Dorians who came from the common cradle of Indo-Europeans, and who had not yet become differentiated in central Europe following their migration from central Asia. These Dorians, who possessed the use of iron, were formidable warriors and colonized the Acheans of the Minoan Bronze Age civilization, a people of herders and planters. But in religious and sociocultural terms, this concerns the disappearance of the tellurian cult worship represented by Python, image of the sanctified Earth, and its replacement by a solar cult, all of which came from the north, from Hyperborea, where the sun played a primordial role that was regarded as essential for human survival.

This Nordic aspect of the Apollo cult was in evidence for the ancient Greeks themselves. Citing the revelations of the Phocaean navigator Pytheas, Diodorus Siculus even established a close relationship between the Delphic cult and the Isle of Britain. In fact it was in Britain that Latona-Leto was born, "which explains why the islanders venerated Apollo in particular. They are all, so to speak, priests of this god. There can also be seen in this island a vast enclosure dedicated to Apollo, as well as a magnificent, round temple, and numerous offerings. Apollo is supposed to come down to this island every nineteen years" (Diodorus, II, 47). It should be noted that Pytheas, a Greek from Marseilles, was not at all astounded to discover on the Isle of Britain an Apollonian cult similar to the Greek cult. Also, if questions were asked on the subject of the large enclosure dedicated to Apollo, namely in regard to its location (perhaps this is one of the Amesbury enclosures on the Salisbury Plain), it is quite conceivable that the magnificent temple could be the monument of Stonehenge, whose connection with the solstice sunrise is beyond doubt. But the problem lies in the fact that *Stonehenge isn't Celtic.* It was constructed in the Megalithic era, around 2000 B.C., and then reworked twice—on separate occasions—during the Bronze Age. It often appears in Celtic tradition, however, if only through the legend that presents this monument as the magic work of Merlin, or in the Arthurian tales that place Arthur's last battle in this immediate vicinity.[10] This incontestably raises the question of Celts, and therefore the druids, incorporating into their culture a tradition that preceded their arrival. Moreover, the solar cult's period of triumph must be sought not within the Celtic Iron Age, but within the Nordic Bronze Age.[11] As for

Apollo's descent to Stonehenge every nineteen years, this leads to numerous speculations. Nineteen years is in fact a cycle at the end of which the lunar calendar coincides with the solar calendar. It is also the cycle adopted, under the name of the cycle of Denys le Petit, by the papacy in the seventh century to determine the dating of the movable feast of Easter. But it is precisely this cycle of nineteen years that the Christianized Celts obstinately refused to accept.[12] All of this remains somewhat unclear.

In any case, it is within the Celtic framework that the origin of druidism should be sought, because, as we have said, druidism could have only existed within the structures of a Celtic society, which condemned in advance all hypotheses concerning a vague, autochthonous predruidism that the Celts would have found among the people they conquered, and which they would have modified and improved according to their own conceptions. This is not so much a question of rejecting the influence or participation in the establishment of druidism by these autochthonous populations, as it is a matter of claiming that druidism took shape within a society that was structured by the Celts, but that did not consist solely of Celts. It is in western Europe that the origins of druidism must be sought, because it was only western Europe that received the indelible mark of Celtic civilization, thus giving proof that, historically speaking, it became implanted there very early.

Here again we must appeal to Caesar's testimony, which is the oldest available. In speaking of the druids he asserts that "their doctrine was established in Britain, and from there, it is thought, brought to Gaul" (VI, 13). He also adds that during his time, it was still necessary to go to the Isle of Britain if one wanted to perfect his grasp of this doctrine. This doesn't prove that druidism originated in Great Britain, but simply implies that the most renowned and most competent schools of druidism were located there. But this constitutes an important indication that is corroborated by numerous Irish sources. For the Gaelic Irish, among whom, so it would seem, druidism was not only the most fully developed but also the best maintained, have never claimed that the druidic doctrine and institution were indigenous. Quite the contrary, when a druid or young person wished to complete their studies, he went to Great Britain—either to Scotland, Wales, or Britain itself. This was the case for the Ulsterman hero, Cuchulainn, who met up with several of his companions again in Scotland. This was also the case for the children of Calatin, who at Queen

Medb's instigation and to avenge their father on Cuchulainn, went to study in Alba (a term that indiscriminately means Scotland or the whole of Great Britain) and there learned "magical and diabolical teachings"; then they sought out "all the druids of the world, and received their teachings until they had attained the overpopulated regions of hell" (*Ogam,* XIII, 509). Taking into account the bias of the Christian transcriber, who clearly intended to liken druidism to diabolical magic, this testimony shows us that the ancient Irish didn't believe that their isle was the cradle of druidism.

The Battle of Mag Tured, another Irish text, and without doubt one of the most archaic, brings to light an interesting detail that has the merit— or inconvenience—of opening the door to a larger debate. It concerns the Tuatha de Danann, or "Folk of the Goddess Dana," a mysterious people who, in the pseudohistoric Irish tradition, are supposed to have immediately preceded the Sons of Milhead, the Gaels. "The Tuatha de Danann were in the Isles of the North of the World, learning science, magic, druidism, sorcery, and wisdom, and they surpassed all the sages in the pagan arts."[13] Two essential notions should be taken from this short passage: first, the Tuatha de Danann were the people who introduced druidism; second, they learned druidism in the Isles of the North of the World.

The Isles of the North of the World pose a problem. If their existence is taken literally, this places the emphasis on the Nordic character of druidism, which in any event appears to be incontestable. But in such a case, where are these isles located? It could be answered that for the Irish, Scotland is a northern island, all the more so as Scotland is surrounded by a multiple number of small islands, of which certain of them, like Iona, became monastic centers (thanks to Saint Colum-Cil), were certainly druid sanctuaries once upon a time. This term could further designate the entire Isle of Britain, or even certain islands more to the south but still in the "north of the world," such as the famous Mona (Anglesey), described by Tacitus as an important druidic center, and of which the historiographer Solon makes mention when describing the Isle of the Siluriens: the isle is "separated by a strait, that is difficult to cast off from, occupied by the Breton people of the Domnonii; the inhabitants still observe the old customs; they don't use money, they honor the gods, and men and women both practice all the sciences of augury" (XXII, 7). One could also see Sena here, the famous Isle of Sein, where priestesses, who in truth were more fairylike than real, resided, and who, according to Pomponius Mela, "reserved their remedies and their predictions for those who only journeyed and sailed there with the aim of consulting them" (III, 6). Why not also envision the sacred Isle of Heligoland on the eastern side of the North Sea? Many curious traditions persist concerning this isle located in a region once occupied by the Celts. Some have considered it to be a remnant of Atlantis.[14] The Isles of the North of the World wouldn't be the Isle of Oesel in the Baltic, once named Abalum *(Insula Malifera),* in which both the name of Apollo and that of the Isle of Avalon are found. And one can go back as far as the remote Thule, the Ultima Tulé of which Greek authors such as Polybius (putting the accounts of the navigator Pytheas in doubt) have left us such fantastic descriptions as follows: "Pytheas has misled the public . . . about Thule and the neighboring countries by declaring that there is neither, earth, sea, nor air in those places, but a blend of all three elements quite similar to a marine lung lying under the earth, sea, and air that links them together in such a way that it is impossible either to sail or walk over this matter" (Polybius, XXXIV, 5). It's probably in these latitudes where the strange Dead Sea is located that the Cimbri called the Marimaruse (Pliny, *Natural History,* IV, 27). Taking into account the fact that the Cimbri in question were Celts, the etymology of the word Marimaruse is correct from a Celtic standpoint, but Thule smacks of the Germanic realm, dating back at least from the high Middle Ages, and it is difficult know what to make of this.

It is more than likely that the Isles of the North of the World should be taken symbolically. Islands, as well as the North, are traditionally the abode of the gods, supernatural beings, or just simply "those who know." In the mind of the Irish storytellers, druidism, which in any case didn't originate in Ireland, could have come only from these mythical isles located in a no-less-mythical North. We will come across this theme again in regard to the Otherworld, such as the Celts conceived it. This process can only guarantee druidism's letters of nobility, which, as a sacred doctrine, must necessarily have a sacred origin.

We have seen that the tale *The Battle of Mag Tured* views the Tuatha de Danann as being the ones who introduced druidism to Ireland. There is an essential point that must be made clear here: the Tuatha de Danann, the fourth people to occupy postdiluvian Ireland, at least according to the traditional pseudohistory told by the Irish of the Middle Ages, and who were the immediate predecessors of the Gaels, and played a considerable role in the mythology and religion not only of Ireland but of all the Celts. As their name indicates, the Tuatha de Danann (Folk of the Goddess Dana), were a people of the gods. It was they who made up the Irish pantheon, and certain of them were encountered in Great Britain and on the continent, sometimes under identical names such as Lugh and Ogma-Ogmios, or under different names that didn't prevent them from being recognized, such as Dagda-Sucellos or Dagda-Taranis, not to speak of the countless deities known only under local cognomens.

Thus, we are in the heart of myth, almost in total theogony. But in all mythological tradition—and this is even more true when speaking of the Celts—one must always ask if the myth doesn't overlay a certain historical reality, either by a process of ephemerization, or else in order to be understandable and transmissible, myth must incarnate, must materialize in fiction, as well as in history. To limit ourselves to declaring the entire Irish tradition mythological, and that not even the slightest historical reference can be brought to bear upon it, is a logical position that allows us to better examine the motives proper to myth, but it is also deprives us of an opening into the real. By stressing the dichotomy between the real and the imaginary, one arbitrarily disassociates two tendencies that coexist within the human being that can, when studied conjointly, provide strong explanations for quotidian behavior. It is through refusing to accept the opposition between myth and reality, myth and history, that we can learn more about the adventure of the spirit.

There is no doubt about the Nordic heritage, even if only symbolic, of the Tuatha de Danann. Tradition makes them the descendants of Nemed, whose race was the second occupant of postdiluvian Ireland. The meaning of Nemed is "the sacred," which indicates the existence of a divine genealogy for the Tuatha. According to the *Leabhar Gabala*, the Book of Conquests, a large mythico-historical compilation from twelfth-century Ireland, the ancestors of the Tuatha were located in Scandinavia, but from the time of the invasions of the Vikings Scandanavia had become a convenient locale for the Otherworld. According to John Keating's *History of Ireland*, it was in Greece that the Tuatha were settled, but that they had sojourned seven years in Scandinavia, then in the north of Scotland, before making landfall in Ireland. In any case, the majority of texts are clear: the Tuatha de Danann first set foot in Ireland on the Monday of Beltane (the first of

May, the second great festival in the Celtic year), and they burned their ships, which encircled them with a halo of smoke, rendering them even more mysterious. This is an allusion to the fire rituals of Bel that are characteristic of the May Day festival. These Tuatha arrived with the four fundamental talismans that constantly reappear in Celtic mythological tradition (even in the versions as recent as the Arthurian romances): the Stone of Fàl (or Coronation Stone), the fiery Spear of Lugh (which is perhaps the same as the one in the famous Grail Procession), the Sword of Nuada, which can only be wielded by its rightful owner (as with Arthur's Excalibur), and the Dagda's inexhaustible cauldron (an obvious prototype of the Grail).

All of this, it is well understood, signifies that the Tuatha brought with them a religious doctrine, a mythological tradition, and also a ritual that was characterized by magic or sacred objects of which later literary tradition would make great use. As was said of the Tuatha in the short text of the fourteenth-century manuscript *Yellow Book of Lecan,* "science, druidism, and deviltry were at their service" (*Mythological Texts,* I, 80)— the term *deviltry* obviously incorporating all those practices that medieval Christians could not accept.

There is a very strong temptation to see the populations of the Bronze Age—more accurately the Megalithic era—in the Tuatha de Danann. They are after all peoples that preceded the Celts, just as the Tuatha are the predecessors of the Gaels. And we will look at everything that druidism could have harvested from the legacy of these peoples. Another temptation, is to see these Nordic people as the common ancestor of both the Germans and the Celts. There is no shortage of arguments for such a theory. First, both Celts and Germans are of the Indo-European tradition stemming from the same beginning, but traveling into Europe by different routes. Second, the writers of classic antiquity have often confused them with the Scythians: the Celts all came from regions located east of the Rhine, probably from Harz, and they long neighbored the Germans on the shores of the Baltic and North Seas.[15] If we compare the vocabularies, it is clear that the Celts, more evolved than the Germans in an earlier era, have contributed to the social constitution of the Germanic group.[16] Last, Celtic mythology and Germano-Scandinavian mythology offer numerous points of convergence, the later influence of Ireland upon Iceland, and vice versa, being taken into account.

There is one thing of capital importance that can be said in oppostiion to these attempts of pre–Indo-European identification of the Tuatha de Danann: druidism can only exist within the structures of a Celtic society. Because of this, it is impossible to consider the Tuatha de Danann as a pre-Celtic populace, since they brought druidism to Ireland, even if only in a symbolic manner. The argument will be made that if this concerns both a pre-Celtic and pre-Germanic population then its social structure could only be Indo-European. But this has nothing to do with the absolute Celtic nature that we are obliged to recognize in druidism. If the Tuatha de Danann were really—or mythically—the people who introduced druidism into Ireland, they must necessarily have been Celts.

We've said that the Tuatha disembarked in Ireland on the day of Beltane. Their Celtic festival calendar is thus already fixed. This in itself doesn't constitute solid proof because the other mythic invasions of Ireland also took place on festival dates of the Celtic calendar—at least this is what was asserted by the Irish of the Middle Ages who refused to envision the ancient peoples of Ireland in any sociocultural context other than the traditional one of the Celts. The first postdiluvian occupant of Ireland, Partholon, had three druids. One of the four chiefs of Nemed, the second invader, was Iarbonel, the "diviner," or, in other words, a druid. And when the third invaders, the Fir Bolg, took possession of Ireland, they apportioned it into five sections, strictly in accordance with the Gaelic principle of "five-fifths," or of "five kingdoms." Whoever the successive invaders of Ireland may have been, they are all presented within the tradition gathered together during the Middle Ages as entirely Celtic, and more precisely Gaelic. Not a single Irish person of the Middle Ages would have doubted this. It is true that people of the Middle Ages never entertained the notion of anachronism, but the Irish had, as did other Celts, a very decided tendency to consider history anachronistically, never having had any reason to think otherwise. This hardly makes the job of the modern historian any easier.

Moreover, if one follows the course of the stories about the different invasions of Ireland, an absolute coherence emerges. The first invasion in antediluvian times, which was bought about by a woman named Cessair, stands entirely outside of history. The first postdiluvian invasion was that of Partholon, who symbolized the creation of the new human being. But the reign of Partholon was primitive, unreservedly down-to-earth and disorganized. This invasion was followed by that of Nemed, the "sacred," whose kingdom was governed by religions norms. It was Nemed's sons who went into exile, separated into two groups, and who, each in their turn, returned to invade Ireland, first as the Fir Bolg, and next as the Tuatha de Danann. The Fir Bolg or Bolg Men, who were often represented as the "Men of the Sack," following an analogous etymology, and who historians have often attempted to declare as Belgians (again because of the same etymology), were in reality "regulars," warriors, the word *bolg*'s provenance in all likelihood from the same root as the Latin *fulgur,* "thunderbolt."[17] Irish society appears to have been policed, structured by a warrior caste that established order. For as in Greek or Germano-Scandinavian mythology, the giants were always very close by. And the giants symbolized the Chaos against which human beings struggled. In this instance, Chaos is represented in Irish mythology by the strange people called the Fomor, a people with whom all the new invaders of Ireland inevitably clashed and who either had to be defeated or appeased by means of treaties. Finally the Tuatha de Danann appeared, the other branch of Nemed's descendants. They were the gods, and they brought with them both the doctrine and practice of druidism, which is to say the social structure that was indispensable so that humans, the Sons of Milhead (otherwise known as the Gaels) could land there in their turn. These Gaels had no other task but to enter into a practical divine framework, since that was the motivation behind the druidic religion: to make the kingdom below just the same as the kingdom on high.

The cohesion and logic of this tale will be noted, whether expressed in its entirety as in *The Book of Conquests* or Keating's *History,* or in the more fragmentary accounts found in other texts such as those about the two Battles of Mag Tured, the first recounts the combat between the Tuatha and the Fir Bolg, the second that of the Tuatha against the Fomors. If all these elements are taken together and put in the form of a table, some interesting conclusions can be drawn:

First Stage: before the Deluge. Cessair, the primordial woman.
   First draft of the world and humanity.
Second Stage: after the Deluge.
First invasion: Partholon. Re-creation. Materialism.
Second invasion: Nemed. Appearance of the Sacred. Spirituality.

Third invasion: Fir Bolg. Warriors. The upholding of order.
Fourth invasion: The Tuatha de Danann. Gods. Druidism. Spiritual and material science.
Fifth invasion: The Sons of Milhead. Current era. Application.

An examination of the three postdiluvian invasions shows that they were complementary. Parthalon represented the regeneration of the human species, for he in some respects is Brahma, if one wishes to draw from Indian symbolism. But then the spiritual principle appeared, that being the Varuna aspect that corresponded to the "sacred" Nemed. To this soon would be joined the warrior principle, the Mitra aspect, that overlays the Fir Bolg. The world—that of the Gaels, was therefore governed by the divine couple Varuna-Mitra (representing spiritual magic and warrior magic, respectively), after they had been created by the god of beginnings. The principle of the divine couple (priest-king) seen here is in perfect conformance with one of the most widespread Indo-European structures.

Considering that the first invasion was a period of creation, and the fifth one of putting the principles into practice, the great lines of the trifunctional division of Indo-European societies can be recognized in the three intermediate invasions. In fact, Nemed represents the sacerdotal class, the Fir Bolg the warrior class, and the Tuatha de Danann the third class. This third proposition may appear shocking: How could the gods be symbols of the third function, that of the producers? The answer is simple. The Tuatha de Danann were not only experts in religion, wisdom, and magic, but in science as well. To say science is to say craft—even more true for a people who had always refused to conceive of a dichotomy between the sacred and the profane, and who had always done their all to glorify manual labor (one of the reasons, incidentally, for their painless conversion to Christianity). The gods of the Tuatha de Danann appeared not only as brilliant warriors, but also as specialists of all the arts, medicine, carpentry, metallurgy, and so on. The greatest of them all, the god Lugh is represented as "knowing how to do everything." He is the "Master of All the Arts." The Tuatha de Danann, therefore, arrive to crown the edifice; they alone will allow the divine plan to be put into action. They are the gods incarnated. Now the Sons of Milhead can come to occupy the lands.

By themselves the Tuatha de Danann represented the entirety of Indo-European society, that is to say its idealization in the spirit of the druidic tradition—*the divine model that humankind must apply.* And it is not contemporary mythologists or sociologists who are saying this. It is Geoffrey Keating, the author of the very valuable *History of Ireland.* Keating breaks up the three terms that make up the name of the Tuatha (on his own authority or is he handing down an older tradition? We do not know). This gives us three categories: Tuatha, the nobility, De, the druids, and Dana, the artisans. The etymologies are correct: the Tuatha are obviously in the business of warrior noblemen; the gods being druids, the druids are also gods; the people of the artisans constitutes a class called the *aes dana.* So it probably is not useful to seek the origin of druidism anywhere but among the Celts themselves. And why not trust Caesar when he declares that the druidic doctrine was elaborated on the Isle of Britain, and from there spread to Gaul, and then, of course to all the other Celtic countries?

5

GODS AND MEN

Every religion has its system of absolute reference, in this instance one or several deities whose personality, practice, and behavior are exemplary. There is no question of trying to establish if this god or these gods are real entities existing outside the human world where they govern and advise living individuals in accordance with a predetermined plan and precise finality, or if they are simply idealized projections of the human mind tormented by the desire to perfect the world through the justification of its own existence. In this type of debate the theme of Pascal's wager is always relevant, and, whatever the solution chosen, all that can be spatially and temporally established is the presence of deities in whom human beings have believed, and with whom they have—in reality or symbolically—established interdependent relationships, mainly in the form of acts of worship. In the same vein, it should be noted that tales exist that place these deities on stage and call for them to act out a series of significant actions—tales that, for lack of a better word, are qualified as "mythological." It is these deities that it is advantageous to examine through what history, archaeology, and tradition tells of them.

Druidism, like other religions, had its gods, even though we still often find it necessary to ask what the real significance was that the druids gave to this word: did *gods* signify personalized gods or specialized functions of the deity? But that's another issue. We know of these gods through the testimony of ancient authors, votive and funerary inscriptions, artistic representations, and, above all, the Irish and Welsh tales that later on give us a more fully fleshed-out picture rather than one transformed that merely gives heroic proportions. This hardly facilitates exact pinpointing. "Gallic deities have often remained little more personalized than the *numina,* those mysterious forces to which it is possible to attribute certiain characteristics. . . . Many of these deities often are merely names to which we attribute characteristics in a fairly arbitrary manner, starting from comparisons contrived by the Romans with their own gods, or through hypothetical mergers."[1] It is impossible not to think of these heroes from epic Irish tales who often utter the famous saying: "By the god my tribe swears by!" But the names of these gods differ from one country to the next, and even if certain consistencies can be discerned, they are not reliable.

> The linguistic group to which it is possible to attach the name of a god is not proof that the deity bearing this name actually belongs to the old pantheon of the people speaking the tongue. Such is the case for all those Apollos of the Gallo-Roman era whose names are substituted for other names, which are not always Celtic—covering the original names of these ancient indigenous deities.[2]

As in similar instances, we are again obliged to look at Caesar's testimony as it is the oldest and the most precise on record.

> Among the gods, they most worship Mercury. There are numerous images of him; they declare him the inventor of all the arts, the guide for every road and journey, and they deem him to have the greatest influence for all commerce and travel. After him in importance are Apollo, Mars, Jupiter, and Minerva. Of these deities they have almost the same concept as all other nations: Apollo drives away disease, Minerva supplies the first principles of arts and crafts, Jupiter holds the empire of heaven, Mars controls wars." (Caesar, VI, 17, 341)

Note the privileged place held here by Mercury underscored by his multiple duties, followed by the clearly secondary triad represented by Apollo–Mars–Jupiter. Comparatively, this last grouping contains an anomaly in that Jupiter, master of the gods, does not appear to have received special esteem. Last, there is Minerva in the role of artisan. But when Caesar claims that the Gauls have almost the same conception of the gods as other peoples, essentially meaning the Greeks and Romans, some skepticism is understandable. Caesar's attempt at this kind of interpretation is itself proof to the contrary.

> For a Roman, the universe stops at the borders of his country's possessions. Beyond that universe exist only ignorant people of whom all that matters is that they are exploited for Rome's benefit. These peoples had original religious conceptions, but in his pride and in his belief that Rome was uniquely civilized, Caesar took the Roman gods as the measure by which to base his description of the Gallic religion. It would not be objective to believe that the Gauls had beliefs similar to those of the Romans.[3]

In other words, this attempt at interpretation by Caesar should not be taken literally; nevertheless, the fact remains that in describing Gallic religion, Caesar cited the existence of a great god (who wasn't Jupiter), three other gods of lesser standing, but who were still a source of great veneration, and a goddess. Already this outlines a divine hierarchy.

And this hierarchy was essentially Indo-European.

> Caesar, the friend of several druids, had excellently defined . . . the five principal gods of the Gauls; he defined them by social criteria, he disbursed them—as patrons and not as symbols—throughout the great activities of social life: the first, incorporated into Mercury, was the inventor of the arts, the master of roads, and the regent of commerce and profit; another god, a Jupiter, had celestial sovereignty; a Mars figure presided over war; an Apollo drove off illness; and, finally, a Minerva was the teacher of vocations. This corresponds to the overall theory of the world that can be found in the Irish epic.[4]

Indeed it is the Irish epic that allows us to understand and explain Caesar's testimony, principally the second version of *The Battle of Mag Tured* in which the general staff of the Tuatha de Danann constitutes an almost complete list of the Celtic pantheon.

6

THE GOD
ABOVE THE GODS

The Gallic Mercury of whom Caesar wrote and of whom he said there were numerous statues (simulacra) spread throughout Gaul during his time doesn't have much in common with the Roman Mercury or the Greek Hermes except for patronage of roads on one hand and commerce on the other.[1] Caesar did not provide us with the Gallic god's indigenous name, but we can easily reconstruct it from Lugos or Lugu, a name that has served to form toponyms as important as those of Lyon, Loudon, or Leyde, all of which are *lugudunum* (Forts of Lugu). This is also the Irish Lugh from *The Battle of Mag Tured*.

The presentation of Lugh, which is very complete, enters into the framework of the narration of events that occurred in Ireland between the first and second battles of Mag Tured. With the aid of the Fomor, the Tuatha de Danann vanquished the Fir Bolg, those mysterious giants who are a representation of Chaos, or the disorganized powers. But, as a consequence of the incapacity of their king, Nuada, who lost an arm and could no longer govern, the Tuatha fell into a state of dependency upon the Fomor, who, in turn, greatly exploited them.

But provided with a silver arm, Nuada again becomes king and invites the leaders of the Tuatha to a banquet. The banquet room is carefully guarded by a porter who does not let anyone enter who doesn't possess an art that is original and different from those already inside (we are in the domain of specialization to the extreme, and no duplication is permissable). The banquet gathers together only the intellectual, warrior, and artisanal elite of the Tuatha de Danann. It was at this point that a young warrior by the name Samildanach (Master of All the Arts) appears, "good-natured and handsome, with all the accoutrements of a king."[2]

The young warrior demands to enter. His name is requested and thus it is learned that he is "Lugh Lonnandsclech, son of Cian, the son of Diancecht, and of Ethlinn, the daughter of Balor."[3] The two grandfathers of Lugh are from the paternal side, Diancecht, healer-god of the Tuatha de Danann, and from the maternal side, Balor, the formidable one-eyed warrior giant whose single eye can strike anyone down dead when its heavy eyelid is lifted with a polished hook by four men.[4] Balor, who possesses this obvious cyclopean and titanesque character, is one of the chiefs of the Fomor—a fact that is not gratuitous. Being both of the Tuatha and the Fomor, Lugh shares a unique double nature that gives him his exceptional character and in the end places him beyond all classification. In fact not only does he have the organizational power of the Tuatha, one socialized and spiritualized to the extreme, but in addition he possesses the instinctive, disorganized, but terribly effective, brute strength of the Fomor. Lugh is a veritable synthesis of these two combative and opposi-tional forces. He is the very incarnation of a philosophical monism, the personalized declaration of the Celtic refusal of the principle of duality. On another level Lugh can be considered the most striking example of what surrealists would strive to carry out based on the discoveries of Freud.[5]

When the young warrior insists on entering, the porter asks him: "What art do you practice? For no one comes to Tara without an art."[6] Lugh answers that he is a carpenter. The porter replies that they already have one. Lugh then says in succession that he is a smith, champion, warrior, harper, poet-historian, magician, physician, cupbearer, and a fine crafts-man. To each of these the porter responds that there is already one there and refuses Lugh entry to the feast hall of Tara. Then Lugh says, "Go and ask the king if he has any one man that can do all these things, and if he has, I will not ask entry into Tara. The porter then goes to find Nuada and tells him of his conversation with the Samildanach. The king can only agree that in fact there is not a single "master of all the arts" at his banquet.

But this is not sufficient to allow Lugh's entry. The king challenges Lugh to a chess match, and only when Lugh wins is he then permitted to enter. But the god Ogma subjects him to another trial. Ogma, a clearly Herculean character, pulls up an enormous stone "that requires four times twenty yoke of oxen to move" and shouts a challenge at Lugh. In response Lugh picks up the stone and hurls it across the house. This is not the end of it, however. Lugh next has to play the harp. "The young warrior then played a tune of sleep to the king and his troops that first night. He cast them into a deep sleep that lasted from that hour to the same hour of the following day. He played them a smiling tune, and they were all put in a state of joy and gaiety. He played a tune of sorrow with such skill that they wept and mourned."[7] Thus Lugh passed his tests, and Nuada took counsel with the other chiefs of the Tuatha. In the end "Samildanach . . . sat upon the throne of the king and the king stood there before him for thirteen days."[8] This was a triumph for Lugh, and this triumph, accompanied by the temporary effacement of the king, is reminiscent of certain Indo-European traditions, Germanic ones in particular.[9]

All this gives Lugh the appearance of a figure who is outside of all categories and outside of all duties because he simultaneously assumes them all—which his answers to the porter clearly throw into relief. He belongs to the sacerdotal class as a harpist, a poet-historian, magician, physician, and cupbearer; to the military class as a champion and hero; and to the third class, that of producers, as a carpenter, smith, and artisan. The claims he flaunted at the entrance to the chamber of Tara were put to the test inside. By the trial of the stone he manifested his strength, thus his membership in the military class. His sacerdotal character was made evident through the trial of the harp. There was no artisanal trial (although perhaps there was one in an earlier version of the tale), but the trial of the chess match made Lugh's royal ability obvious. Chess was a game reserved for the king and, by the intrinsic value of the game itself, constituted a theoretical and symbolic exaltation of royalty's functioning.[10] In short, by winning the match Lugh was chosen from among the military class to occupy—even though it was but temporarily—the royal office. Through this same test he proved his worth as a tactician, showing himself capable of assuming the duties of the commander-in-chief, duties that he would assume during the preparations for, and the unfolding of, the Battle of Mag Tured. Through his double affiliation (Tuatha and Fomor) and by his position without class, Lugh allowed the world to find its balance, favoring the organized forces (the Tuatha) and mastering the unconscious, instinctive forces (the Fomorian giants). This was what Odin never successfully achieved in the much more pessimistic Germanic mythology in which the equilibrium between the gods and the giants was always threatened.

In another version of the second Battle of Mag Tured, Lugh is described with all the splendor belonging to his rank. As his outer garment, he

> donned his marvelous and never-before-seen apparel from beyond the sea, to wit his linen shirt embroidered with gold thread over his white skin, and his well-known and comfortable tunic with its customary multicolored satin from the brilliant Land of Promise.[11] He also put on his large and handsome smock of very pure gold, with its fringe, its clasps and borders, his solid war belt with its buckle. He put on his new cuirass of gold with its beautiful carbuncle stones and beautiful gold encrusted knobs from which echoed the calls of a multiform and unknown army. He took the large and terrible gold shield made of purple-red wood with a gold point that was very sharp and terrible, a magnificent umbo of pale bronze, and a perfectly set gold boss with taut and interlacing chains of old silver and splendid straps inscribed with numerous signs. In one hand he took up his long, dark, and very sharp sword and, in the other, his large, cruel, empoisoned lance with its thick and heroic five-point shaft. He seized the slingshot to break the shields of the heroes who were swift with their weapons. He sought out his battle club with the heavy head to use against those with hard skulls.[12]

And his comportment was no less impressive: "It was the anger of an enraged lion, the noise of the sea with large waves, the grumbling of the blue-fringed ocean, the anger of the speedy hero, Lugh, massacring the enemies, fighting against their tributes and defending Ireland."[13] Certainly there is a great difference between these enthusiastic descriptions—in which the "patriotic" Irish spirit comes to light—and the plastic representations of the Gallo-Roman Mercury, the god of the exchange, who, with his petty bourgeois, nouveau-riche countenance, pales beside Lugh. The Romanized Gauls saw Lugh only in his character of the guardian of commerce attached to his third office. This is hardly compatible with Caesar's assertion that Lugh was ranked above all the other gods.

The Gallic Lugu obviously had been the object of a very important religious worship. His name, as we have said, is connected to the city of

Lyon, which, incidentally, was a kind of sacred city for the independent Gauls. A legend retold by the psuedo-Plutarch recounts that the city was founded at a site designated by a flock of crows. Interestingly, the crow is the symbolic animal of Lugh, which could appear paradoxical—the name of Lugh refers to a root word signifying "light" and "whiteness" (Greek *leukos,* white, and Latin, *lux,* light) and the crow, by its black color, seems to express more the night or darkness. But it is a fact that Lugh is linked, in one way or another, to the crow through tradition in artistic representation, as is clearly alluded to by the myth of the founding of Lyon. In any event, the sacred symbolism of Lyon is attached to the worship of Lugh. We know that the great Celtic festivals took place four times a year—forty days after a solstice or an equinox—the first of November, February, May, and August. In Ireland the August festival is called Lugnasad, "the nuptials of Lugh," and tradition explicitly states that it was Lugh himself who instituted this festival that consists of a great gathering on the plain of Meath in honor of his adoptive mother Tailtiu (an ancient version of Talantio), a kind of telluric deity. When the Romans organized Gaul, or rather the Gauls, they made Lyon the intellectual, political, and religious capital of this large group.[14] In Lyon, Augustus instituted the feasts of the first day of August—his month—feasts obviously consecrated to the worship of Rome and its Emperor. And it was was not by chance that it was at Lyon that the Gauls held assemblies known as the Concilia Galliarum. Nor should we be surprised that Lyon was the first Gallic city to be affected by Christianity. And let us not forget that in the nomenclature of the Roman Catholic Church, the metropolitan archbishop of Lyon always bears the official title of "Primate of the Gauls."

Lugh, both poorly and successfully incorporated into Mercury, endured in the devotions of the Gallo-Romans. Archaeology has brought to light more than 450 inscriptions dedicated to Mercury, and more than 200 representations, statues, or bas-reliefs, many more than for other gods in Gaul. He often bears diverse surnames that indicate a more specified function or the site of the worship, thus the Mercurius Arvernus, whose legend poses no problem, or again the Mercurius Iovantucarus literally the "Protector of Youth." From the onset of Christianity numerous sanctuaries became Mount Saint Michaels, sites that transferred the luminous and solar duties of Lugh to the luminous archangel. At times this Mercury is represented by the classic Roman image with the petasus and the caduceus. Other times he is accompanied by an animal who takes on more importance than in the Roman tradition, or the specifically Gallo-Roman image of the ram-headed serpent appears. And other times still again, instead of being a young man or an athletic adult, Mercury is an aged, bearded man clad in a woolen garment and holding a staff (possibly the traveler's staff). A Strasbourg bas-relief represents Mercury with a hammer, likening him to a deity of a Martian nature, or, if an Irish reference is used, of the Ogma or Dagda type. Finally, certain representations associate Mercury with phallic worship, while others depict him in the company of a goddess, the latter found mainly in eastern and southeastern Gaul where that goddess bears the name of Rosmerta, "the Provider," a characteristic of the third office. It must finally be noted that one of the scholias in Lucan's *Pharsalia* identifies Mercury with Teutas, a deity who forms part of the triad enunciated by Lucan himself, but a god who may or may not have been a regional diety.[15] And in Reims there is a three-headed Mercury, which brings us back to one of the characteristics of Celtic tradition: the importance of the number three and of trebling.

At the least, however, it can be said that Lugh, such as he is described in the Irish epics, is greatly removed from the Mercury conceived by the Romans. He has more affinity with the Greek Hermes, perhaps, if only because he protects roads and travelers, but moreso because as the master of all the arts he is the repository of the gods' secrets. Lugh also bears surnames: Samildanach, Lonnbeimenech (he who knocks furiously), Lamfada (of the long hand), or even Grianainech (a name in which the Irish word meaning "sun" or "heat" can be recognized). This, linked to the meaning of the word "lugh" (luminous), gives a solar character to this figure, and it is not surprising that worship of Lugh was replaced by that of Saint Michael. But Lugh doesn't seem comparable to the Greco-Roman Apollo, even though his attributes are the crow (like Apollo) and more importantly the lance brought from Gorias (one of the towns of the Isles in the North of the World) by the Tuatha de Danann: "No battle was won against it or he that held it in his hand."[16] This lance could very well symbolize the rays of the sun that bring heat, illnesses, and death, but also healing, as every divine object is ambivalent in nature.[17]

In reality the sole Indo-European god with whom Lugh is most like is the Germanic Odin-Wotan. The two even have features in common. Lugh, like Odin, is superior to all the gods, even though he may not be the primordial god. Lugh, like Odin, is the commander-in-chief of the army of the gods who war against the giants. Like Odin, he is the owner of a marvelous spear, and also like Odin, he wages war not only in a heroic manner but also in a magical one (a Varunian theme). Like Odin, Lugh has an affinity with the crow and like Odin, master of runes and protector of poets, Lugh is a master-poet and musician. Finally, if Odin is one-eyed, Lugh is the grandson of a one-eyed man with a deadly glance, and, to work his magic during combat, Lugh closes one eye. Only the very Varunian aspect of Odin—his magical powers—doesn't appear, with one exception, in Lugh. This role in Irish mythology is more often held by the Dagda, or Ogma, and by Gwyddyon, son of Dôn, in Welsh mythology. This latter, the hero of the fourth branch of the *Mabinogian,* has even more direct connections with Odin: he is an expert in magical combat and plant battles.[18] He is sneaky, hypocritical, and a false witness as is Odin; and like Odin he transforms his appearance and also knows all the world's secrets as well as its hidden treasures. Gwyddyon's name refers to the root word that indicates knowledge, divine fury, and wood, all at the same time. And Gwyddyon is outside of all classes: he is druid, warrior, and multiple craftsman, and his incestuous son Lleu Llaw Gyffes, the "Lion of the Sure Hand," has etymological connections with Lugh of the long hand and with the spear that never misses its mark.

Summing up Lugh's personality as it corresponds to that of the Gallic Mercury noted by Caesar, it suffices to say that he was absolutely outside of all class. He was not the primordial god. He was not the god of the beginning times. He was not even the king of the gods. Yet he was above all the others, incarnating within himself alone the entirety of divine duties that, from the druidic point of view, are also fundamentally the duties humanity must perform to realize the unity of the world above with the world below, a unity without which Chaos—in this instance the Fomor—will dominate.

7
THE PHYSICIAN
AND THE SUN

Following Mercury, Caesar next lists in importance the god Apollo who cures disease, undoubtedly because of the wide worship he enjoyed. It is, therefore, not the solar aspect of this god that is put into evidence but his healing aspect. In fact the figure of Apollo doesn't belong to Roman mythology. He was first introduced by the Etruscans who made him into a disturbing deity linked to plague and epidemics, and then by the Greeks for whom the solar character of the deity was most important. But Apollo is not even of Greek origin—despite the success of his cult at Delphi and on Delos—but a hyperborean deity, probably of Scythian origin, that infiltrated Greece at the time of the Dorians' movement into that land. The name Apollo undoubtably refers to the Indo-European root word from which apple is derived: *malum* in Latin, *pomme* in French, *apfel* in German, and *aval* in Breton and Welsh.

Later references can be found to the famous Isle of Avalon, the *Insula Pomorum* of Geoffroy of Monmouth's *Vita Merlini,* the *Emain Ablach* or "Land of the Fairies" of Irish tradition, the *Insula Malifera* of classical antiquity situated in the Baltic where the tree and the apple were symbolically commingled, as well as the famous fable of the golden apple in the garden of the Hesperides.[1] It was on the Isle of Avalon that Morgan and her nine sisters knew the magic spells that could cure mortal wounds, like those of King Arthur. And it was at Emain Ablach, as on Avalon, that none were afflicted with illness, old age, or death. This fact is of enough significance to claim the presence, though he is not named, of Apollo the Healer, or of a completely different but equivalent deity on these isles.

The healer Apollo exists in Irish tradition, appearing as a member of the general staff of the Tuatha de Danann under the name of Diancecht. And when Lugh asked him about the extent of his abilities, he answered: "Every man that is wounded, provided that his head has not been cut off, or at least that the membrane of his brain or spinal cord has not been cut, will be completely healed by me for the combat of the next morning."[2] This means it is easy to understand why the Celts cut off the heads of their enemies, even those who were apparently dead. They had no desire to see them back on their feet thanks to the skill of their doctor-wizards. Incidentally, it was Diancecht who gave Nuada his silver arm "that held within it the movement of each arm." But the son of Diancecht, Miach, went even further: "He went to the lopped-off arm of Nuada and said 'joint upon joint' and 'nerve upon nerve,' and he healed it in three times nine days."[3] Envious of his son, Diancecht struck Miach with a sword, cutting the skin upon his head, but the boy healed himself with his art. A second time, Diancecht struck him with a blow that cleaved to the membrane of the brain, but the boy healed again. Diancecht struck him a third time, this time reaching the brain. "Miach died. Diancecht said that the physician himself could not have cured him from that blow."[4]

The follow-up to this tale of jealousy is quite curious. Miach was buried and "plants sprout from his tomb, to the number of three hundred sixty-five, identical to the number of his joints and nerves."[5] Then Diancecht's daughter Airmed harvested the plants and ranked them according to their qualities. But Diancecht "comes to her and mixes the plants together so well that their individual effects could not be known unless they were to be subsequently revealed by the Holy Spirit."[6] This comment by the Christian transcriber reinforces the fact that no one, save Diancecht or Airmed, knew the universal medicine of plants, and this knowledge could only be a gift from the divine, thus affirming the divine nature of medicine. This episode also brings Germano-Scandinavian mythology to mind, specifically that concerning the blood of Kvasir and the head of Mimir. It was following a bloody, if only symbolic, ritual and the dismemberment of a mythical character, that the possibility of knowledge of the great secrets of life and death is offered. The worship of the Eucharist like that of the Precious Blood (helped by the Christianized

Grail), goes back through various historicizations to the same origin.

All of this nevertheless needs to be connected to the Tuatha de Danann's Fountain of Health. As would be expected, during the course of the Battle of Mag Tured there were numerous casualties. "This was then done: a fire was set in the warriors who had been wounded there so that they would be more dazzling on the morning of the next day. It was for this reason that Diancecht and his two sons and daughter—Octriuil, Miach, and Airmed— sang incantations over the spring named Health.[7] Mortally wounded men were cast into it, and when they emerged, their mortal wounds had been cured by the strength of the four healers gathered around the fountain.[8] Another name of this fountain is Lake of Plants, for Diancecht planted there a blade of every grass that grew in Ireland.[9] This is encountered again in Welsh tradition, namely in the second branch of the *Mabinogian*. It is the cauldron of Bran Vendigeit "whose virtue is this: if a man is killed today, you have only to cast him inside so that on the morrow he will be as good as ever, save that he will no longer have the power of speech."[10] In practice a fire was lit beneath this cauldron following a battle. "Corpses are thrown inside of it until it is full. On the next day they arise as warriors who are as formidable as ever, save that they cannot speak."[11] This ritual is reminiscent of the strange depiction on one of the engraved plates of the famous Gundestrup cauldron.[12] On the lower portion defeated soldiers march to the left; in this left area a giant is dipping a warrior headfirst into a pool. On the upper area the soldiers, this time on horseback, go back in the right direction.[13] Is this a question of a sacrificial ritual in honor of Teutas such as is presented in one of the scholias of Lucan's *Pharsalia,* that is the immersion and suffocation of a victim in a cauldron, or an illustration of that tradition concerning the Fountain of Health and the Cauldron of Resurrection?[14] Or is it that, at the least, the sacrificial ritual honoring Teutas has been poorly understood, and that it concerns, as in certain Samhain rituals, a simulated act intended to strengthen military valor? In any event it is this same cauldron that Peredur speaks of in the Welsh version of the Grail saga: "He saw a horse coming that bore a corpse on its saddle. One of the women arose, lifted the corpse from the saddle, bathed him in a tub filled with warm water that was lower than the door and applied a precious ointment to him. The man came back to life and greeted him with a face animated with joy. Another two corpses arrived carried on saddles. The woman reanimated both of these men in the same manner as she had the first man."[15] The presence of the daughter of Diancecht at the Fountain of Health and the role of this mysterious woman in the tale of *Peredur* should be noted. And as Peredur is the Welsh Perceval, the Grail can hardly be overlooked, nor the fact that the wounded Fisher King only survived, in certain versions, by virtue of the Grail.[16]

That which concerns the activity of Diancecht at the Fountain of Health and the ritual of immersion in the cauldron does not appear to be an isolated element specific to mythological tradition, but seemingly an experience from real life, namely in Gaul and Great Britain during the time of their independence, and long after. I am speaking of the practice of thermal cures, attested to among the Gauls, propagated by the Romans, and proof of which is constituted by the existence of temples seeded with votives at the location of certain river sources, particularly those of the Seine.

The Gauls, convinced of the beneficial effects of water, used certain springs for medicinal purposes, a practice from which the Romans greatly profited. For example, beneath a Roman emplacement at Saint-Père sous Vézelay (Yonne), the substructure of a Gallic installation was discovered that, while certainly more rudimentary, was quite as effective as those of the Romans. The same was true in numerous other sites: some of these springs had been abandoned for a long time, like that of the Herse in the forest of Bellême (Belisama is one of the cognomens of the Gallic Minerva) on which a Latin inscription reveals a dedication to the "infernal gods" (in the pagan sense of the term). Other springs are known worldwide and have been used with unquestioned success. Such is the case with Vichy, but in regard to this there is a curious folk tradition claiming that the springs of Vichy were once located in Rougères, toward Varennes-sur-Allier, and that it was because of a curse by the guardian fairies of these springs that they dried up there and henceforth gushed at Vichy.[17] In truth, remains of thermal installations were discovered at Rougères in 1850. In fact if one wanted to compile a complete list of the ancient thermal springs in Gallic territory, as well as in Great Britain, one would be facing an immense task.

Vichy is located in the Bourbonnais region. Along with the Pyrenees, Bourbonnais and Auvergne have the richest selection of thermal springs from the ancient Celtic domain. And the name of Bourbonnais has something in common with these springs. The word Bourbon, in fact, comes from the Gallic name Bormo or Borvo that means "bubbling" or "boiling."

This name can be found not only in the various Bourbons, but even in Bourbouilloux, the name of several different rivers, in Bourbonne-les-Bains, and in La Bourbole. That said, Bormo or Borvo is also one of the names Apollo bears in Gallo-Roman statuary and epigraphy. As the word is related to the Irish *berbaim* (I boil), and to the Latin *fervere* (to cook), it means a bubbling produced by heat as well as by the release of cold gases. But we cannot avoid recalling the text of *The Battle of Mag Tured* that, in this instance, although not terribly clear, says that a fire was lit in the corpses and next they were thrown into the Fountain of Health. The connection between fire and water is undeniable. In the Welsh *Mabinogian,* as in *Peredur,* a fire is lit beneath the cauldron before the wounded and dead are placed inside. And what should be said about the famous Fountain of Barenton (which really exists and which even today can be seen just as it was described in the ancient texts, and which, as Chrétien de Troyes says, "boils though 'tis colder than marble.[18] The numerous sacred fountains that existed in western Europe at that time must also be taken into account, especially those located in Armorican Brittany. These fountains were generally dedicated to a "healing saint" who was, in short, the guardian genie, the *deus loci.*

It is not by chance that these fountains were Christianized in a fashion that permitted ancient practices to be maintained with the blessing of church authorities. Examples of this are countless, but following are two characteristic examples. The fountain in Bieuzy-Lanvaux en Pluvigner (Morbihan) cures headaches and toothaches if one drinks of its water and says a prayer to its patron saint. It should be remembered, however, that as legend has it Saint Bieuzy, having been struck in the skull with an ax, continued stoically to perform the Mass, then went on a long journey, the ax still embedded in his skull, to die next to his master, Saint Gildas. In several parishes of Morbihan, fountains exist that are dedicated to Saint Gobrien; pilgrimages are made to these sites for the healing of boils— "nails" as they are called—and it is customary to throw an iron nail in the fountain (or on the presumed tomb of the saint). It should be noted, however, that the name Gobrien comes from an ancient Breton root word that served as the origin of *gov* or *goff* (Plogoff), meaning "blacksmith," which it is almost the exact name of the blacksmith-god of the Tuatha de Danann, Goibniu, and his Welsh equivalent Govannon or Gobannon. This speaks to the permanent nature of these medico-religious practices that were placed under the protection of a saint who had replaced a pagan deity.

In this case, the Gallic Apollo was the patron of the majority of beneficial springs in Gaul and Great Britain, either directly, or in his name accompanied with a cognomen, or by simply the cognomen alone. We have already seen that Borvo is one of those cognomen, and that there are quite a large number of others, the principal ones being Grannus and Belenus, not including the Maponos of great Britain.

This last name is interesting in that it exactly corroborates a mythological British legend whose outline is preserved in a passage from the Welsh tale *Culhwch and Olwen*. It concerns Mabon, (an evolved form of Maponos), the son of Modron (the evolved form of Matrona, "maternal," the name of the Marne river), who was imprisoned in a mysterious location beneath the town of Kaer Lloyw (Gloucester), a name meaning "City of Light." Following Mabon's disappearence his mother went into mourning and the world was no longer what it was. He was freed by the companions of Arthur who, to achieve this, passed through a river "riding on the backs of salmon."[19] It is evident that Mabon, whose name means "filial," represents the young sun as night's prisoner. This Mabon can be seen again under the name of Mabuz, in the archaic version of the legend of Lancelot of the Lake.[20] Lancelot, the son of the Lady of the Lake, was a prisoner in a strange city. The Lady of the Lake made off with Lancelot, raised and educated him, then sent him into the world with the mission of liberating Mabuz, for this was the price he had to pay to find out his true name. In Irish tradition this Mabon character is recognizable in the person of Oengus, called the Mac Oc, (literally the "Young Son"), the adulterous child of the god Dagda, and he plays an important role in several mythological tales.[21] But the Maponos label attached to the name of the Gallic Apollo caused him to spill over and out of the purely medical role that he appears to have assumed in the eyes of Caesar and in Irish myth (even though Diancecht was the grandfather of Lugh). Oengus was not only a doctor and guardian of the fountains of health, he also had a relationship with youth and the sun and was in this role that he seems to have been worshiped among the island dwelling Britons, namely among the Brigantes and at Carlisle.[22]

With Grannus and Belenus the solar aspect is even more clear-cut. Grannus has given his name to Grand in the Vosges region, as well as to

Aix-la-Chapelle, an ancient *Aquae Granni* (from which the German Aachen is derived), one of the main centers at which he was worshiped. Inscriptions concerning Apollo Grannus are numerous and have a relationship with medicinal waters. Yet it is possible that the name Grannus comes from a word that was also the root of the Irish *grian* (sun). The name Belenus that Apollo bore among the Nordic people in Aquilia, in northern Italy, southern Gaul, and several other regions such as Beaune (Côte-d'Or), which was the ancient Belenate, is an indisputably solar term. In fact it is necessary to connect the name of Belenos to the name of the Irish May Day festival, Beltane (Fires of Bel), where its meaning would be the "shining one." The famous Fountain of Barenton in the forest of Paimpont-Brocéliande, once bore the name Bélenton, in which can be recognized a Bel-Nemeton, that is a "sacred clearing of Bel." It is probably this same divine figure who appears in the mythologies and (fantastic) genealogies of Wales, under the name of Beli the Great, taken up again by Geoffroy of Monmouth in his *Historia Regum Britannia* under the form of Belinus. Some genealogies have made him into the husband of a certain Anna, who is identified with the grandmother of Jesus, and who could well be the Irish Dana (and the Welsh Dôn). He probably is represented in the *Chanson d'Apremont,* as the Saracen Balan, and appears as Balin, the knight of the two swords, author of the "Dolorous Stroke" in the Arthuruian romances that flowed from the pen of Robert de Boron.[23] And what of those places called Bel-air or Bel-Orient, or even Peyrebelle (a particularly sinister spot that has no relationship with *pierre belle)* and Aiguebelle? The Signal of Bel-Orient on the mountain of Bel-Air, in the Côtes-du-Nord region, appears more a site of worship (with a chapel that more than likely replaced a previously existing structure) than a name connected to the geographical location. As for Mont-Saint-Michel du Péril de la Mer, it was once named Tombelaine, a name that was shifted over to the neighboring islet. It so happens that Tum-Belen is none other than the Mound of Belenos. The replacement of the "shining" god by Michael, the archangel of light, is surely not by coincidence.

But under his Belenos incarnation, the Celtic Apollo, still presents several problems. It does not seem as though the Greeks, and the Latins even less so, had a true sun god. For the Germans, the existence of a true sun god is even more vague and it is hardly enough to claim that such and such a figure was a "solar hero." It is no more clear-cut with the Indo-Iranians, despite the presence of the Indian Surya (who is of recent introduction) and of Ahura-Mazda who, within the framework of Zoroastrian philosophy, was mainly the ontological light opposed to Ahriman of the darkness. And the Mithra of the Roman era, who had nothing in common with the Vedic Mitra, was content to borrow his symbolism from the sun. As for the Scythians who remained much more archaic, they had a solar goddess, the famous and cruel Scythian Diana, the driving force in the legend of Orestes and Iphegenia, a goddess who the Greeks made into their Artemis through a considerable softening of her character as well as by a kind of astrological transfer that transformed her from a solar goddess into a lunar one. A myth comparable to that of Osiris does not exist among the Indo-Europeans. Does this then mean that the solar cult is not Indo-European?

It is difficult to categorically respond in the affirmative although everything leads one to think so. The monument of Stonehenge in Great Britain, of which we have already spoken, dating from the Megalithic era and the Bronze Age, is very revelatory in this regard. Noted by the authors of antiquity as a solar temple, it is without doubt that Stonehenge was built in connection to the sunrise on the summer solstice.[24] The same holds true for the megalithic alignments of Carnac whose directional lines appear in relation with the rising of the sun. But contrary to stubborn misbeliefs, these monuments have strictly nothing to do with the Celts. They are the product of earlier inhabitants—not Indo-Europeans. And archaeological discoveries have shown that the Nordic Bronze Age was the culminating point of solar worship in Europe.

All of this information could sweep away a series of false notions about druidic religious services and beliefs. "As for Belenos, there is a strong possibility that he is the Celticized representative of the Bronze Age solar religion.[25] Belonos, Grannus, Maponos-Mabon, and to a certain extent the Irish Mac Oc, are quite likely images borrowed by the Celts from the native populations they subjugated. According to the *Book of Conquests*, when the Sons of Milhead (the Gaels) invaded Ireland, they found themselves in the presence of the Tuatha de Danann. At that time the Tuatha had three kings, Mac Cuill, Mac Cecht, and Mac Greine, grandsons of Dagda, and married to three queens, Banba, Eriu, and Fotla. The names of these three queens are eponyms of Ireland. But the names of the three kings are interesting: "Mac Cuill, that is to say Sethor, the hazel tree was his god; Mac Cecht, that is to say Tethor, the plough was his god; Mac Greine, that is to say Cethor, the sun was his god."[26] As "Son of the Hazel Tree," Mac Cuill is represents the druidic office as the hazel tree *(coll)*, a tree often used in magic and divinatory practices. As "Son of the Plough," Mac Cecht represents the producer class, in particular that aspect of it that concerns agriculture. He would therefore be a ploughman-god, which is quite exceptional among the Irish who are a people of herders rather than farmers, and this would constitute the sole mention of such a god in Irish mythology. Finally, as "Son of the Sun," Mac Greine can only represent the second class, that of the warriors. Here again we come across the functional tripartition. The essential thing to know is why the military class is placed under the patronage of the sun.

The fact that must first be understood is that Mac Greine is not himself the sun. His god is the sun, and he is the "Son of the Sun."

In Gaul, Belenos had a feminine equivalent whose name, Belisama, a Celtic superlative meaning "very brilliant," also provided the name for the town of Bellême (Orne). An inscription in Greek characters to Belisami has been discovered in Vaison-la-Romaine, in the country of the Gallic Voscons. Another Latin inscription, *Minervae Belisimae sacrum,* in Saint-Lizier (Ariège) makes Belisama the surname of Minerva. But in Bath, England, a goddess named Sul is worshiped, who the Latin writer Solinus also compares to Minerva by specifying that an eternal flame burns in her temple, which is reminiscent of the fire maintained at Kildare (Ireland) in honor of the goddess Brigit, and later in memory of Saint Bridget at the Christian abbey. From all the evidence Sul is a sun goddess. So why then is Minerva referred to? It has been suggested that this is connected to the lightning personified by Minerva, daughter of the god of the sky, altough this is not a very convincing argument.[27] Perhaps it would be better to look at the problem from the angle of the Celtic Minerva, who unquestionably is Brigit of the triple face. This triple Brigit, who appears under different names in Irish mythology, is at once poet (therefore a druid), warrior, and master of crafts, thus covering the three functions by herself, which easily explains her solar component, a component linked to the military class.

An intrusion into Germano-Scandinavian tradition allows us to consider this complex idea, it being understood that it is not a question of explaining it by a Germanic origin, nor of insisting upon the Irish influence on the skalds of Iceland, the transmitters of this tradition. The theory is quite simply that the Germano-Scandinavians, like the Celts, had inherited indigenous non–Indo-European and Nordic assumptions dating back as far as the Bronze Age. The legend of Siegfried-Sigurd supports this. When the hero Siegfried, after killing the dragon Fafnir and his intiator Regin, and thereby coming into possession of many marvelous powers, delivers the sleeping Valkyrie—a Sleeping Beauty archetype—the myth becomes very explicit, even if the various versions of the legend differ in the small details. This Valkyrie, clad in a warrior's cuirass, is in the middle of a fortress surrounded by a rampart of flames. The hero crosses through the flames and frees—or conquers—the Valkyrie, who is named either Brunhilda or Sirgdryfa. Consequently the destiny of Siegfried-Sigurd is inexorably linked to that of the Valkyrie, as Tristan is linked to Iseult in Celtic legend after the trial of the love potion. The symbolism is clear: the fortress surrounded by flames is the sun, and the Valkyrie at its center is the sun goddess. Siegfried-Sigurd, who has been passed off as a solar hero, is really a moon-man who receives his light from the sun, which is to say his strength and even his life, just as Tristan cannot live longer than a month—the time of a lunar cycle—without finding Iseult again.[28] Now the Valkyrie has explained to the hero that because of her duty as a Valkyrie, she was once clad in the plumage of a swan. Thus she is a swan-woman. Countless examples of swan-women exist in Celtic tradition, particularly the Irish, and notably it was a distinctive feature of the women of the *sidhe*, the goddesses of the Tuatha de Danann, to transform themselves into swans.[29] And the swan, a Nordic hyperborean beast, is also a solar symbol linked to Apollo. Iseult the Blond, the Celtic equivalent of Brunhild-Sirgdryfa, has a preminently solar character. Iseult's prototype in Irish mythology is a certain Grainne whose name is derived from *grian,* the "sun." In Celtic tradition the solar role is not held by a man but by a woman. The moon is masculine in Celtic (and Germanic) languages, and the sun is feminine. The Celtic calendar is a lunar one, and the Gauls "measured lengths of time not according to the number of days but according to the number of nights" (Caesar VI, 18).[30]

In short, the Valkyrie, the woman-warrior, is also the woman-sun, which perhaps explains the identification of Belisama to Minerva-Athena, who sprung fully formed and armed from the brain of Jupiter-Zeus, and also why Mac Greine, "Son of the Sun," represents the military office in the *Book of Conquests* triad. But this especially demonstrates that the so-called solar hero, the mythologist's pride and joy, is in reality a moon-man who is dependant upon the sun-woman, to whom he is either son or lover. On the mythical plane, no difference exists between the two roles because its only aim is to establish an intimate rapport between these two symbolic figures.

Thus if one truly wants to accept the existence in Celtic tradition of a feminine figure who inheirited the prerogatives and duties of an ancient Bronze Age solar goddess (one in the mold of the Sythian Diana, both luminous and dreadful), then it must be assumed that Mac Cecht is the "Son of the Sun Goddess." Using this as a point of departure then, Mabon-Maponos is the son of the ancient sun goddess Modron-Matrona. The Greek Artemis—and the Roman Diana—was stripped of her solar attributes, which were transferred to Apollo, who has been made into, no doubt mistakenly, her brother. This same tendency is observed in Celtic tradition: it is the son or lover who bears the solar coloration to the detriment of his mother—or mistress. Therefore Modron-Matrona represents one of the faces of the ancient sun goddess, she who was called Sul in Bath and whose medicinal character is evident in that it is she who protects the healing waters. A connection seems clear to the "white ladies" of Pyrenees folklore and their possible connection to the apparitions of Lourdes, or even those of the numerous fountains, or wells in close proximity to churches dedicated to the Virgin Mary in Brittany and elsewhere. Moreover, in Welsh tradition Modron is the equivalent of Morgan the Fee in the Arthurian romances, who is the mistress of the Vale of No Return, a site surrounded by flames where she imprisons faithless knights. She is also the Queen of the Isle of Avalon, the isle being the image of the sun upon the ocean, which is the universe, and the apple, the fruit par excellence of Avalon and all islands of that type, being the symbol of knowledge, light, and immortality. Morgan is also a healer, which brings us back to the Diancecht aspect of the Celtic Apollo, most particularly the daughter of Diancecht, Airmed, whose name means "measurement." In Welsh tradition, as in the Arthurian romances, Modron-Morgan has a son Owein-Yvain, the winner of the trial of the fountain dedicated to Belenos in Barenton, from which he sent the Black Knight, the symbol of nocturnal darkness, fleeing. Owein-Yvain is also a moon-man chasing the darkness in the middle of the night, but one who receives his strength and light from the sun-woman. And when Modron wishes to aid her son when he is in danger, she sends him a flock of ravens who in reality are herself and her nine sisters. They are capable, as Geoffroy of Monmouth tells us, of transforming themselves into birds.[31] In the Irish epic, *The Courtship of Finnbais,* the fairy woman Befinn (Beautiful Woman) who is presented as the sister of Boinn (Bo-vinda, White Cow), acts in the same fashion when her son Fraêch (heather) is in danger.[32] It so happens that Fraêch appears to be the double of Oengus, the Mac Oc, son of Boinn and Dagda.

In sum, the Celtic Apollo is especially characterized by the medical function, the sole characteristic of those usually attributed to the Apollo archetype that Caesar retained, and the only one that has a real importance in Irish tradition where Diancecht is a person of considerable significance.[33] But he also has a youthful aspect and, as youth and health go hand in hand, he is a protector of the young. Is not the Otherworld often qualified as the "land of youth," or the "country of eternal youth"? It is on this account that the god appears in the aspect of Mac Oc and his equivalents, Mabon-Maponos, Fraêch, Mac Cecht, and even Owein-Yvain. This is the "young son," or the "young lover." But visible in the background is the shadow of an ancient goddess-sun, inheirited from the Bronze Age whose dominant traits can be rediscovered on one hand in epic heroines such as Grainne or Iseult, and on the other in the mythical lovers-sons such as Grannus, Maponos, or Belenos.[34] In reality the solar characteristics of the ancient goddess are often scattered among the multiple individuals of Celtic mythology.

8

THE WARRIOR DEITY

Caesar's nomenclature placed Mars third in importance among the gods and attributed the customary military duties to him. There are Gallo-Roman statues in the territory of Gaul that represent him in a very Roman style. There are an equal number of inscriptions (in the neighborhood of 250) and temple sites, such as the Fanum Martis of the Armorican Curiosolites that must be Corseul or Erquy. One fact in all this is quite bizarre: on the frontiers where numerous legions were stationed, inscriptions relating to Mercury are predominant, while the majority of inscriptions concerning Mars are located in the center of Gaul.

The Gallic Mars had multiple names, according to case and to region. At Trêves he was Iovantucarus, meaning "dear to the youth," Vellanus, "the best," in Wales. He was also Alborix, "master of the world," Lucetius, "luminous," or even Olloudius, "very powerful." But the most interesting names are Smertrios, Segomo, Camulos, and, at times, Toutatis.

Mars-Smertrios is represented on the famous altar of the Nautes of Paris (Cluny Museum) as a man raising his club against a serpent. This is more akin to Hercules than the classic Mars, who, let's not forget, was originally an agrarian god for the Romans. In any event, the name of Smertrios—which can be seen again in that of the goddess Rosmerta, the "provider"—contains a root indicative of the redistribution of goods. Smertrios therefore would have been the "providence-god," the god of distribution. The main point to know is whether it is the bounty of the earth he distributes or the booty of war. In contrast, the surname of Segomo, which can be found in southern Gaul, is in no way ambiguous. It was he who gave victory, an image that conforms to what we expect of Mars.

Mars-Camulos is vouched for throughout the entire Celtic domain. He gave his name, Camulodunum, to the principal city of the Trinovantes of Essex in Great Britain, and that of Camulogenos to the military head of the Gauls in Lutece in the A.D. 52. It seems that Camulos was quite well known and revered. The name contains the root *cam*, "curve," and can signify the "tortuous" or "crooked," which is perhaps an allusion to a sophisticated military tactic. In any case, this Camulos appears again in Irish epics, more precisely, in the so-called Leinster cycle, or Ossianic cycle. He is, in fact, under the name of Cumal, the father of the hero Finn, king of the Fiana, the half-historical, half-legendary wandering band of warriors. Under the pretext that the tales about the Fiana are relatively recent—and even still living in oral Irish and Scottish tradition—this cycle has been kept on the sidelines of all mythological study. However, even if the composition of the tales was recent, their foundations appear particularly archaic, even related to pre-Celtic eras, probably those of the reindeer hunters. This implies that Camulos-Cumal, of whom we don't know much except that he was the rival of a certain Morna who killed him during the Battle of Cnucha, is an important figure. But he is surely not originally Celtic, and must incorporate a more ancient deity, perhaps the mysterious Cernunnos.[1]

As for Mars-Toutatis, identifying him doesn't pose any real problem. Toutatis is identical to the former Teutas, and the name signifies "father of the tribe" or "father of the people." The scholias of Lucan's *Pharsalia* identify him once with Mars and once with Mercury. In Great Britain he is likened to Mars at York and Carlisle. There are several inscriptions of Mars-Toutatis, or Mars-Teutas, in different regions under Celtic domin-ion. In fact this name can be taken as a common modifier. Mars, therefore, is considered as the "father of the tribe" that he protects. This is reminis-cent of the saying found in Irish epics: "By the god my tribe swears by." Toutatis-Teutas, it seems, can be the cognomen of any god. The true problem lies elsewhere, for without comparison Lucan cites Teutas as being a god who stands alone in his famous triad that also includes Esus and Taranis. But this triad goes beyond the framework of Mars.

It is within the general staff of the Tuatha de Danann that we rediscover the Celtic Mars, but here he is divided in two. This is similar to what the original Mars of the Romans must have been, both guardian god of peace and the god who conducts war, a somewhat clear picture of which is provided by the double-face of Janus. In this instance this division concerns King Nuada and his champion Ogma, a pair that appears to represent the Mitra-Varuna couple.

Nuada was the titular king of the Tuatha de Danann, even if he had to temporarily cede his title to Lugh at the time of the latter's entrance into Tara, and even if he had to abandon his duties for a time because of his severed arm. But with the silver arm set in place by Diancecht, and with the graft performed by the son of Diancecht, he was again able to fully assume his role as king. This brings to mind the Germano-Scandinavian Tyr (and the Mucius Scaevola of Roman pseudohistory) who is one-armed. It also resembles the Fisher King of the Grail Quest who could no longer maintain his kingdom's equilibrium because of his wound. He was, however, the institutional king, jurist, and warrior, characteristic of the miltary royalty of the Mitra type. Nuada was also known outside of the Gaelic world, an idea supported by Latin inscriptions concerning a certain Nodens or Nodons. Notably, there is a ruined temple in Lydney Park near Aylburton on the Severn that dates from the fourth century A.D., an era during which the Celtic religion endured beneath a Roman veneer that was happily tolerated by the imperial authorities of the British island. In this temple that adjoins the thermal baths, a small monument was discovered, the dedication of which reads "D. M. Nodonti, Devo Nodenti, Deo Nudenti," and upon which is depicted a figure slaying a large salmon. Is this a fisherman? Was Nodens a fisherman-god? Taking into account Nuada's wound and his inability to rule, there has been a desire to see him as an equivalent of the Fisher King from the Grail Quest.[2]

Welsh tradition tells of a figure by the name of Lludd Llaw Ereint (Lludd of the Silver Hand), the mythical founder of the city of London, which in Welsh is Kaer Lludd. This Lludd is probably a distorted form of the older Nudd who corresponds to Nodens and to Nuada, at least if he isn't a distorted form of Lugh. But a Nudd also exists in this same Welsh tradition, a man who was the father of two sons. The first is Edern (the Latin Aeternus) who, under the name of Yder in the romances of the Round Table figures as one of Arthur's companions, and even as Saint Edern in the Armorican Breton hagiographic tradition. The second son is named Gwynn, and Welsh Christian tradition, undoubtedly unable to co-opt him, turned him into a demon guardian of Hell. Now Gwynn (meaning white, hand-some, thoroughbred, or sacred) is the linguistic equivalent of the Gaelic Finn, the son of Cumal-Camulos. A poem on the Fiana places Finn as the grandson of Nuada, making these coincidences too striking not to take into account.[3] And it depicts how the Welsh tradition and the Arthurian romances, even if they have undergone alterations and transformations, still reveal important elements of Celtic mythology that are just as valuable as those preserved in Irish tradition.

The first face of the Celtic Mars looked like that of Nuada. Before the second Battle of Mag Tured, when Lugh asked Nuada what he would do against the Fomor, he replied: "I will be ready to feed your armies and in addition I will feed whoever is the same age as me."[4] It might seem suprising that the great Nuada should have been reduced to a head sutler's role in a major battle, a battle in which his very kingdom was at stake. But upon reflection, this portrayal has merit. First of all because he was king, the apportioner of wealth, he was the nourishing father of his people. It should be noted that this response by Nuada corresponds perfectly with the role of the Fisher King who caught food for his people (basically this was all he could do). The Celtic type of king was an indispensable hub for his society. But a hub does not move and if Nuada was wounded during the first Battle of Mag Tured, losing his arm as the Fisher King lost his virility, it could only have been in a symbolic fashion. It was not a question of an actual wound, but one of a much stronger attack on his sovereignty. For Nuada clearly assumed the Mitra aspect of royalty.

This leaves us to discuss the second face of the Celtic Mars. In this instance we are dealing with Ogma, the champion of the Tuatha de Danann. He is a curious figure who posseses Herculean features. He is also the god of eloquence, the presumed inventor of the so-called "Ogmic writing," by which a person bound his listeners with his magically accented speech.

It is a Greek of the second century A.D., the mocker and skeptic Lucian of Samosata, who has left us with the best portrait of Ogma, a portrait that was made into images by the odd Albrecht Dürer in a drawing in his *Kunstbuch*.[5]

> Our Hercules is known among the Gauls under the local name of
> Ogmius; and the appearance he presents in their pictures is truly

grotesque. They make him out as old as old can be: the few hairs he has left (he is quite bald in front) are dead white, and his skin is wrinkled and tanned as black as any old salt's. You would take him for some infernal deity, for Charon or Iapetus—any one rather than Hercules. Such as he is, however, he has all the proper attributes of that God: the lion's-skin hangs over his shoulders, his right hand grasps the club, his left the strung bow, and a quiver is slung at his side; nothing is wanting to the Herculean equipment. However I have yet to mention the most remarkable feature in the portrait. This ancient Hercules drags after him a vast crowd of men, all of whom are fastened by the ears with thin chains composed of gold and amber, and looking more like beautiful necklaces than anything else. From this flimsy bondage they make no attempt to escape, though escape must be easy. There is not the slightest show of resistance: instead of planting their heels in the ground and dragging back, they follow with joyful alacrity, singing their captor's praises the while. . . . Nor will I conceal from you what struck me as the most curious circumstance of all. Hercules' right hand is occupied with the club, and his left with the bow: how is he to hold the ends of the chains? The painter solves the difficulty by boring a hole in the tip of the God's tongue, and making that the means of attachment; his head is turned round, and he regards his followers with a smiling countenance.

The narrator's distress before such a graphic composition is easily understood. His natural tendency to scorn the barbarians—he accused the painter of not knowing where to hang the chains—is offset somewhat by his curiosity. A Greek has a completely different conception of the world and the heavens. He couldn't understand it. Luckily a Gaul who seemed to understand the Greek mentality quite well came to his aid:

We Gauls connect eloquence not with Hermes, as you do, but with the mightier Hercules. Nor need it surprise you to see him represented as an old man. It is the prerogative of eloquence, that it reaches perfection in old age; at least if we believe your poets. . . . Hence, if you will consider the relation that exists between tongue and ear, you will find nothing more natural than the way that our Hercules, who is Eloquence personified, draws men along with their ears tied to his tongue. Nor is any slight intended by the hole bored through that member: I recollect a passage in one of your comic poets in which we are told that "There is a hole in every glib tongue's tip." Indeed we refer to the achievements of the original Hercules from first to last, to his wisdom and persuasive eloquence. His shafts, as I take it, are no other than his words; swift, keen-pointed, true-aimed to do deadly execution on the soul. And in conclusion he reminded me of our own phrase, "winged words."[6]

Here is testimony that is quite clear and precise. It allows for making allowances and considering the epic tales of Celtic origin a little differently. In appearance they seem to be merciless battles in which the heroes kill one another off, but in a majority of instances these battles are symbolic, testifying to internal struggles and oratory jousts. Examples of this abound in Irish epic literature, and Lucian's text only confirms the impartial observations of not only the Irish and Welsh texts, but of even the Arthurian romances.

This said, the description of the Gallic Ogmios, god of the "powerful eloquence," allows for a better understanding of certain Latin and Greek texts that mention the Celts' unbridled passion for eloquence. "In their speech they are threatening, lofty, and given to the tragic" (Diodorus Siculus, V, 31). They have moreover "an eloquence that is characteristic of them" (Pomponius Mela, III, 2). It is also easy to understand why the Romans were terrified at the sight of an approaching Gallic horde, for the latter made a great din of "harsh songs" and "discordant clamor" (Titus Livy, V, 37). In addition "the image of the Gallic army and the noise they made froze them with fear. The number of horns and trumpets were incalculable; at the same time the entire army emitted such a clamor that not only were the sounds of the instruments and the cries of the soldiers to be heard, but the surrounding area that sent back their echo seemed to be adding their own noise to this din" (Polybius, II, 29). We can only think of the Irish hero Cuchulainn: "Cuchulainn seized his two spears, his shield, and his sword, and from his throat gave forth the shout of a hero. . . . He let out a cry that was the equal to that of one hundred warriors" *(Tain Bô Cualngé)*. Underneath it all, this eloquence is *magical,* and it is through its magic power that men are enchained. It is from this that the image of Hercules is derived. For the Celtic Mars was a warrior who had to be strong, even if that strength was not that of arms but of the Word. And contrary to Nuada-Noden who was the royal warrior and prisoner of the law—for the Celtic king was not above the law, he was its slave—the face of Ogmios as described by Lucian is clearly Varunian. It was by the magic Word, the ruse, as was the case with the Germanic Odin, that he defeated his enemies. Ogmios is not unknown to the Irish. He also can be found in the general staff of the Tuatha de Danann, under almost the same name— he is the champion, Ogma.

This Ogma, who also distinguished himself in the Battle of Mag Tured, is a complex individual. His demeanor as champion indisputably made him a warrior, a strong man. But in Ireland he was also thought of as the inventor of the writing known as *ogham*. This writing, which consists of a series of horizontal signs arranged around a vertical axis is in fact an adaptation of the Roman alphabet and can date back no earlier than the beginning of the Christian era. In any event, there is nothing to justify the interminable glosses that seek to interpret the ogham—and Scandinavian runes that date back no further—from soley a magical perspective. There is nothing esoteric about ogham writing and if it seems obvious that it served druids and satirists for magical purposes that is because all writing, according to Celtic thought, had magical powers. If we take this as our starting point, it is a waste of time to think of Ogma as a kind of Hermes Trismegistus, the keeper of great Celtic secrets. In addition the name Ogma probably has nothing at all to do with the ogham. Yet it is significant that the invention of writing has been credited to this Varunian god, binder, and charmer; moreover, tablets of execration have been discovered in Bréganz on which Ogma is invoked against individuals listed by name, somewhat similar to the acts of sorcery in which the Devil is in sum the executor of the Great Works. By this token the act of writing a curse on wood or stone, an act comparable to the fabrication of certain Scandinavian runes, was a very serious thing. An ancient Irish text tells us: "The father of the *Ogham* is Ogma, the mother of the *Ogham* is the hand, or knife of Ogma."[7] And the author of the text took advantage of the occasion to give a more detailed description of Ogma as "a man who is very learned in language and poetry and who invented the *ogham*."[8] And we come back to Lucian's Ogmios, with this statement: "This language must remain the property of the erudite and not that of the shepherds and farmers."[9] This is all very clear.

In fact the name of Ogmios is not Celtic at all, but derives from the Greek *ogmos,* meaning "path." From this he therefore would be the "leader,"[10] which corresponds to the portrait drawn by Lucian of the aged Hercules leading his troops by little golden chains, these being the charms that the Word animates and compels to act. This Mars-Varuna therefore forms a counterpart to the Mars-Mitra represented by Nuada, showing with one stroke that royalty for the Celts, which comes out of the military class but is under the control of the sacerdotal class, is nothing without the sacerdotal influence.

If we summarize all that has been said about the Celtic Mars, we must define him as double: he was both the warrior-king who watched over his people in times of peace and who led them to victory in times of war, as well as the warrior-druid who could utter spells and captivate by the power of the Verb, rectifying mistakes and unforseen situations with one stroke. Once again this is the druid-king pair, but idealized to the extreme and deified. And this pair can again be seen during the final throes of the Celtic tradition, as the well-known partnership of Arthur and Merlin.

9
THE FATHER OF ALL

It is suprising to find that in Caesar's nomenclature, Jupiter ranks only fourth in importance. It seems that Caesar made his classifications based on the level of worship bestowed upon the deities of whom he spoke. It is necessary to state explicitly that this concerns Gaul of the first century B.C. What was the case in Gaul before that time? And especially what was it in the isle of Britain and in Ireland at the same time? Celtic civilization endured from the fifth century B.C. to the twelfth century A.D. in territories that did not all evolve in the same way. In the twelfth century, outside of the rapid growth of the Arthurian romances, the ancient Gallic territory no longer had much in common with the Celts. But Ireland was still Celtic. And so it is necessary to be extremely careful that we not take Caesar's testimony as absolute. It remains a testimony—a very valuable one certainly and very convenient to use as a base of discussion—limited both in space (Gaul) and time (first century B.C.).

There is, however, one confusing fact that needs to be mentioned: in Romanized Gaul, Jupiter was worshiped and represented as the Roman Jupiter and cases are quite rare where the inscriptions make mention of a any other name. Is this then to say that among the Gauls there wasn't a celestial god, father of the other gods, like the Zeus-Jupiter of the Greco-Romans? This would be quite surprising, and all the more so in that Caesar makes mention of one. It is highly likely that the name of an indigenous deity has been replaced with the Roman name of Jupiter almost everywhere, but it is impossible to know which indigenous deity this would have been. Luckily Ireland has preserved the Irish name of its celestial god, the "father of all." He of course belongs to the general staff of the Tuatha de Danann. We are speaking of the Dagda whose most frequent name is Eochaid Ollathir—"father of all," or "all powerful father."

During preparations for the second Battle of Mag Tured while, under Lugh's "chairmanship," the allotment of tasks is being discussed, each individual expresses his opinion and brags of having accomplished the greatest of deeds. It is at this point that Dagda takes the floor: "Those great things you are boasting you will do, I will do them all with only myself." "It is you who are the great god," they all replied, and henceforth the name the Dagda remained his.[1] Such is the explanation given in *The Second Battle of Mag Tured* for the most widely known name of the god in Ireland. Dagda in fact comes from the ancient *dago-devos,* which literally means "good god," and by extension "very divine." The episode recounted here is quite significant; the Dagda does more than the other Tuatha de Danann, without however attaining the plenitude of duties reserved for Lugh. Dagda is therefore a god superior to the others. This is his Jupiterian aspect. And by his other name of Ollathir, the Irish equivalent of the Scandinavian Alfadir, Odin's cognomen, he is the "father of all," or the "omnipotent father." He is certainly a member of the military class, as he shows in battle. But one of his attributes—a club that kills with one end and resuscitates with the other, an attribute that at first view seems Herculean—is much more ambiguous. This club makes Dagda into a kind of god who is master of Life and Death. *He would therefore be both Jupiter and Dispater,* the famous Dispater (or Dis Pater), Pluto's equivalent, the master of the land of the dead who, according to Caesar, masks a Gallic deity of great importance. "All the Gauls claim to be descended from Dis Pater. This, they say, is a druid tradition. Because of this belief they measure the duration of time, not according to the number of days, but according to those of nights. In their observance of birthdays and the beginnings of months and years day follows night" (Caesar, VI, 18).

Caesar's text is important, because it not only confirms a certain number of nocturnal Celtic customs, but because it permits this double aspect of Jupiter, master of heaven and life, and of Dispater, master of the underground world and death, to be seen in the Irish Dagda. This interpretation is fully justified by the dual nature of this figure's club, and it has the merit of explaining this "magical" object by its symbolic value.

This image of Dagda went on to have a great posterity, and is often found in certain Irish epic tales, like those of the Ulster cycle, that in principle, the Tuatha de Danann have no role—except to sow discord and disorder among the Gaels who have banished them from Ireland. Thus, in the famous tale *The Drunkenness of the Ulaid*, it is learned that three Tuatha have inserted themselves among the Ulstermen.[2] One of them is "a man with one large eye, enormous thighs, of prodigious stature, and covered with a large gray cloak (and holds) a large iron club in his hand."[3] And this character strikes the nine men accompanying him with the malefic end of his club, killing them with one blow. But placing the beneficial end of his club upon their heads, he resuscitates them immediately (a good description of the Dagda). The supplementary note here is that he is one-eyed, like Odin. In the Welsh tale *Owen, or the Lady of the Fountain*, as well as in the corresponding tale *The Chevalier of the Lion* by Chrétien de Troyes, this character reappears as "A dark man, as big as two men of this world; he has but one foot and one single eye in the middle of his forehead; he carries an iron club in his hand."[4] This time not only is he one-eyed, but also one-legged. In addition he reveals himself to be a master of wild beasts who he is in charge of guarding in the forest. He is recognizable again in many other Arthurian romances.

This club of the Dagda is indicative of the military function in Celtic society. But as it has both beneficial and malefic qualities, it gives a Varunian aspect to the Dagda that Nuada doesn't have. This is why the Dagda can be considered as the second component of Celtic double royalty. It is with Ogma that he is then interchangeable, the Dagda and Ogma both being described as Hercules.

But the Dagda is far from being simply a warrior. He owns a magic harp that he alone can play, and that is capable of moving on his command. When, after the Battle of Mag Tured, Lugh, the Dagda, and Ogma go into the banquet house, the harp is hanging on the wall. "It was within this harp that the Dagda had bound all melodies and it would not resound until the Dagda, by his call, had named them. . . . The harp sprang from the wall and toward the Dagda, killing nine men on the way. He played [the Tuatha] the three airs by which harpists are recognized: the sleepy tune, the laughing tune, and the crying tune."[5] A harpist and magician, the Dagda is a druid and so belongs to the first social class, the sacerdotal class.

But this is not all. The Dagda possesses a third attribute, a cauldron "that no one went away from ungrateful."[6] This means that the Dagda's cauldron is a cauldron of abundance, an inexhaustible source of food, an obvious prototype of the Grail that, when it appears in the room housing guests, gives each of them the food and drink of their choice. But abundance is inseparable from divine inspiration and resurrection. Earlier we spoke of the cauldron of the Welsh hero Bran Vendigeit and the tub in which Peredur witnessed the resuscitation of dead youths, as well as of the scene depicted on the Gundestrup Cauldron of the warriors marching into a cauldron. It is also necessary to mention the Cauldron of Ceridwen, in which this strange character, who is both sorceress and goddess, boils a beverage "of inspiration and science." In the Welsh legend of Taliesin it is by improperly absorbing three drops of this beverage that the young Gwyon Bach obtains supreme knowledge, the gift of metamorphosis, and after a ritual death and new birth, he becomes the bard Taliesin.[7] This theme of a cauldron that offers abundance, wisdom, and rebirth is widespread in Irish, Welsh, and Arthurian tales, and it also frequently appears in the folktales of western Europe.[8]

Because of his association with this cauldron, the Dagda clearly belongs to the third social class, that of the producers. As the "Father of All," the Dagda is druid, warrior, and provider. He holds the three Indo-European offices, which places him above the other gods. His attribute of being the god of prosperity is quite evident in the tale of the second Battle of Mag Tured, for when Lugh sent him to spy on the Fomor, these latter people forced him to eat:

> The Fomor also made porridge. This was to mock him, as his love for porridge was great. They filled the king's cauldron, which was as deep as five giants' fists, with porridge for him. Eighty gallons of fresh milk went into it and the same quantity of oats and lard. Goats, sheep, and swine were thrown in and cooked with the porridge. It was poured into a trench dug in the ground and Indech told him that he would be put to death if he did not eat it all.[9] The Dagda swallowed down this enormous amount of food with a grunt of approval. When he was done his belly was larger than the cauldron of a house and the Fomor made fun of him.[10]

The following portion of the tale turns into an obscene farce in which, leaving the Fomor the Dagda can hardly walk

> because of the size of his belly. His attire was indecent: a brown tunic fell just to the bulge of his buttocks. His virile member was long and erect. He wore two horseskin breeches with the hair left on the outside. Behind him he carried a forked branch that took eight men to lift and whose track was large enough to serve as the borderline of a province; this is called the track of Dagda's wand.[11]

From what can be understood of the following pages—for the manuscript has been altered, no doubt intentionally—the Dagda meets a young girl. "The Dagda's desire went toward her," the narrator prudishly says. But because he has overeaten, he cannot carry out his intention. For this the young girl, with no lack of scorn, vigorously criticizes him, which unleashes a vain burst of anger from the Dagda.

It would be a mistake to take this burlesque and smutty episode as a simple diversion. By insisting on the gluttonous and hypersexual nature of the Dagda the anecdote wishes to draw attention to the characteristics of the third office; but because the equilibrium between sexuality and nutrition is ruptured; to the benefit of the latter, nothing works. Note that the Fomor, the representatives of original Chaos, are the cause of this. For the most part the Dagda is in full digression. He has returned to the original oral stage of sexuality. Gorged on porridge, he is nothing more than a big baby, a prepubescent. But this temporary impotence, due to an external intervention, emphasizes (thanks to its aspect of contrast) the ordinary sexual activity of the Dagda, which is prodigiously intense. The Dagda is always presented as having a rendezvous with a woman, and even at times when it is expected that he will concern himself with serious matters, he always finds time to keep this type of engagement. Such is the case during the preparations for the Battle of Mag Tured. We are even told that this rendezvous was set for the day of the feast of Samhain, and that the woman with whom he couples was none other than Morrigan, a sort of goddess of carnal love and war. This is not by chance. In addition, as the Dagda is the "Father of All," he must assume his duties. He has numerous children: in particular Oengus (sole choice), the Mac Oc (the young Apollonian figure), and Brigit (the triple goddess) who also fulfills the three offices. Brigit reappears under the name of Boinn, wife of her brother Elcmar, another name for Ogma, but in his negative aspect. It is from the adulterous union of the Dagda and Boinn that Oengus is born. But because Boinn is Brigit it is with his own daughter that the Dagda assures—in a sacred and symbolic incestuous union—the continuity of the race of gods. This doesn't, however, prevent him from being dispossessed of his domain of Brug-na-Boyne (the megalithic mound at New Grange) by his own son, the Mac Oc. The latter, counseled by his adoptive father, Mider (or Mananann in another version), seals a pact with the Dagda, the terms of which lend to him the domain during a period of a day and a night. Unfortunately the Dagda didn't heed the fact that symbolically a day and a night express the whole, the negation of time—in other words, eternity. So he was obliged to abandon his realm to his son. It should also be mentionned that the conception and birth of Oengus was also a challenge to time. The Dagda had in fact sent Elcmar on a mission so that he could profit from his absence and get close to his wife. Having placed an enchantment on Elcmar, this latter individual believed himself to have been absent for a day and a night whereas in reality Boinn had time to give birth to a son "symbolically conceived and born in the space of a whole day."[12] In short, the Dagda is a kind of regulator of time, which he arranges to his taste, an office that conforms perfectly with that of the Gallic Jupiter of whom Caesar says, "He controls the empire of heaven."

But it is necessary for a moment to return to the gluttonous and hypersexual aspect of the Dagda. The character of Bran Vendigeit in the Welsh tradition of the *Mabinogian* offers certain similarities with the Dagda. First, he owns a cauldron of resurrection. Second, he is a giant capable of stretching between two river banks so that his army can cross—which allows him the right to say: "Let him who is chief be a bridge."[13] This is Bran's paternal aspect. Following a disastrous battle in Ireland in which he was wounded in the foot by a poison spear, he asked his companions to cut off his head and take it with them. The head of Bran presided over a strange banquet of immortality in which the existence of time was abolished.[14] This Bran the Blessed (who some think can be recognized in Ban de Benoïc of the Arthurian romances) brings to mind the semihistorical Brennos, the leader of the Gallic expedition to Delphi in the second century B.C., who, when wounded, had himself killed by his companions.[15] In fact, this Bran who was wounded in the foot has many features that correspond with the Fisher King and Pelleas, as well as with another Welsh hero from the *Mabinogian*, Pwyll Penn Annwfn, husband of the goddess Rhiannon, the "great queen."[16] Let us not forget that the Fisher King, notably in the German version by Wolfram von Eschenbach, is struck by a blow from a spear that wounds his virility, following his transgression of a taboo that is of a sexual nature.[17] Having become impotent, the Fisher King could no longer govern his kingdom, which consequently withered and became sterile. It was thus necessary for Perceval (or Peredur) to appear on the scene before this situation could be normalized. But it is Perceval who became king of the Grail in place of the Fisher King. Might this not be another version of the transference of sovereignty at work in Brug-na-Boyne when the Mac Oc takes possession of his father the Dagda's realm? This is much more than simple coincidence.

It is not forbidden to see this element of giantism that characterizes the Dagda—from the sexual and alimentary point of view, as well as from the simple physical perspective also, singularly highlighted in another well-known character in literature and folklore, the famous Gargantua.

It is true that Gargantua is not the creation of Rabelais who extracted his hero from medieval tradition so as to make him into a symbol of the New Man in accordance with the conceptions of the Renaissance. Gargantua, by his gigantic aspects—his appetite, his sexuality—is indisputably of the same nature as the Dagda, an opinion that is in no way belied by the anonymous tale that appeared in Lyon in 1532 entitled "The Great and Inestimable Chronicles of the Great and Enormous Giant Gargantua" which establishes a relationship between Gargantua and the Arthurian legend (Gargantua's father and mother were created by Merlin with the help of his magic).[18] In any event Gargantua is a mythological Celtic character who has become part of folklore. In his *Historia Regum Britannia*, Geoffroy of Monmouth co-opts him as king of Britain under the name of Gwrgant of the Swine's Beard,[19] and the French toponymy is rich in places named "Pas de Gargantua" (Gargantua's Straits), "Tertre de Gargantua" (Gargantua's Mound), and other such names. This mythical figure is even found in ancient names such as the Monte Gargano in Italy, the Mont Gargan in Limousin, or Livry-Gargan in the Parisian region. In all his works Henri Dontenville has shown the exceptional importance of Gargantua in this "French mythology" that he has attempted to cull from a slew of incongrous documents.[20] For Henri Dontenville, Gargantua is unquestionably an ancient Gallic deity who has endured in popular memory in spite of all the attempts to repress or Christianize him.

There appears no reason to doubt this. It also should be compared with several Greek texts that tell of Hercules, the founder of Alésia, who married a native princess and sired Galatia, the mythical ancestor of the Galatians and the Gauls. In any event we are dealing here with a god of gigantic aspects with respect to strength, abundance, and sexuality, characteristics that are those of the Dagda, in both his military and producer aspects, as is indicated by the numerous local legends concerning him. Should we perhaps see him in Gargan—or Gargano—the name borne by the Gallic Jupiter as referred to by Caesar? This is possible, especially considering the frequency of toponyms—which are not all recent, nor from after Rabelais—where Gargan-Gargantua comes in is an argument in favor of this hypothesis. That said, what does this name mean? The current interpretation, joined to that of the names of Grandgousier and Gargamelle, his parents, or to the name of Badebec, his wife, tends to view it as a derivative of *bouche* (mouth), or *gueule* (jaw or mug) that comes from an older word—that on the one hand gave us the word *gargouille* (gargoyle), and on the other, the Latin *gurgem,* from which *ingurgiter* (ingurgitate, gulp down), as well as other words of the same family are derived. It is unfortunate that this interpretation gives more weight to the Rabelasian nature of the character than to the very origin of this deity, who is, let us repeat—Gallic and Celtic. Certainly Rabelais did everything to emphasize the *grand gueule* (big mouth) side of Gargantua. This isn't contradictory to one of the Dagda's aspects, but it was because of his own desire to create in this figure a "well of knowledge," who was a symbol of the voracity of the Rennaisance humanist on the material as well as on the intellectual plane. If Gargan, or Gargano, is originally Celtic, why not look for the significance of his name in the Celtic languages? This would seem logical, but strangely enough no one seems to have ever thought of this.[21]

It is an Armorican Breton folktale collected at the beginning of the century in the Forest of Camors (Morbihan) that gives us, if not the solution, then at least a valuable piece of information.[22] The collection is linked to the legend of Konomor, the Breton Bluebeard. The figure is a "salt seller" named, interestingly enough, the Gergan. In coming to the aid of the wife of the evil lord of Kamorh, who was trying to capture and kill her by unleashing his dog upon her, the Gergan took a handful of salt and threw it at the lord's castle, causing it to be swallowed up by the Earth. This is a gesture of execration that certainly has a druidic tone to it. It is a magic gesture, and brings to mind Pantragruel, son of Gargantua (according to Rabelais), and also a demonic character of medieval mysteries, who made his enemies thirsty by throwing salt on them—furthermore showing that Rabelais was not completely innocent of reusing part of the tale. The coincidence is too close to be chance. As for the name of Gergan, it is the High Vannetais dialectal form of the classical Breton Gargam, which literally means "curved thigh," or in other words "the lame man." The term *gar*, "thigh," is, moreover, not only Breton, but also existed in ancient French in that it is the root for the French words *jarretière* (garter) and *jarretelle* (suspender) as well as the English word *garter*. Now the word *gargamelle* that so many have incorrectly tried to make mean "big mouth," is nothing but a French diminutive of Gargam, and her son Gargantua simply borrows his mother's name in a somewhat more masculine form. Gargamelle and Gargantua are originally figures with "curved thighs," in other words lame deities, which brings us back to certain descriptions of the Dagda, and gives evidence, as in the examples of Odin and Tyr—the one-eyed and one-armed dieties respectively—to a characteristic of the god noted for his physical handicap or peculiarity. Indeed, in mythological symbolism quite frequently the all-seeing one is blind or one-eyed, for example, the god of eloquence has a stammer, the god of plenty and distribution has one-arm (Nuada), and the strong and fleet deity is lame or one-legged. By this reckoning, Gargantua, like his mother Gargamelle, is a fast and powerful supernatural being. Such describes the Gargamo of the Gauls who Caesar associated with Jupiter, a being simultaneously endowed with great physical strength, a prodigious appetite, an unrestrained sexuality, and who, like the Dagda, pitted all of that against such forces of darkness and Chaos as the Fomor.

To be more specific, the relationship of this Dagda-Gargantua with the statues of the Gallic Jupiter figure is quite confusing. Paul-Marie Duval notes in regard to the Gallic Jupiter that

> [He is] depicted in a particulary militaristic fashion on a series of numerous Gallo-Roman monuments, especially those in the northeast region that have no equivalent elsewhere. In these the columns of the mounted god strike down a monster with the tail(s) of a serpent

or a fish (what is traditionally called the *anguiped giant*) or are held up by this tail. So whereas no Roman gods (except for the Dioscuri in exceptional cases) have been represented on horseback, here the god of the sky is even depicted as a mounted warrior, holding the thunderbolt, and sometimes the wheel. The dedication consistently names this figure as Iupiter Optimus Maximus.[23]

This famous monument called "The Rider of the Anguiped" has not ceased to intrigue commentators. While it is certainly a Jupiter, it is only Roman in name, and most probably masks a Gallic deity. Celtic scholar Paul-Marie Duvall continues,

> The symbolism of these monuments is visibly of a cosmic, metaphysical order. As for the group itself that crowns the ensemble, it expresses the triumph of celestial light that sees all, over the hidden, subterranenan forces (as the giant who appears to be emerging from the ground and his serpentform nature that emphasizes his chtonian character—day getting the best of night, pure forces over impure, perhaps eternal life over death, and, occcasionally, the imperial peace over the barbarian world). At present it is only in Gaul that this expression of the complex power of Jupiter has been found.[24]

It is not strictly necessary to fall back on any kind of proposals phrased in Manichean terms that see everything in terms of black and white. It is a metaphysical, not a moral question. But in this instance the vision proposed by Paul-Marie Duvall seems justified: "The Rider of the Anguiped," the authentic Gallic Jupiter, is none other than Dagda-Gargantua, fighting against the Fomor, the personification of original Chaos. And why couldn't the anguiped be Balor? And if this is not exactly what this statuary group signifies, it must be something relatively close.

This Anguiped Rider is sometimes the holder of a wheel, and it so happens that Gallo-Roman statuary is rich with representations of a mysterious unnamed god, holding a wheel. The best representation of this is the Gundestrup Cauldron on which the god is bearded, his arms in the air, half-hiding a wheel, held by a helmeted warrior. In some cases the god with the wheel is identified as Jupiter. This suggests that this wheel should be viewed as the major attribute of the celestial god, as thunder without the bolt of lightning, not as a luminous flash of lightning, but instead connecting the sound of thunder to the sound made by chariot wheels. And the wheel has been proposed as a solar symbol, Jupiter's domain. What is most important is to know the exact significance of the association between the Celtic Jupiter and the wheel. The wheel is not the attribute of the Dagda, but there is in Irish tradition an interesting character who is the hero of the extrordinary epic tale *The Siege of Druim Damhgaire*. In it we meet the druid Mog Ruith whose magical exploits against the druids of King Cormac are quite hallucinatory. The name Mog Ruith means "servant of the wheel," which can only bring us back to the god of the wheel in Gallo-Roman statuary, and therefore to Jupiter. Mog Ruith is a kind of vaguely historicized doublet of the Dagda with whom he shares every characteristic.[25] But, in addition, Mog Ruith transports himself on a bronze chariot that has the appearance of a flying chariot. He also flies like a bird himself, further emphasizing his celestial aspect. He has power over the other elements in that he frees the waters that the druids of Cormac had bound, and he fights these same druids with fire and the druidic wind. He is one-eyed like Odin and embodies druidic omnipotence. The wheel—of which he is the servant, and with which certain Gallic deities are adorned—is perhaps the symbol of the knowledge of the past and future, the "Wheel of Fortune," that only the druids—and the druid-gods (which are are the same thing)—are capable of mastering because of their all-seeing abilities.

Moreover, the god with the wheel has often been identified with Taranis, whose name contains the word *taran*, meaning "thunder." This Taranis is mentioned by Lucan in the *Pharsalia*, in the company of Teutas and Esus. It clearly seems that this triad of Lucan's could be a sort of Christian-style trinity. The three names likely designate the same individual, each seen under a different function. As Taranis, it is the function of the thundering Jupiter that is most dominat. The scholiast Lucan states explicitly that the victims offered to Taranis were broken in containers of wood, which obviously brings to mind those willow mannequins of which Caesar spoke (VI, 16) and in which prisoners were burned alive as sacrifices. Obviously linked to fire, the name Taranis could very well be a metathesis of Tanaris, or Tanaros, the equivalent of which is the German Donar, and which contains the Britainnic term *tam*, or "fire." Indeed the name Tanaros is affirmed by an inscription discovered in Chester, Great Britain, and substantiates that Gallic

Jupiter-Taranis is the aspect of the Dagda that most conforms with the Indian example of Indra. All the more so as at the beginnings of the historical era, Indra, is clearly linked to the caste of the military aristocracy.

As Esus, it is the aspect of the "good god" that predominates. Indeed the name of Esus is the exact equivalent of the name Optimus that is attached to Jupiter. In the Cluny Museum, on the altar of the Nautes of Paris, Esus is represented as a woodchopper. He seems to be linked to the tree—perhaps the oak as is Jupiter—and Lucan (who identifies Esus once with Mars, and another time with Mercury), informs us that the victims offered to the god were hung down from a tree, probably upside down, and that they were bled. This cruel rite, which was perhaps a simple simulation intended to obtain regeneration, curiously enough can be found again in a version of the Grail Quest with regard to the vengence exacted by Perceval against his father's murderers.[26] Nevertheless this god presents himself as a simple laborer. On the Nautes altar he is pruning a tree with a long billhook. On a bas-relief in Trêves he is attacking the tree trunk with a hatchet, but what is most surprising is that the tree's foliage is arranged in such a way as to allow a bull's head to be seen while three birds perch on its branches. Now a bas-relief on the Nautes altar, which neighbors that of Esus, represents a bull in the forest with three large birds on his head and rump that the pure Gallic inscription allows to be identified as *tarvos trigaranus,* that is, the "bull with three cranes." This tarvos trigaranus has inspired a great number of commentaries, and it can be found, curiously enough, in the chansons de geste, in particular the *Song of Roland,* under the name of Tervagant who the Saracens worshiped at the same time as Apollo and Muhammed. It should be noted that several examples of three-horned bulls exist in Gallo-Roman statuary, and that the idea of the triad, or trinity, is familiar to all of the Celts. That said, it is obvious that the god Esus, woodchopper and woodsman who brings to mind the woodsman encountered in Chrétien de Troyes's *Knight of the Lion,* is linked in one way or another to this bull with the three cranes. The Armorican coins of the Osismi people, representing a horse, topped by a bird—probably the leader, or the celestial guide—who is leaping over a bull, help confirm this connection. This image on the coin can only concern a legend of which Esus is the hero. D'Arbois de Jubainville proposed this as an illustration of an episode from the *Tain Bô Cualngé,* the great Ulster epic in which the hero Cuchulainn fights against three Irish kingdoms to defend the Brown Bull of Cualngé. The divine bull, the object of so much covetousness, is harassed by the goddess

Morrigan who takes the form of a bird (Morrigan is also a triple goddess). This interpretation is no worse than any of the others and none any more satisfying has been provided. In this case it is necessary to see in Cuchulainn a sort of heroicized and somewhat historicized doublet of the Dagda, the Dagda in his aspect as a protector of the people and their property that which in this case is the sacred bull.

This protector of people and property aspect can be found again in the last term of Lucan's triad. This is Teutas to whom, Lucan asserts, victims are sacrificed by suffocation, their heads plunged into a cauldron. Teutas, or Toutatis, a name given at times to Mars—and at other times to Mercury—is a name worthy of Jupiter. The name means "Father of the People," or "Father of the Tribe." A name almost equivalent to the Dagda's Ollathir. Certain commentators claim that it is a question of a common name and can be applied to any guardian deity of a social group. This is not only a common name but a periphrastic label. And all the names of the god are of this variety. Why not consider Teutas-Toutatis as a personalized entity, at least among certain peoples?

This in no way prevents the Gallic Jupiter from having other cognomens and other attributes. It is for this reason that the god accompanied by the ram-headed serpent can be classified as a Jupiter-Dagda figure. Such a god is depicted on one of the plates of the Gundestrup Cauldron. He is holding a torque in one hand and in the other grasps a ram-headed snake by the throat. But he has stag's antlers, which connects him to Cernunnos, the horned god, who doesn't seem Indo-European. On the Mavilly Pillar in the territory of the Santone people in what is now France he is a kind of warrior-god accompanied by a serpent with the head of a ram. This motif appears no where else among the Gauls. It must be said that the serpent theme had little chance of spreading in Ireland, where snakes are practically unknown. Yet another divine attribute seems to have met with great success in Gaul: the mallet.

The god with the mallet exists nowhere other than in Gallic territory. The inscriptions name him Sucellos, which literally means "smack-hard," or "he who strikes well," a name that perfectly suits his sculpted representation, just as it fits the description of the Dagda carrying his ambiguous club. Generally he appears to be bearded and of a ripe age, and clad, Gallic style, in a short tunic, breeches, and a *capuchon*. Sometimes he holds his mallet very high in one hand, as if it were a scepter, and a very pot-bellied vase in the other, and at times he is encircled by two small Gallic casks, or at other times accompanied by a dog. In that nearly two hundred representations of this figure have been discovered, variations of it are numerous. In certain cases the mallet looks more like a cask than a hammer; in others this god is often accompanied by a crow, which can't help but bring to mind the goddess Morrigan-Bodbh who often appears in the form of this bird. Whatever the case, this mallet is intriguing. Is it a symbol of death? One is tempted to believe so as various usages and traditions of western Europe refer to him in regard to funeral and prefuneral rites. Even today in Ireland, a hammer is placed in the coffin "for knocking on the door to Purgatory." In certain parishes of Brittany, namely Guénin (Morbihan), there is a common custom concerning "the hammers of the good death." When the agony of death for someone persisted too long, the oldest woman of the village would seek a stone at the priest's house—a kind of club or hammer that was reserved for that purpose—and hold it above the dying individual's head while telling him to prepare to die.[27] In certain regions of Great Britain the same hammer, the *holy mawle,* was hung behind the church door, and it was said that a son whose father had reached the age of seventy had the right to kill him. In short, it was another way of "shaking the coconut palm."[28] It is believable that such things were apparently put to practical use, especially in societies that couldn't allow themselves any useless mouths to feed. In any event all of this is in conformance with the image of the Dagda, whose club could kill and resuscitate, who was the master of time and space, and community guardian as Teutas, the provider of goods as the master of the cauldron, the master of fire as Taranis, the father of all and the celestial father as Jupiter, the master of life and death as Dispater, intoxicated with food, drink, and sex as Gargantua yet, nonetheless, the sworn enemy of monsters as the anguiped rider. He was also the master of beasts as Esus the Very Good or the Man of the Woods, lame because of his fleetness, one-eyed because of his sight and, therefore, a druid-magician-prophet, poet and philosopher, legislator who stood for surety of contracts even when he was their victim, the master of fates as the god of the wheel, participating in every function and transcending all of them, the best of all, since this is the definitive meaning of his name of Dagda. The least that can be said of the Celtic Jupiter is that he is an extremely complex individual.

10

THE THREE-FACED GODDESS

A fifth deity who had some importance to the Gauls, according to Caesar's nomenclature, is Minerva, the goddess who "teaches the principles of arts and crafts" (VI, 17). Regarding her, Caesar uses the word *opus*, which has the general meaning of all work resulting from human activity, and the word *artificium*, which designates technique, métier, the means of proceeding. It is not necessary to confine this Gallic Minerva to a purely material role for it is quite obvious that she is the patron of both artists and artisans, as well as of warriors—a fact too often forgotten—since war is an "art." Contrary to what one would think, this Minerva is not exclusively of the third function. It is undeniable that, like the Jupiter-Dagda, she shares the three Indo-European functions.

We do not know her Gallic name, although she sometimes bears the name of Belisama, the "Very Shining One," namely in Saint-Lizier (Ariège), and at other times she is referred to as *medica*, which indicates her connection to the first function. One of the best representations of this Gallic Minerva (Gallo-Roman, actually) is that of a bronze head wearing a helmet that has owl-like features and wears a crest in the form of a swan—one recently discovered in Kerguily en Dinéault (Finistère) and is currently in the Museum of Brittany in Rennes. Inscriptions concerning this goddess are numerous throughout the entire Celtic territory, further underscoring her importance. The Gauls had the reputation for being skillful artisans and artists of merit, even when the Greeks and Romans didn't understand the meaning behind their thought processes.

In Ireland this figure is indisputably the famous Brigit, daughter of the Dagda (like Minerva-Athena is the daughter of Jupiter-Zeus), the patron of poets, the fili, and doctors (first function); artisans, blacksmiths, and bronze workers (third function); and she often appears with the features of a warrior (second function). Moreover, certain Irish texts make mention of three different Brigits, implying that she is a goddess of three faces, or a triple goddess. It is she who presided over the feast of Imbolc on the first day of February. It is on this same day that the Irish pay hommage to Saint Bridget of Kildare, who for Christians seems to have replaced the pagan deity. In truth the Irish have made Saint Bridget into their great patron saint, following only Saint Patrick in importance. And when it is said that Bridget maintained an eternal fire at the abbey of Kildare, of which she was abbess, it brings to mind the eternal fire maintained in Bath, Great Britain, to honor the goddess Sul who Solinus identified precisely with Minerva. We also can see in this a certain analogy with the worship of Vesta in Rome.

The name Brigit comes from the radical *bri* or *brig* meaning "high," and by extension "strong," as is recognizable in certain continental toponyms such as Bregenz (Brigantia), Briançon, or even Brech (Morbihan), a name that despite its consonance is not Breton but Gallic in origin. The word also can be seen in the Breton *bré*, in the sense of "height, hill," or utilized as a prefix (Brélevenez, Bréholo). It has also provided a number of quite ancient names for fortresses located on high ground.

But the name Brigit disappeared quickly from Irish tradition, hidden because it was troubling for the Christians and and cast a cloud over Saint Bridget. This has not prevented transcribers of the Gaelic tradition from presenting her in their tales but under varying names. She can be recognized in Boinn, in Eithne, in Etaine, as well as in Bodbh and Morrigan, all of whom also are interchangeable triple goddesses. In addition it is a strong possiblity that she could be the Irish Macha, who is also the Welsh Rhiannon and the Gallo-Roman Epona. She is most surely Tailtiu, the Irish Earth goddess, the mother Earth goddess of Lugh, in honor of whom the latter instituted the feast of Lugnasad on the first of August, six months after the feast of Imbolc of which Brigit is the patron.

Boinn (or Boyne, or Boann) literally means the "white cow" (bovinda). The name appears quite commonly in a society of herdsmen who measured their wealth in heads of cattle or sheep. In this sense Boinn represents prosperity, and the color white (attached to the idea of beauty and racial purity) reinforces that function. She is the wife of Elcmar, brother of the Dagda, but is also a black double, a negative of that individual meaning "envious" or "jealous." By sending Elcmar away and coupling with Boinn, the Dagda is not committing adultery as the texts—anxious to respect Christian morality—would have us believe, but turns his dark side into nothing, magnifying his white aspect of "the good god," and thus thanks to prosperity engenders the "young son" (Mac Oc) who is also the "sole choice" (Oengus). This is the story told to us by a tenth-century poem by Cinead ua Hartacain in which it is learned that Elcmar also bears the name of Nechtan, a Gaelic tranposition of the Latin Neptunus, and that he owns a marvelous fountain known as the Well of Segais. After Oengus's birth, Boinn wishes to purify herself—and undoubtedly restore a kind of virginity—and she says: "I will go to the beautiful Well of Segais so that there is no doubt concerning my chastity. I will walk widdershins three times around it living without lie."[1] We are dealing with a circumnambulation ritual here that can still be seen today in the customs of certain healing springs in Brittany. It should be noted that Boinn claims to perform the ritual in the opposite direction of the sun's course, an indication of an intent toward regeneration, of a return to the past, which implies that the Well of Segais can be considered as a sort of fountain of youth. But as the *Dindshenchas* recounts in prose, this was "a secret spring in the prairie of the Sidhe of Nechtan. Whoever went there did not return without their eyes bursting, at least anyone other than Nechtan and his three cupbearers."[2] The magical operation of rejuvenation and regeneration is therefore dangerous.

> Once Boinn went there out of pride, to experience the powers of the spring, and she said that there was no secret power that could touch the power of her beauty. She made a complete circle of the spring facing toward her left, three times. Three waves emerging from the spring broke over her. They took with them a thigh, a hand, and an eye. She turned toward the sea to flee her shame, and the water followed her to the mouth of the Boyne.[3]

And it is since that time that the river to which Boinn gave her name has existed: the Boyne.

The etiological legend is one thing. The current procedure of using myth to explain the name of a river, hill, or valley does not mask the original fable. Boinn wishes to go backward and restart the previous cycle. But this is an impossibility and an error.[4] In the eternal becoming, which seems to be the druidic conception of the world, one cannot go back. On the contrary it is necessary to go forward, and rejuvenation and regeneration are *ahead,* not behind. Boinn disappears as the "white cow,"[5] but reappears later as Etaine, the heroine of one of the most beautiful love stories of Ireland.[6] Etaine, the daughter of the king of Ulster, the wife of the god Mider, then, following a rebirth, the wife of King Eochaid, is the ancestor of a royal line. In Ireland she bears the name of Be Finn, the "beautiful woman," or the "white woman." This mythological figure, who is of the highest importance, does not simply sink into oblivion, but crossed the sea, as did the greater part of Irish legends, and she was incorporated into the Arthurian romances. Indeed, Boinn-Be Finns will be seen again under the name of Vivian in the legend of Merlin. It is also she who will become the Lady of the Lake, the initiator of Lancelot of the Lake.[7] As we have seen, the gods never die, they merely transform.

But under the aspect of Etaine, Boinn is humanized. She gradually loses her quality of a primordial goddess to become sovereignty incarnate. And in one variation of the legend she takes the name of Ethne or Ethlinn, and is then stripped of her Tuatha de Danann aspect, renounces her pagan divinity, and has herself baptized by Saint Patrick.[8] The fable is quite eloquent, and despite the change of religion, the deity never truly dies but transforms according to new conceptions. Boinn-Brigit not only becomes Saint Bridget of Kildare, but because she is the mother of the gods of druid Ireland, she can just as easily be viewed as the Virgin Mary, mother of the Christian god, and as elsewhere, both his "wife" and "daughter" simultaneously. If one digs beneath appearances the theological content of the two is identical.

But if Brigit-Minerva is representative of the third function, that of procuring fecundity and abundance, she is also a *banfile,* which means "woman-fili," or "woman-poet," or even "woman-prophet." Sometimes this word is improperly translated as "druidess," for it is the term *banrui* that literally means "woman-druid." Therein lies the problem of the existence of druidesses. But it is not because Brigit is a banfile that she is a druidess. The term is quite recent and susceptible to having been adopted by Christianity in order to classify Brigit in a purely literary domain that has less "fire and brimstone" than that of the druids. In actuality it is impossible to affirm if druidesses existed at all. No text—insular or continental—tells us, and so it is equally impossible to assert that there weren't any. The only certainty is that women belonged to the druidic sacerdotal class without their exact duties being specified. As for Brigit, if she is a druidess it is because she is a goddess, and by definition every druid is a god and every god a druid. Brigit embodies druidism as the art of poetry—in the most sacred sense of the word—and it is this qualification of the muse of poetry, the mistress of the arts, that is analagous to the definition that Caesar gives of the Gallic Minerva. And as medicine is an "art," with a good deal of incantatory magic, it follows that Brigit was also the muse of physicians. It is probable that Airmed, the daughter of Diancecht, is another name of Brigit. In any event Brigit possesses all the offices, thereby affirming her connection to the sacerdotal class.

It is perhaps by this artistic (poetic or medicinal) aspect that the Gallic Minerva is Belisama, the "very shining one," which would indicate that she is also the Sirona of Gallic inscriptions whose name refers to the star shining in the sky. She is also the Arianrhod of Welsh tradition, the heroine of the fourth branch of the *Mabinogian.* Her name means "silver wheel," and among the Welsh, Caer Arianrhod, literally "city of Arianrhod," designates the constellation Corona Borealis. It is not too far a stretch to compare this Brigit, pagan goddess turned Christian saint, to the fairy Melusine, a diabolical being turned conditional Christian who was also mistress of arts and crafts (numerous endowments for churches, abbeys, and castles), a generous donor, and the mother of a large progeny.[9] In any case Melusine, like Brigit, Boinn, Etaine, and Tailtiu (the Earth mother of Ireland), is the mythical founder of a lineage, and like them, she manages to transform without ever disappearing.

But without her warrior aspect, the Celtic Minerva would not be complete. If she teaches crafts she also teaches the military art. Celtic literature and literature of Celtic origin is filled with examples of women-warriors who are also magicians, as well as the initiators of young men, from a military, sexual, and magical vantage point—perspectives that could not be envisioned separately. In Gallo-Roman statuary she sometimes is presented as the warrior Athena. Certain Gallic coins, mainly the Baïocasses of Normandy, show images of naked, armed women who are disheveled and seem to charge into combat like Furys. According to Dio Cassius (LXII, 6–7), in revolt against the Romans the British queen Boudicca, offered sacrifices and acts of thanksgiving to the goddess Andrasta or Andarta, the goddess of war. It so happens that there is a goddess Andarte, who was worshiped by the Voconces of the Drôme. But in Ireland, again in the general staff of the Tuatha de Danann, she is Morrigan, the daughter of Ernmas, which means "murder."

The etymology of Morrigan's name has been a subject of controversy. "Queen of Nightmares" is one interpretation it has been given, but it is more likely that it just simply means the "great queen" (the augmentative prefix *mor* is similar to the Gallic *ver* of Vercingetorix, and *rigan*, derived from *rig*, "king"). Her name immediately brings to mind that of Morgan the Fee of the Arthurian romances to whom Morrigan is connected by numerous elements, even if only those coming under the aspects of fury and sexuality. But the British Morgan is derived from the ancient *morigena*, "born of the sea," for which the corresponding Irish term would be *muirgen*. In any event the Irish Morrigan clearly has a triple aspect: she is sorceress and prophet, warrior, and inflamer of sexual desires. In the *Tain Bô Cualngé* she offers herself to the hero Cuchulainn in the form of a woman, then returns later to goad him into battle in the form of a cow and especially a crow (bodbh). At the time that preparations for the Battle of Mag Tured were being undertaken, she coupled with the Dagda and prophesied the arrival of the Fomor, which didn't prevent her from entering into the battle herself. "She went to Scene to kill the king of the Fomor. . . . She would steal the blood from his heart and the valor from his kidneys."[10] In the course of the action Morrigan "encouraged the Tuatha de Danann to throw themselves into battle with fervor and passion."[11] And she inflamed the passions of the combatants with a song. At the end it is she who announced the victory to all of Ireland, and finished by prophesying on the world to come. In this instance she is clearly identifiable with Bodbh, whereas a second version of the tale places her in the characteristic triad: "The three druidesses, Bodbh, Macha, and Morrigan, said that they would be the cause of showers of hail and clouds of poison that would befall the Fomor to such an extent that they would be rendered weak and confused, and that the druidesses would deprive them of their intelligence and good sense during the battle."[12,13] This is an excellent example of warrior magic.

The word *bodbh* means "crow," and it is often in the form of this bird that the Morrigan appears, especially on the fields of battle. But the word, *bodbh*, is ambiguous in that it also means "victory" as in the name of the British queen Boudicca, "victorious." As for Macha, we are dealing with the deity who caused the famous illness of the Ulaid (similar to labor pains) by the curse she cast over them because their king had forced her, while she was pregnant and ready to give birth, to run a race with his horses.[14] This Macha has something in common with horses, and can be considered as a mounted goddess, or even a mare-goddess, like Rhiannon, the heroine of the first and third branches of the *Mabinogion*.[15] The name of Rhiannon (Rigantona) can mean "great queen." The Gallic, or rather Gallo-Roman goddess, Epona, who is quite often represented in statuary as a mounted figure accompanied by a foal, or even as simply a mare and its foal, seems to have the same nature or origin as Rhiannon and Macha, although it is possible that she may not be Celtic.

The triad of Bodbh-Macha-Morrigan is in fact the representation of a single goddess in three different forms. The same holds true for the triple Brigit. There are numerous representations in Gallo-Roman statuary of three maternal figures, the Matrae or Matronae. Often these groups of mother goddesses bear names that make them the guardians of a well-defined social group of a town or city. Nor should we forget either that Ireland is sometimes incarnated by a triad of feminine personas such as Eriu, Banba, and Fotla. The number three, which symbolically speaking is the number of eternity and wholeness, was particularly favored by the Celts. The ancient mythico-historical traditions of Wales are presented in the form of triads (Triads of the British Isles) consisting of groups of three people who embody the characteristics of a function, of three striking events, or of three principles. We should also think of the triskelion—a symbolic ornament that, although not of Celtic origin, has become in some way the emblem of Celtic civilization—given the frequency with which it appears in Gallic and especially Irish plastic arts.

This does not prevent certain feminine deities in Gallo-Roman statuary from being accompanied by or even accompanying masculine dieties. This is an indication of functional complementarity, a method we find used in Irish tradition as well.

Keeping this in mind, even though Brigit in some way may be the goddess of medicine, there is also a god of medicine—Diancecht. In the same way, although there is a goddess of crafts, there is also a master artisan named Credne and a master smith named Goibniu both in the general staff of the Tuatha de Danann. Goibniu, whose name is derived from the root for the English word *goblins* and the French word *gobelins* (small fanciful beings who live underground and who are experts in the blacksmithing art), is a remarkable individual. "Goibniu the Smith was in his forge making swords, spears, and javelins, and because he made these weapons in three turns: the third turn was a finish and he would set it in the ring of the spear. And when the spearheads were stuck in the side of the forge, he would throw the shaft and the rings the way they would go into the spearhead and they would want no more setting."[16] This allowed the Tuatha de Danann to have new weapons every day. Of course this sacred smith, who has a corresponding figure in Welsh tradition under the name of Govannon, son of Dôn, is in the Vulcan-Haphaistos registry. He is the master of fire and metal and, therefore, knows the secrets of the Earth's interior. This theme has been fully explored, namely in the mythic German legend of Siegfried.[17] In Celtic stories he is also an intiator, the figure who reveals to the young hero how he should behave, in addition to being the one who forges invincible weapons for him. This is the case with Cuchulainn who obtains his name (Dog of Culann) from the smith Culann,[18] and with Finn Mac Cumail, who is initiated by the smith Lochan.[19] The character of the smith—always quarrelsome, ambiguous, intentionally demoniac, disturbing, and more or less a sorcerer—is well known in folktales in which he often plays an essential role.[20] It is said that in so-called primitive societies, the smith, by his knowledge and craft, is the master of agricutural works and the arts of war since he manufactures farm instruments as well as weapons. He is an authentic "master of the forges," and as such he represents a nonnegligible power in the society. It is for this reason that the knowledge of secrets that extend far beyond his craft are attributed to him and, in fact he should be referred to as a druid-smith. This is the case for Goibniu who as a god is also a druid.

For Goibniu is not satisfied with just his role as smith. After the Battle of Tailtiu, which witnessed the victory of the Gaels over the Tuatha de Danann, the latter are forced to content themselves with underground mounds and far away islands for their homes and their territory. But it is somewhere in this Otherworld that the Banquet of Goibniu is held—a banquet of immortality. It is very interesting to note that this banquet is held in the name and under the chairmanship of Goibniu. It is true that like Diancecht he was remembered for a long time, and indeed he is found cited in the company of Christ in an incantation against wounds that is preserved in a manuscript from the Saint Gall Monastery: "Quite strong is the science of Goibniu, quite strong is the point of Goibniu, the sharpened point of Goibniu, away from here!"[21] Brigit has perhaps disappeared from the tradition, but surely not Goibniu. And what about the Breton Saint Gobrien who cures boils (nails), and whose name is derived from the same root as Goibniu and Govannon?

Surrounded by formidable and efficient auxillary gods, clad in multiple names and faces, participating in the three Indo-European functions, mistress of poetry, magic, and prophecy, learned in various crafts, mother of all the gods, somewhat of a nymphomaniac and animated by the fury of a warrior, a triple goddess, but always single, probably the heir of the Great Goddess of prehistory, such is how the Celtic Minerva presents herself. Her complexity is as great as that of the Dagda.

11

In the Depths
of the Sanctuary

Despite its fragmentary and often contradictory pieces of information, Celtic mythology reveals a fairly strong underlying structure. Under whatever names they appear the deities can be relatively classified by function in accordance with the model provided by Caesar. But Caesar did not claim to have listed all of them, and many divine entities can only be integrated into his nomeclature with difficulty. It is not that they are less important, but perhaps of an origin or nature different than that of the Indo-European gods. In any event they pose a problem.

Consequently, we have not yet spoken of Cernunnos, a well-known deity thanks to the Gundestrup Cauldron and several Gallo-Roman monuments. He is the "horned god," the "god with stag antlers." The Gundestrup Cauldron presents him seated, Buddha-like, holding a torque in one hand and a ram-headed serpent in the other. His head is crowned with enormous antlers and he is encircled by four animals. On the Altar of the Nautes in Paris he appears with his legs bent back, and on a monument discovered in Reims he is spilling out a bag full of coins in the presence of a stag and a bull. In Nuits-Saint-Georges (Côte d'Or), he is three-headed, has antlers, holds a purse on his knees, and is accompanied by two goddesses, each of whom carries a horn of plenty. A tree, a bull, a dog, a hare, a boar, and a stag can be seen beneath him. The oddity in this depiction is the figure in the middle. By all evidence it is a woman with a naked torso who has a tower on her head and who has a male sex organ, making her androgynous. What is she doing next to Cernunnos and what is the exact signification of this god? As characteristics he has the Buddha pose, the three heads, and a symbol of abundance. The three heads indicate, by ternary symbolism, eternity and wholeness, an idea which, in the case of the Nuits-Saint-Georges monument, is reinforced by the presence of an androgyne who is more female than male. Would Cernunnos be a deity of abundance? Most assuredly he belongs to the third function—but is he Celtic? There is reason to doubt it.

There is no corresponding figure for Cernunnos among the Tuatha de Danann. On the other hand, the Leinster, or so-called Ossianic Cycle, does provide us with figures that may compare to him. The true name of Finn, the king of the Fiana, is Demne, which means the "deer." With a wife, Sadv, who lives half the year in the form of a doe, he has a son named Oisin, meaning "fawn," and a grandson named Oscar, "he who loves the stags." By way of comparison it should be noted that Cernunnos (pronounced Kernunnos) probably means "he who has the top of a stag's skull." Let us recall that the Fiana troop is a kind of itinerant knighthood whose activities consist of making war (on behalf of a king), and hunting. The fact that the texts concerning Finn and the Fiana are relatively recent has provided a pretext for those seeking to deny these tales any documentary value in Celtic mythology. In their view the adventures of the Fiana are adaptations of the stories concerning Ulster, although there is no proof for this whatsoever. The Leinster Cycle contains archaisms and situations that have nothing at all to do with the epic of Cuchulainn, Conchobar, and the Ulaid. To the contrary, it would seem that the primitive outline of the cycle, constantly reworked and rejuvenated in its expression, has its roots in a pre-Celtic past.

Indeed the Celtic legends (Ireland and Britain taken together) can be divided into three categories, each marked by an essential activity. The first of these categories is represented mainly by the Ulster Cycle: the protagonists are part of a society of cattle raisers. All these epic tales revolve around ruthless raids on cows and bulls, and the domestic animal used to guard the herds seems to have been the dog in that countless heroes have the word *dog* in their name such as Cuchulainn, Curoi, Conchobar, or Conall. The second category contains the Welsh *Mabinogion* (especially the first and fourth branches) and the Arthurian Cycle in which the protagonists belong to a society of boar hunters and pig breeders. Its most significant myth is that of the hunt of the boar Twrch Trwyth.[1] This society represents an evolution with regard to the example cited before it, one that has paved the way to an agrarian society. It is therefore less ancient, or more localized to Great Britain, which was beginning at that time to detach itself from primitive pastoral customs. The third category includes the Leinster Cycle, which deals with a society of deer hunters. Of the three, this one is most likely the oldest. In its basic outline the Leinster Cycle could date as far back as the prehistoric times of the reindeer hunters. This, of course, is only a hypothesis, but it is plausible and logical.

This timeframe would allow us to better situate Cernunnos in history. Representing abundance, surrounded by various animals, and wearing antlers he could be an ancient prehistoric deity who was recuperated by druidism, a deity who has recieved much subsequent worship. Breton hagiography is rich in anecdotes on Saint Edern (the son of Nudd, or Nuada) and the stag.[2] The stag, whose ambiguous moral nature has been strengthened (either good or evil depending on the circumstances), was exploited in the Arthurian romances.[3] Finally, under different metamorphoses, he became the god of the sorcerers, otherwise known as the horned, sulphurous, medieval Devil who presided over the famous Sabbat.[4] This shows the means by which the image of a deity can cross through the centuries, even if its exact meaning is no longer known.

Nonetheless, a statuette of a goddess wearing stag's antlers and holding a cornucopia and a patera was found at Broyes-les-Pesmes (Haute Saône), and now is housed in the British Museum. Is this a feminized version of Cernunnos? Does it have something to do with the woman-doe who was the wife of Finn and the mother of Oisin? There are other representations of goddesses accompanying animals, the most remarkable being that of the goddess Artio in the Bern Museum, in which a seated woman, an enormous bear, and a tree are shown. Artio comes from *arto,* one of the Celtic names for bear, the other name being *matu.* Is this a goddess of the bears or a goddess-bear? The bear is the symbol for royalty and sovereignty and King Arthur's name comes from the same word *arto,* and the name of King Math from the fourth branch of the *Mabinogion* comes from *matu.* But the Celtic king is nothing without "Sovereignty," which is most often represented by a woman who one weds or with whom one has sexual relations—Guinevere particularly for King Arthur. Wouldn't the bear-goddess of Bern be the symbolic depiction of the king-bear, in the shelter of the druidic tree, before divine

Sovereignty? According to the *Mabinogion,* King Math cannot live peacefully unless his feet are resting in the lap of a young virgin.[5] Queen Medb of Connaught, whose name means "drunkeness," and who represents Sovereignty, as it was symbolically imagined by the Celts extremely well, was quite generous with, as the texts say, "the friendship of her thighs," not only to her husband King Ailill, but to any warrior to whom she took a fancy. Before courtly romancers froze her into a single affair with Lancelot, Queen Guinevere had this same nature, and her relations with the Knights of the Round Table are rather ambiguous. It must be said that the *refined love,* or *courtly love,* if it is an exaltation of femininity, is also and especially the recognition of the idea of Sovereignty incarnated by the woman.[6] All of this is the memory and quite powerful resurgence, at certain times, of a social state that precedes the arrival of the patriarchal Indo-Europeans, in which the gynocratic principles were at least as important, if not more so, than the androcratic principles.

But there are other representations of goddesses accompanied by animals. A bronze from Ardennes, housed at the Bibliotheque Nationale of Paris, shows a woman who is believed to be the goddess Arduinna astride a boar, eponym of the Ardennes. By virtue of the boar's symbolism she would be more a deity of war than of the hunt. In Welsh tradition the thematic link between a divine woman and the boar appears quite often, particularly in certain episodes of the archaic tale of *Cuhlwch and Olwen.*[7] There is also the goddess of the birds as can be seen on one of the plates of the Gundestrup Cauldron. This brings to mind Morrigan-Bodbh, Morgan the Fee, and the Rhiannon of the Welsh tradition whose birds put the living to sleep and woke the dead.[8] And then of course there is the Gallo-Roman Epona whose name indicates her kinship with the horse, in that the word *epona* seems to be a British transcription (with replacement of the *kw* sound by *p*) of a Latin term derived from *equus,* meaning "horse." It is true that traditionally, the majority of Irish kings, historical or mythological (even the Dagda, Eochaid Ollathir), bore the name of Eochaid, which seems to derive from the ancient Indo-European *ekwo,* thereby signifying a king-horse or king-cavalier.[9] Nevertheless this Epona is linked in one way or another to an equine theme, just as are the Welsh Rhiannon and the the Irish Macha.[10]

In any case, the relationships between Celtic deities and animals are constant, and it will be necessary to return to this point later in regard to possible totemism among the Celts as well as to probable shamanic components of druidism. But on a strictly sociological level, this familiarity with the animals is explained because overall the Celts were a people of hunters and cattle breeders, especially in Ireland where there wasn't representation of a god of the third function, one who specialized in agriculture. Moreover, it doesn't seem as if there was one in Gaul either, unless Cernunnos fills that office. In Welsh tradition the character of Amaethon, son of Dôn and brother of the smith Govannon, can be considered as an image of the agrarian deity. But almost nothing is known about him except that his name means "laborer," which doesn't prove very much as this also could be said about the Irish Mac Cecht, the "son of the plow," whose mention constitutes the sole allusion to agriculture in the pantheon of the Tuatha de Danann. The name of Amaethon, however, provides a valuable clue for it comes from the same word as the Gaulish *ambactos* (Caesar, VI, 15), which means "servant." This quite clearly suggests that agriculture was regarded as a subalternate function, which is entrusted not to citizens but to servants, who are not to be confused with slaves. It is even possible to claim that the Celts, an intellectual, artisanal, and warrior elite, abandoned the work in the fields to the autochthonous populations they had subjugated in western Europe. This would help explain the remarkable absence of an agrarian god in Celtic mythology.

But there is no god of the sea either. The Gallo-Roman representations of Neptune concern only the patronage of springs and rivers. There is not a single mention of the maritime realm. In Ireland one can certainly come across the name of Nechtan, which is the Gaelic transposition of Neptunus, moreover, this is one of the cognomens of Elcmar who himself is a black double of the Dagda. Now Elcmar-Nechtan is the master not of the sea, but of the marvelous Well of Segais. It seems that the Celts, particularly the Irish, ignored the sea, and in fact, contrary to popular opinion, all the Celtic peoples except for the Veneti were land dwellers who either scorned the sea or feared it. It will be necessary to revisit this point in regard to the hypothetical legacies of an Atlantic civilization (not to say Atlantean).

Irish tradition does present us with a god who adds to this confusion. This is Mananann mac Lir, who appears in Welsh tradition under the name of Manawyddon ab Lyr. *Lir* or *Lyr* means "waves" or ocean," but the name of Mananann-Manawyddon is linked to that of the Isle of Man, appropriately meaning the "manx." It often has been said that he was the god of that island—located halfway between Great Britain and Ireland—which is currently still very Gaelic.[11] But, conversely, it may be the isle that gave its name to the character and not vice versa. He belongs to the general staff of the Tuatha de Danann, and though he does not participate in the Battle of Mag Tured, he does appear in numerous Irish tales as a character of considerable importance. He himself says to Oengus Mac Oc: "I am the king of your kings, the elder of your armies, the light of your batallions, and the prince of your champions."[12] He also declares that he is the adoptive son of the Dagda. After the Battle of Tailtiu, which witnessed the defeat of the Tuatha de Danann at the hands of the Gaels, he becomes the supreme chief of the Tuatha. "They were brought before the noble High King Mananann so that they could take counsel and advice. Mananann's advice to the warriors was for them to disperse into the sidhe and establish themselves in the beautiful plains and hills of Ireland. Mananann would divide among the nobles their dwelling places in the sidhe. And he created the *feth fiada*, the Banquet of Goibniu, and the Pigs of Mananann for the warriors. As a result of the feth fiada the princes could no longer be seen, by the Banquet of Goibniu the supreme kings became ageless and did not grow old, and that the Pigs of Mananann could be killed for their food and yet survive for their sustenance. Mananann tought the nobles how to install their fairy homes and how to arrange their fortresses in the manner of the households of the Land of Promise, Emain Ablach."[13] In this manner Mananann is the supreme chief of the Tuatha de Danann who reside both in the sidhe, the megalithic mounds of Ireland, and the more or less mythical islands that surround that country. He governs the Land of Promise, a common name of the Celtic Otherworld, that has nothing of the Beyond about it. It is truly an *other* world, one with which it is possible to communicate under certain conditions. He also presides over the Banquet of Goibniu, a banquet of immortality to which he assigns the marvelous pigs who are perpetually reborn. Finally he is the embodiment of the feth fiada, a magic charm that gives the Tuatha the gift of invisibility to use when they wish to circulate among humans and remain unseen. Numerous folktales have retained the memory of this feth fiada, mainly in Brittany, and in connection with fairies.[14] Mananann resides most often in the Land of Promise where he is married to the goddess Fand, whose name means "swallow," but he experiences some conjugal mishaps, mainly because of Cuchulainn.[15] He frequently intervenes in human affairs, like a kind of Odin-Wotan, or Merlin. In particular he is the father of the hero Mongan whose curious story is recounted in certain tales.[16] The hero Bran, son of Febal, meets him at sea and Mananann gives him an admirable description of Emain Ablach.[17]

The Welsh Manawyddon, it seems, does not have the same importance. He is the hero of the third branch of the *Mabinogion* in which he is shown to be a magician and master craftsman. He married the goddess Rhiannon.[18] He is often cited in poems attributed to the bard Taliesin. In a more recent tale he becomes the oracle of the hero Caradawc, who is perhaps the historical Caractacos of Tacitus or the Caradoc of the Arthurian romances.[19] He constructs a strange, round-shaped prison with all the bones of the Romans killed in Great Britain, a prison intended for traitors, Picts, and Saxons. In this Welsh tradition he is the brother of Bran the Blessed, the master of the Cauldron of Resurrection.

Mananann-Manawyddon ab Lyr always appears as coming from "elsewhere," that is the Land of Promise, traditionally located beyond the sea. This is why he has been made a "son of the waves" (Lyr or Lir, who should not be confused with the king whose misfortunes are recounted by Geoffroy of Monmouth in his *Historia* and who later became Shakespeare's King Lear), a name that indicates his kinship with the Otherworld. By the same token he has been given the name of the Manx, because the Isle of Man is symbolically beyond the sea for the Britains as well as for the Irish, and is from all the evidence, a central point between the two countries. Moreover Mananann-Manawyddon is no doubt only a relatively recent cognomen. It is perhaps necessary to seek the name he bore before, which is Mider, master of the sidh of Bri-Leith, one of the Tuatha de Danann who does not appear very often but who is indicated, however, as being king of Mag Mor, the "great plain," a variant name for the Otherworld.

Indeed, the different versions of *The Courtship of Etaine* show us these two interchangeable personalities (Mananann and Mider), and it is the most Christianized version that features Mananann.[20] It is more than likely that Mider was the original name, more so because a name is found on Gallo-Roman statuary and epigraphy in eastern Gaul. A bas-relief from the Haguenau Forest depicts a warrior holding a spear in his left hand and resting his right on the head of a bull. The inscription reads: *deo Medru Matutina Cobnerti filia.* This assumes the existence of a god Medros, whose name could come from the root word *med,* "measure," or *mid,* "hydromel," "mead," or, by extension "intoxicated." This would be an allusion to the banquet of immortality that was maintained by virtue of the pigs who were perpetually reborn. That is if it doesn't mean the "mediator," a role Mananann seems to play among the Tuatha de Danann. This Medros is also found in another bas-relief of Gunstett, near Wurth, in which he is wearing a helmet, and also on an inscription in honor of Toutatis Medros discovered in Rome. In one version of *The Courtship of Etaine,* Medros loses an eye following a blunder for which he holds his adoptive son Oengus responsible (although he is ultimately healed by Diancecht). Losing an eye makes him unsuitable for royalty, but like Nuada, and again thanks to Diancecht, he regains his power at the same time that he recovers his dignity. Undoubtedly this is a trial of initiation or regeneration similar to that undergone by the Fisher King of the Grail Quest. In any event, Mider becomes the husband of Etaine, a double of Boinn and, therefore, of Brigit. He temporarily loses her because of tricks played by his first wife, the sorceress Fuamnach, but the tale ends with his recovery of Etaine from King Eochaid, a double of the Dagda, and flying away with her in the form of a swan.[21]

Mananann-Mider appears to be a great god, but instead of reigning over a triumphant divine society he is content to balance out a group of defeated gods who have been literally occulted into an Otherworld. Again, this Otherworld is not a kingdom of the dead, but an "elsewhere" that is concomitant to this world, with the possibility of movement between the two. This is the reason that Manannan must balance out the relationships between his people (the Tuatha) and human beings. His most characteristic aspect, therefore, would be the mediator, a fairly accurate translation of Mider. But within this tripartition framework he can hardly be attributed a precise function. Unlike the majority of Celtic deities, he is no longer a social god; he is outside society, in a waiting stance, extending the life and activity of the gods and awaiting the propitious moment at which to reappear in the light of day and reestablish divine power. This is the meaning behind the gift of invisibility that he gave to the gods. The gods are still there, and always present, but one does not see them. They are, in some sense, repressed within the unconscious mind. But it takes but little to cause them to resurface.[22]

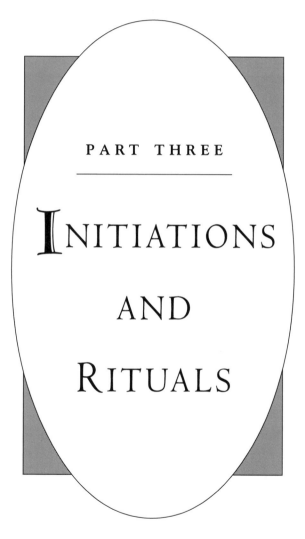

PART THREE

Initiations and Rituals

$\mathcal{M}$ythological tales constitute support for the beliefs of a people for the same reasons as the Gospels do for the Christian church. Easily retold, literally intelligible because of their concrete nature, capable of being interpreted for a deeper reading, they are indispensable reference points for a religious life. But they also express in a narrative, almost novelesque fashion, a certain number of rituals that originally were experienced as dramatic representations. Every theatrical work has something of the sacred in it. Every theatrical representation puts into play a dramatic activity whose outlines belong to the myth it embodies and materializes. Greek tragedy has retained something from much older religious rituals, if only through the idea of sacrifice, and comedy, by its derisory aspect, highlights cultural archetypes. The same holds true throughout the world.

The Catholic Mass is a dramatic representation and every dramatic representation is a sacred game similar to the Catholic Mass. But when a religion loses its ritual, whether because the ritual weakens, as is currently the case in the Catholic churches, or whether because the religion itself has disappeared, the dramatic representation becomes profane or conceals itself within a narrative description.[1] This is what happened with the Celts. The druidic religion no longer being practiced, its worship, which became little more than a memory, has become an object of curiosity, a thing of the past, even a superstition of our naive ancestors.[2] Ritual practices, therefore, have been *retold*—often being distorted in the process—instead of being *lived,* and these "tales" were quite naturally integrated into the ancient stories with their mythological structure. To a large degree this accounts for the origin of the epic—historical as well as mythological.

Thus it is important to pay the closest attention to these mythological tales if we wish to discern the great lines of druidic worship, for historical testimonies are rare and archaeological evidence almost nonexistent. This does not mean that everything should be taken literally, especially in regard to ruthlessly waged wars and fantastic combats, as well as human sacrifices. The majority of these tales were transcribed, if not composed— and often retouched—by clerics anxious to affirm, at times *a contrario,* the grandeur and primacy of Christianity. But such as they are, the Irish, Welsh, and Arthurian tales are documents, and it is up to us to analyze them in a critical fashion by comparing them with what history and archaeology tells us.

12

THE DRUIDIC SANCTUARY

We no longer live in a time that sees druidic altars on every small dolmen poking out of the bushes, or tables for bloody sacrifices on the famous and so particularly abundant basin stones. But it is important not to go to the other extreme and see a Gallic temple in every Roman brick construction.

The reality is that before being conquered by the Romans or assimilated by the Greeks, *the Celts never built temples.* There is never a mention of the existence of temples in Irish or Welsh epics, nor have Latin and Greek authors ever made mention of any existing Gallic temples before the conquest. The temple of Apollo that is mentioned as existing on the Isle of Britain is Stonehenge. It dates from the Bronze Age and, therefore, is not Celtic; moreover, it is an open-air sanctuary and not a constructed, covered temple. Titus Livy alludes to a temple of the Boii tribe, and Polybius mentions a temple of the Insubre people, but each reference is made to a location in the forest with no specifications concerning shape or architecture. Caesar himself wrote only of a *locus consecratus* (VI, 13 and 16), which in no way designates a Roman-style temple. As for archaeology, it has nothing to teach us in that there were no buildings. The only cultural buildings that can be attributed to the independent Celts are restricted to the Mediterranean region where, as in Entremont near Aix-en-Provence, they had been in contact with the Greeks and Romans and were influenced by them.

Constructed temples, mainly square ones, appeared after the conquest. But these were devoted to Roman deities and had nothing to do with druidic religion. Furthermore, the isolating of the druids, made legal during the time of Tiberius, forbade any druidic association with temples constructed after the conquest and Romanization. If sites of druidic worship still existed at that time they were carefully concealed, as Lucan reveals in the *Pharsalia*. But round and octagonal temples are also seen appearing on Gallic soil even though they are not to be found in Roman territory (outside of that of Vesta), proof of something—a memory, a habit. It has been suggested that the round temples are from an ancient ritual of circumambulation, which has been proven to have existed around the tomb of a hero. Thus the first temples would have been built around a tomb, which would explain the ambulatory of the later Christian churches. It certainly needs to be noted that numerous Christian sanctuaries were erected on the site of the tomb of a saint or martyr. But what does that prove? According to epic tales, the Irish had the custom of raising a funeral pillar of wood or stone on the site where a hero had met his death (although not necessarily on his tomb), and to sing praises in honor of the deceased around this pillar. It is a funeral rite and homage rite that has nothing very specific about it, except that in Ireland no constructed temples have been found; the ceremonies took place outside on sacred mounds or in the center of woods, which certainly doesn't prevent the site from having been marked by a pillar or rocks set in a circle. And the underground chambers of the megalithic mounds (dolmens and covered aisles), which the pagan Irish saw as the dwellings of the gods, certainly have never been the sites of worship, since in principle these chambers were reserved for the gods, and because for the most part the entrances were filled in and no one could enter.[1] It has also been proposed that the temples were built of wood and as a result no traces of them were left.[2] But not a single Irish tale mentions a temple, which in itself is quite remarkable.

In Great Britain the problem is somewhat different. Under Roman occupation great tolerance was shown toward the British who thus were able to practice their worship more than those in Gaul. A few temples of a more druidic spirit have been found, but their architecture bears a Roman imprint nonetheless. Moreover, at the end of the fourth century when Saint Ninian set out to convert the southern Picts (in the Scottish Lowlands), he built a church that caused a sensation. It was a *candida casa*, a "white house," which is to say it was built of stone, a detail that proves that the idea of a temple built of stone was foreign to the Celtic world. And when Dio Cassius noted that during the time of the Britains of Boudicca sacrifices were offered to the gods in the temples, he used the word *hiera,* which in Greek, means nothing other than the Latin *locus consecratus* of Caesar. On the other hand, like many others he mentions "sacred woods," and for that he uses the term *alsos,* the equivalent of the Latin words *lucus* and *nemus.*

The word *nemus* appears again specifically in its Celtic form as one of the mythical invaders of Ireland, a certain Nemed, which means "sacred." The word comes from the same root as *nemus,* a root meaning "heaven" and which has spawned the Gaelic *niam,* the Welsh *nef,* and the Breton *nenv* (pronounced nan). The preeminent Celtic sanctuary appears to have been the *nemeton,* a word designating the celestial, sacred clearing in the center of the forest. According to what we know, the druids had a predilection for forests and all the druids of Gaul reunited once a year in the forest of the Carnutes. In Great Britain the druidic establishment on the Isle of Mona (Anglesey) was in a forest. When Lucan speaks of a Gallic sanctuary near Marseilles, he places it in a forest; it is there, he says, that horrible sacrifices were performed and that crude statues representing the gods *(simulacra maesta deorum)* were to be found. A priest officiated in this remote and secret sanctuary in honor of the *dominus loci* (master of the site). "The people never come within proximity of the site of the cult and have abandoned it to the gods. The priest himself dreaded entering the surrounding area for fear he might come upon the master of the sacred wood" (*The Pharsalia,* I, 339 ff). Lucan specified other things as well: "The druids live in the deep woods *(nemora alta)* and withdraw from inhabited forests. They practice barbarous rites and a sinister worship" (I, 452 ff). And he adds, "They worship the gods in the woods without the use of temples." And he uses the term *nemus* bringing us back to *nemeton.*

A text of Strabo (XII, 5) indicates that the Galatians of Asia Minor "had a council of three hundred members who gathered together in a place called *Drumeton.*" This is not the only example of a place-name known to be derived from *nemeton.* Nanterre (Hauts-de-Seine) is an ancient Nemetodurum. The Nevet Forest, near Locronan (Finistère), bears a name that results from the word's evolution in modern Breton. Neant-sur-Yvel (Morbihan), in the Brocéliande Forest, as well as the hamlet of Pertuis-Nanti in Paimpont (Ille-et-Vilaine) are also derivatives that were attached during the twelfth century in a country that was once Celtophonic but has been French speaking since. And the ancient name of the Fountain of Barenton, Belenton, clearly appears to be a Belnemeton, a "clearing consecrated to Belenos."

What does the *nemeton* represent exactly? "The druidic sanctuary is more linked to a symbolic or effective idea of 'center' than to a form or material aspect since it is expressed in its totality by a word that designates the *sacred*: as a precise geographic location, as a moment in calendar time, and as a person, an individual distinguished from the rest of society."[3] The Celts were of the opinion that it was vain to enclose the area in which the gods resided. To the contrary, they thought there were places, whether symbolic or real, where the world of humans could open to that of the gods, and vice versa. The nemeton is this site of sacred exchange. It is the clearing in the forest as well as being the forest as a whole, the top of a mound, or an isle in the middle of the sea. How many Christian sanctuaries, whether church or modest chapel, have been erected on the location of an ancient nemeton? As for wells, and the area that surrounds them, these were also privileged sites, since in addition to the communication of Earth with heaven *(nem)*, contact with the vital and fecund powers that surge up mysteriously from the center of the Earth could be made there. In this sense the Barenton Fountain illustrates perfectly the idea Celts had of the nemeton.[4]

Every nemeton is the center of the world. The idea of *omphallos* (the navel of the world) coincides exactly with that of the sanctuary, no matter that these sanctuaries may be countless. They are simultaneously unique and multiple, since, in the words of the famous formula, the deity is a circle whose center is everywhere and whose circumference is nowhere. The place where contact is established with the invisible world, the divine world, is necessarily an absolute center from which the forces put in play there can radiate. But it is man who establishes this center, according to what he feels most profoundly. The nemeton is never chosen by chance. Most of the time it is located on the site of a prehistoric sanctuary, for as sacred tradition would have it certain places are privileged. One can talk about telluric currents, magnetic forces, propitious environments, but this is not to fall into the trap of a pseudoesotericism: sacred sites are truly privileged places, whether because supernatural things occur there, or because the psychic energy of the individuals who have practiced rituals there for centuries ended up permeating the site. Tradition lacks neither holy or cursed places.

The idea of a central sanctuary is very well rendered by the Gallic toponym Mediolanum, which is the ancient name of Milan (in Cisalpine Gaul don't forget), of Chateaumeillant (Cher), in the territory that was formerly that of the Biturige tribe (meaning "kings of the world"), and for about 60 percent of the sites in continental Celtic Europe. The word *mediolanum* is literally "the place of the center," lanum (from the same root as the Latin *planus* and the Gallic *landa,* "moor"), having taken on the more exact meaning of "place of foundation." Now, as all foundations are sacred, the place of the foundation is sacred, and becomes a sanctuary. Knowing this it is not surprising to note so many toponyms with *lann* in Christian Brittany. The Breton *lann* simultaneously means both the "moor" and the "furze" that grows there, and a "hermitage" built by a pious individual—the founder of a parish—on the moor, or in a remote area. We see here exactly the same reality as that described by Lucan in *Pharsalia:* an isolated sanctuary in the middle of the woods and its officiating cleric who lives nearby. Celtic Christianity has incorporated a great number of druidic customs. And if Lanmeur is perhaps simply a "great moor," Lanildut is indisputably the "sanctuary of Ildut," as Lannedern is the "sanctuary of Edern," and Languidic the "sanctuary of Kidy." And all these places are centers of the world in that they are theoretical centers around which communities whose bond was the very concept of the sacred, had established themselves. By this reckoning, the least Breton lann, like the least Celtic nemeton, is on a par with the sanctuary of Tara, the mediolanum of Ireland, omphallos of the world, where the Stone of Fal was located, which cried out when a king (necessarily the "king of the world") or future king sat upon it, and where the great seasonal assemblies of the Gaels took place.

All of this refers to the idea of *desert.* Roman Christianity has distorted our comprehension of the phenomenon. The Christianity that developed did so in the context of the Roman empire, that is to say an urban civilization that was Hellenistic at the start and, therefore, under the influence of the Greek *polis.* There was all at once a break with nature. And the first Christian mystics understood this quite well, they who, starting with Saint Paul, went on retreats *in the desert.* Now desert, in the etymological sense of the world, is that "which has been deserted," everything that has not been subjugated by human activity. Even today, in peasant vocabulary, the desert designates any abandoned location in which uncontrolled vegetation has gained the upper hand. But this in no way implies the idea of aridity and desolation, or the lack of water and plant life. To withdraw into the desert is to go back to nature. This is what the first Christian hermits did. But as the most famous of these lived in dry countries where arid regions were predominant, a confused idea of this has seized people's minds: to live as a hermit it is necessary to go to the solitary reaches of Upper Egypt, the Sahara, and Libya. It is to forget that there are deserts outside the gates of the great European cities. This is what was understood by the monks of the Middle Ages when they established their monasteries in areas that were remote but at times close to cities. They did nothing but follow the example of the Irish or Breton hermits who had followed the example set by the druids.

This conception of sanctuary that can be everywhere and nowhere, but which is always at the center of the world and always in touch with untamed nature, is one of the specific features of druidism. It testifies to the realization that human beings are in constant relation with the cosmos, that we are never alone, even in the desert. To the contrary, because there he meets the great *All* who is the deity, whoever it may be and whatever name it is given. This also reveals the imbecility of certain commentaries on the "primary naturalism" of the druids' religion, identified with a group of propitiatory rituals for conjuring up mysterious natural forces. This conception of sanctuary proves, to the contrary, the existence of a large scale metaphysical and theological system of thought.

13

MISTLETOE
AND PLANT RITUAL

Not a single liturgical text has come down to us from the druids. There is nothing very astonishing about this since the Celts did not write down their sacred texts. And even if there had been any, the Christians would have made them vanish. We can only reconstitute certain elements of druidic worship with the aid of various testimonies.

The mistletoe ritual is known to us thanks to Pliny the Elder. "The druids have nothing more sacred than the mistletoe and the tree that bears it, provided that it is a hard-oak" (Pliny, XVI, 249). Pliny expressly states that the druids assumed the tree bearing mistletoe to be an oak. It is not strictly an oak, but mistletoe can only be found on certain limited species of that tree. Its harvesting takes place on "the sixth day of the moon . . . because the moon already has considerable strength though not yet at the center of its cycle." Nowhere is it said that it is the winter solstice, as some wish to believe, as to compare to the custom of mistletoe at Christmas, or New Year's Day (which in actuality has only been a New Year's Day for a short time). Pliny's text mentions only the sixth day of the moon, but doesn't make explicit at what time of the year this refers to. There is surely no reason to specify the time or else Pliny would have noted it. Moreover Pliny never told us that the druids cut the mistletoe *with its berries*, which would have implied winter mistletoe. It is an abuse of interpretation to claim that the mistletoe must be cut with its berries. It means that mistletoe could be harvested at any time during the year, as long as it was the sixth day of the moon. This said, the old custom of the Aguilanée or the *au-gui-l'an-neuf*,[1] a custom still quite hardy in all regions—particularly in Britain—and relying on folk songs, is either much less aged than is said, or quite displaced from its original date. Indeed, formerly, the year began on April first, while the Celtic New Year was the feast of Samhain on the first of November.

All of this points to the belief that the harvesting of mistletoe had nothing to do with the winter solstice, nor with the Christmas holiday. But it did take place under very specific conditions: the druid himself cut the mistletoe "with a golden sickle." The mistletoe was gathered "in a piece of white linen," and the druid was clad "in a white robe." The color white is the preeminent sacerdotal color. This harvesting therefore was a concern of the head chief of the druids. The use that they made of the mistletoe, well, that's another problem. The golden sickle makes one smile as it has become such a cliché image of Epinal.[2] In addition gold is too soft to cut anything. Undoubtedly, what we are dealing with is a gold-plated, bronze or iron sickle. But in any event the solar-lunar symbolism is obvious: the gold is the image of the sun, the sickle is the lunar crescent. This is not by chance. And Pliny adds that this harvesting of the mistletoe was followed by a sacrifice of white bulls, who were very young since "their horns had bound for the first time" (XVI, 249). It is known, moreover, that the bull sacrifice is a ritual of royal enthronement, which would seem to indicate that the cutting of the mistletoe was not an isolated ritual, but a part of a ceremonial series that has remained unknown to us. The specificity of this custom must be responsible for its popularity with the Greeks and Romans, popularity that came at the expense of the other components of the ritual that as a result are unknown to us.

But there are other ritual harvestings. For instance to cut "the plant called *selago*, iron is not used; one extends the right hand from the left side of one's garment, as if to commit a theft; it is necessary, moreover, to be dressed in white, to have one's feet washed and bare, and to have previously made an offering of bread and wine" (Pliny, XXIV, 103). Selago is lycopodium, which is still used today in homeopathy; and it is well known that homeopathic preparations require delicate handling, protection from any contact with metal that would risk the altering of certain properties of the raw or manufactured product. The gold sickle is much easier to understand since gold is a neutral, truly beneficial metal. And the ritual is significant. The right side is that of the light; the left, which is the north since the Celts oriented themselves facing the rising sun, is the mysterious side, that of the shadow. The cutting of the selago is an act of taking possession of mysterious forces. And so as not to alter these forces it is important to be in sacerdotal garb (the white clothing) and to be in complete contact with the earth by means of one's washed, bare feet. But there again this harvesting of the selago is but part of a more complex ritual since it is proceeded by an offering of bread and wine. The *samolus,* a plant of the marshes, is also harvested in specific conditions: "He who cuts it should look neither behind him nor deposit the plant anywhere except there where drinks are stored," and above all, he must perform this operation "with the left hand" (Pliny, XXIV, 104). All of this forms part of a religious medicine ritual of which plants seem to be the principal component. It is good to remind ourselves of the Fountain of Health of the god Diancecht. And Pliny again mentions that the druids used vervain to draw fortunes "while singing incantations" (XXV, 106).

There is a tendency to speak here of "plant magic," but the phrase can lead to confusion.[3] The Gauls have been scorned and the druids held up to ridicule for less than this.[4] Now these plant practices form part of a set, and cannot be isolated from their mythological context, that is to say from the philosophical system of the druids. To say that at the time of the conquest, the druids had degenerated into simple village hedge wizards is to ignore, on one hand that folk medicine exists and that it has often proved its worth—despite the ironic denegations of the medical schools[5]—and, on the other hand, it is to comprehend nothing of druidism, which, being a social religion, necessarily touches upon all aspects of life, medicine included, but also *magic* in the most noble sense of the word.

It isn't for nothing that the nemeton was located in a completely natural location, often at the center of a forest. The relation of the druid with wood is obvious—the name of druids *(dru-wides)* and the name of wood *(vidu)* are linked. *Knowledge* and *wood* are placed parallel to one another, although perhaps only symbolically. The fact of writing, or rather carving, ritual incantations on pieces of wood made the symbol move into the practical domain. The yew, the hazel, the rowan, and the oak are trees that were used by druids. The yew, whose fruits are poisonous, was particularly honored. The druids and the fili of Ireland carved their spells on yew wands. The name Eochaid, which is a royal name par excellence, perhaps signifies he "who fights with the Yew." The Gallic peoples, the Eburovices

(Évreux) and the Eburons (Belgium) have names containing the word *eburo,* "yew." For magical procedures the druids and fili made use of hazel and rowan wood. The oak—a "visible representation of the deity," according to Maxim of Tyr (*Dissertationes,* VIII, 8) who attributes that belief to the Celts—is a symbol of science and power, and it is the tree upon which mistletoe grows. As for the apple tree, it is more than ever "the tree of the science of good and evil" for it is the tree of the Isle of Avalon or Emain Ablach, and the apple is the fruit of immortality, knowledge, and wisdom. When a messenger from the Otherworld presents herself to the Irish hero Bran, son of Febal, she gives him a branch saying: "This is a branch from the apple tree of Emain Ablach that I bring to you; small branches of white silver are upon it and lashes of crystal with flowers."[6] When Condla, son of King Conn of the Hundred Battles, is invited to leave for the Otherworld in the company of a ravishing young girl, she throws him an apple. The druids of Conn drove off the fairy creature with their spells, but Condla kept the apple: "For the space of a month Condla took no drink or food. It seemed to him that nothing was worthy of being eaten except his apple. The apple did not shrink, no matter how much he ate of it, and it remained whole."[7] And the magic of the apple was such that when the fairy appears a second time nothing can retain Condla, who hurls himself into the crystal barge the messenger is piloting.[8] These marvelous apples of Emain Ablach, which are the same as those of Morgan of the Isle of Avalon,

> have the color of polished gold, and the head of a month-old infant is no larger than each of these apples. They have the taste of honey when one eats them; they leave neither bloody wounds or illnesses in those who eat them; they do not shrink when one has eaten them for long and always. He who has made off with one of these apples has performed his greatest feat, for after that, it will come back to him.[9]

In any event, the apples of Avalon are less dangerous than those of the Earthly Paradise. Not only do they procure immortality, but they also are not forbidden to those brave enough to pick them. It is necessary to know how to pick them; as well as how to eat them, something Adam and Eve obviously didn't know.

These plant practices are interesting in and of themselves, but they are only explicable by reference to a fundamental myth of Celtic tradition, *The Battle of the Trees*. This myth appears in its most complete form in the famous *Kat Goddeu*, "Battle of the Trees," a poem attributed to the Welsh bard Taliesin, who in the midst of obscure details recounts how Gwyddyon saved the Britons from disaster by transforming them into trees and having them fight in that form against their enemies.[10] The theme is picked up again in the Irish tale *The Death of Cuchulainn* in which three frightful witches, the daughters of Calatin, are seen phantasmagorically instigating a great battle between two armies of magnificent moving leafy oaks.[11] The same detail is seen again in the tale of *The Battle of Mag Tured* in which two witches say, "We will enchant the trees and stones, and the clods of earth so well that they will become an armed troop fighting against the enemy and put them to flight in horror and torment."[12] Now one can understand from which tradition Shakespeare was drawing his inspiration when he wrote the episode of the witches and the "forest that walks" in *Macbeth*.

The myth has even been rehabilitated and historicized by Titus Livy in his *History of Rome,* but in an obviously rationalistic form. The consul Postumius, with twenty-five thousand soldiers, was engaged in battle in a forest of Cisalpine located in enemy Gallic territory:

> As the Gauls found themselves at the extreme end of the forest and around it, just as the Roman army entered, they pushed over the furthest trees that they had cut at the roots. The first fell on the nearest trees, and these latter were themselves so unstable and easy to overturn that all below were crushed in their confused fall, men, horses, and weapons. Hardly ten men were able to escape. (Titus Livy, XXIII, 24)

The forest in question is named Litana by Titus Livy. Now Litana or Litava are the names of Armorica (Llydaw) among the Welsh, but more often symbolically designate the Otherworld.[13] This is a perfect example of plant-inspired myth.

But Taliesin's *Kat Goddeu,* a text most likely composed of two or three different and earlier poems than those of the definitive compilation, contain a precise reference to another form of plant practice:

> *When I came to life*
> *my creator formed me*
> *with the fruit of fruits . . .*
> *with primroses and the flowers of the hills,*
> *with the flowers of trees and bushes . . .*
> *with the flowers of the nettle . . .*
> *I have been marked by Math . . .*
> *I have been marked by Gwyddyon . . .*
> *by the learned children of Math.*[14]

Except for the plant reference these details have nothing at all to do with the principal subject, and they are only comprehensible thanks to the fourth branch of the Welsh *Mabinogion*. Arianrhod, daughter of Dôn, not wishing to acknowledge the son that she had in a mysterious and incestuous manner, curses him "to never have a wife of the race that now inhabits the world at this time," her brother Gwyddyon, who raises the child, goes to find his uncle, the king-magician Math, who says, "Let us both seek by means of our magic and our charms, to make a woman for him out of flowers."[15] And it is no sooner said than done. "So they gathered together flowers from the oak, broom flowers, meadowsweets, and with their spells they shaped the most beautiful and perfect maiden in all the world."[16] Thus Blodeuwedd, the "flower-daughter," was born, whose life ends tragically when, to punish her for her adultery and crime, Gwyddyon transforms her into an owl.[17] It is true that this isn't Gwyddyon's first attempt, as another poem of Taliesin indeed affirms.

> *The most skillful man of whom I've heard tell,*
> *was Gwyddyon, son of Dôn, of terrible powers,*
> *who made by magic a woman from flowers . . .*
> *With soil from the courtyard,*
> *with chains round and braided,*
> *he shaped fine steeds*
> *and remarkable saddles.*[18]

There again an explanation for the Celtic predilection for plant myth can be found in the fourth branch of the *Mabinogion*. Wishing to make off with the pigs of Pryderi, who are the equivalent of Mananann's pigs, Gwyddyon proposed an exchange for them by giving Pryderi sumptuous gifts, not letting any scruples hold him back: "He then resorted to his skills and began to demonstrate the power of his magic. He made appear a dozen stallions, twelve black hunting dogs . . . twelve golden bucklers. These shields were mushrooms that he had transformed."[19] One cannot help but think of Merlin, especially in the episodes that recount how he wished to seduce the young Vivian, causing the appearance of buildings, wonderful orchards, and human beings that were in reality nothing but tufts of grass and branches.

This would thus be magic—or hypnotism—but let us repeat that it refers to a fundamental myth whose traces are found throughout the entire Celtic world, in Cisalpine Gaul (Northern Italy), in Great Britain, and in Ireland. Not to mention the folktales that repeat altered versions of this same theme. The "fabrication" of Blodeuwedd, the "Battle of the Trees," druidic plant medicine, the pains druids took in the harvesting of certain plants, the relation between *wood* and *knowledge,* the familiarity of druidism with plant nature, plant "magic"—all of this cannot be merely the result of silly superstitions. There must be something behind it.

In 1918 the philosopher Rudolf Steiner wrote,

> During the era of Atlantis, plants were not solely cultivated to be used as food, but also to make use of the energy that slept within them for transportation and industry. Thus Atlantis possessed machinery and equipment that transformed the nuclear energy held in plant seeds into technically ussable energy. This is how the flying vehicles of Atlantis were propelled through low altitudes.[20]

But let us not dwell on such fantasies. Steiner had a reputation for being a visionary, but this is going too far. It really takes some nerve to assert that Atlantis, the existence of which has never been proven, had flying machines some 80,000 years ago. Steiner, no doubt, found himself in that fabulous Atlantis, as a journalist perhaps. If only he could have brought back some color photos! It is true that Steiner believed in reincarnation, but it should be noted that Plato, who, to date was the first author to speak about Atlantis, places the Atlantean civilization as being 9,000 years before Solon, that is to say 11,500 years before Rudolf Steiner. But even though Steiner's text might seem like science fiction for mental defectives, it does force us to reflect.

First of all, it was not standard practice in 1918 to talk about nuclear energy. Second, it must be noted that Rudolf Steiner, completely influenced by Goethe and namely the Goethe little known to non-Germans, was long interested in plant questions, agriculture in particular. In 1897 he published a treatise on the *Metamorphosis of Plants,* and much later, a kind of course for agriculturalists called *Foundations of the Biodynamic Method.*[21, 22] Biodynamics is a method of growing that, with the exclusion of all fertilizers, additives, and insecticides, claims to revivify the soil and improve vegetables in a closed cycle, that is to say it uses the energy contained in the plants themselves. The chief thing is to know how not to lose that important energy and how to cause it to surge at the opportune moment. Numerous practical experiments in biodynamics have been performed since that time, in Switzerland, Germany, Belgium, and France, and it seems that they have provided positive results of increased yields.[23]

The biodynamic principle is not a recent one. Traditional alchemy was not only interested in the mineral realm; there was also a question of a *plant stone* parallel to the mineral stone. And to manufacture this plant stone, it is necessary to concentrate the vital energy of plants, rid them of the gangue that prevents them from being active, in other words to lift the evil spells that seem to weigh upon the vegetation as they do upon the animal domain. The objective is to liberate the energy contained in the plant that is sleeping and, therefore, invisible and unsuspected on the surface. This is what has been done in the mineral realm with regard to atomic energy, but it is perhaps more difficult to tackle with regard to living matter. But these are not utopian fantasies. They are not even dreams. These are daily laboratory experiments in the majority of the so-called developed countries. There is nothing antiscientific about it whatsoever. And it is undeniable that Rudolf Steiner was aware of this kind of energy.

With this in mind, if we go back to the Celtic example it is possible to arrive at some odd conclusions. Could not those trees that walk and fight be the imagined, symbolic representation of the utilization of plant energy? The birth of Blodeuwedd, a being manufactured out of flowers, could this not represent the utilization of an energy contained in the plant world, capable, once it has been brought forth, of giving birth to another being? After all, as the saying goes, we are what we eat, and we are only alive because we borrow from plants (and animals) their vital forces through ingestion and digestion. Why could there not be other methods besides that of the phenomenon of digestion?

The question has been raised. The answer could provide explanations for certain cases of miraculous cures and for certain phenomena that are classified as supernatural or magic. Alchemical tradition claims that the Philosopher's Stone—of which the making of gold, contrary to current opinion, is only a secondary function—is a universal panacea. It so happens that this universal panacea exists in druidic tradition. According to testimony of Pliny the Elder himself, it is mistletoe.

In fact, Pliny says, "The Gauls believed that mistletoe, taken in a drink, would provide fecundity to sterile animals, and that it constituted a remedy against every poison" (XVI, 249). We do not know the Gallic name for mistletoe, but in Irish its name is *uileiceadh,* which literally means "cure-all" "panacea," and the Welsh word *oll-iach,* which is quite close, has precisely the same meaning. The Armorican Breton term is *uhelvarr* (high branch), but in thirteenth-century Vannetais dialect the paraphrase *deur derhue,* meaning "water of the oak" was used, a name that warrants a closer look.

Mistletoe is indeed an extraordinary plant. A parasite, it is some sort of vampire plant that feeds on the blood of others plants. In truth it survives by drinking tree sap, which is truly the "water of the oak." In addition mistletoe is one of the most ancient plants on our planet, perhaps one of the first to have appeared, and in any event is an escapee from a faraway era in which the conditions of life were not similar to those today. From this it can be concluded that mistletoe has survived different stages of evolution and adapted itself to new circumstances as a matter of life or death. Unable to draw its vital energy from the earth as other plants do, it attached itself to plants whose vital energy it made its own. In this sense mistletoe frees the energy of the oak (or any other tree) and uses it. Wouldn't this be the best example that illustrates the theory of plant energy?

These remarks are not aimed at proving that druids possessed the secret for freeing the vital energy of plants and then used it to power machinery. If this had been the case it would be known today. The Celts are not so far removed from us in time, and the Romans, quite pragmatic and ever ready to take possession of the inventions of others, would not have failed to profit from these. Yet all the same it is likely, and even probable, that the Celts understood this principle of plant energy and used certain plants, mistletoe for one, for therapeutic, even magical objectives. But as far as knowing what methods they used, we know next to nothing of them. What is interesting about this in the framework of an overall study of druidism is to see how a myth such as that of the plant dynamic (battling trees, plant birth, universal plant medicine) exists in Celtic tradition. For a myth, whatever kind it may be, underlies a reality, no matter how irrational it may seem in appearance.

Which brings us back to the importance of the mistletoe ritual. The oak that represents divine power and cosmic energy, even when it is symbolically replaced by another tree, the mistletoe—water of the oak—is the very essence of the deity. The care with which mistletoe is plucked, and the sort of "magic potion" that is subsequently made from it, indicates a constant quest on the part of the druids for contact with the higher powers, a contact that manifests itself with an act of assimilation, a veritable digestion of these powers. It is well and truly a question of integrating the deity into the human being, and from that embodying the god.

14

THE FOUR ELEMENTS

Like all other peoples the Celts speculated on the value and identity of the traditional elements as manifested energy. Earth, air, fire, and water were conceived of as "transits" by which energy is transformed and regenerated. This conception virtually leaps out at us from certain spells and, more particularly, from the poems of the Welsh bard Taliesin (or at least those attributed to him) in which the theme of metamorphoses appears. "I have donned a multiple number of shapes before acquiring my definitive form," the poet says.[1] These metamorphoses have often been interpreted as proof that the Celts believed in successive reincarnations. But outside of several well-defined incidences of clearly symbolic cases, absolutely nothing confirms this theory. Metempsychosis of any shade is totally unknown to the Celts. The metamorphoses testify solely to the realization that the individual belongs to every domain, thus to all the elements, and that he or she is inseparable from the cosmos. Without the Cosmos the individual cannot explain him or herself, and conversely, without the individual the Cosmos cannot explain itself either as there is no one to pose the question.

EARTH AND AIR

As a primordial element earth does not seem to have had an exceptional importance in druidic thought. There is not, properly speaking, an earth goddess in Celtic mythology. Tailtiu, the nourishing mother of the god Lugh, is not a telluric deity like the Greek Demeter, and the maternal goddesses more often represent the human community, Ireland in particular, rather than the soil on which that community has established itself. The concept of the earth goddess belongs not to the Celts, but to the megalithic populaces that preceded them. Moreover, the Gaelic word *talamh*, "earth" (related to the Latin *tellus*), is masculine. This is easy to understand if it is considered that all Celtic societies were originally pastoral and not agrarian. The society is nomadic, therefore the earth has little importance. But this in no way prevents the rituals that concern the connections of man with the earth.

Indeed, it is necessary that human beings live on the Earth and reach agreement with her by a sort of contract. What best expresses this idea is the rite of the Fal Stone, that phallic—therefore masculine—stone located at Tara that cried out when a king or future king sat upon it. There is an obvious echo of this in the "Seat Perilous" of the Grail legend. The stone that cries out is the sign that the Earth accepts an individual as king. In other words, acknowledges that person as the privileged intermediary between it and the society that has temporarily settled upon it, to the extent that every Celtic kingdom was dependent upon the king's capability, as well as restricted by what his gaze could encompass. This notion is quite difficult to comprehend for those of us accustomed to an entirely different conception of the nation-state and who are constantly confronted by the notions of the "country" and the "land of our ancestors." There is no direct link between the earth and the people, or the tribe; the mediator is the king, whose legitimacy must be recognized by both the social group (election and sacerdotal approval), and by the earth of which he has been made the contractual occupant. There is no possession of the earth which, by definition, always remains universal.

This is why in funeral ceremonies earth appears as the primordial element at the same time that it appears as the ultimate element. It was customary to wash the corpse in a stream, a practice that was then followed by the actual burial ceremony. Caesar spoke of incineration, but we also know that burial was also widely practiced. Unfortunately it is impossible to determine if one of these practices was reserved for one class or another. Incineration and inhumation existed conjointly, but beyond that it is impossible to draw any further conclusions. But in any event, the deceased was given back to the earth. As in many ancient civilizations, sometimes "everything that the deceased loved is thrown into the funeral pyre, even animals, and it was still not so long ago that slaves and dependents who were dear to the deceased were burned with him" (Caesar, VI, 19). This custom is certainly not unique to the Celts.

Once the burial had been completed a funeral pillar was erected and an epitaph was carved on the stone. Then a poet would sing or chant the funeral lament. We have excellent examples of lamentations in the Irish epic (in particular that for Ferdead given by Cuchulainn in the *Tain Bô Cualngé*), as well as in Welsh poetry.[2] After which the eulogy for the deceased was pronounced, certainly by a druid and without a doubt in poetic form. Following is an example of such a poem accredited to the Welsh bard Taliesin that is considered authentic:

> *Uryen of the cultivated plain,*
> *the most generous of baptized men,*
> *abundance you have given*
> *to the men of the world . . .*
> *Ah! until I am undone by old age,*
> *near the hard agony of my demise,*
> *never will I have joy*
> *if I don't celebrate Uryen . . .*[3]

After this the funeral games took place. These may have been simulated combats, duels in the fashion of medieval tournaments, types of dramatic presentations, as well as banquets that degenerated into drinking bouts. The essential significance of these funerals was to accompany the deceased, not to his final resting place, but to the symbolic spot where, entrusted to the earth, he could begin his journey in the Otherworld.

Other rites that bring the element of earth into play also were practiced. The hagiographic legend of Saint Patrick provides evidence of a bloody cult in Ireland devoted to the horrible idol of Crom Cruaich.[4] All the descriptions of this refer to a cromlech, a circle of stones dating from the Megalithic era. It does not seem that this would have been an element of druidic worship, more a reminder of earlier beliefs and customs that were more or less tolerated by the druids.

The practices performed upon earth by the druids were quite different. For the druids it was not a question of worshiping a sacred earthly deity, or of earning its favor, but of mastering the earth and putting it in service to human will. For this reason what was called the "hedge of the druid" prevented anyone from crossing over a certain border and from either entering into a circle or leaving it. We have many examples of this, particularly in the *Tain Bô Cualngé,* in which Cuchulainn places at a ford a branch forking at four spots and carves ogham on the stone. The enemy army was unable to cross the ford that had served as a stage for this magical operation, which brings to mind the invisible castle or stone (it depends on the version of the legend) in which Merlin is sealed by Vivian. It also happens that druids can claim the power to overturn and transform the landscape, to hollow out the earth or flatten the hills. Before the Battle of Mag Tured, one of Lugh's magician's, Mathgen (born of the bear), says that "with his powers he can throw down the mountains of Ireland on the Fomor until their tops are rolling upon the ground. And the twelve chief mountains of Ireland will be under the orders of the Tuatha de Danann and will fight for them."[5] There is an element in this that is identical to the Battle of the Trees: a liberation of the energy contained in the mineral realm and its utilization for military ends. In the tale of *The Courtship of Etaine,* Oengus, who must obtain the young Etaine for his adoptive father Mider-Mananann, is subject to obligations on the part of Etaine's father. With the help of the Dagda and the Tuatha de Danann, he clears a dozen plains in a single night, and hollows out twelve rivers in the same amount of time. Later, in order to regain Etaine from King Eochaid, Mider is compelled by magic to remove all the stones of Meath and to construct a dike on the marshland.

The second element, air, is the mysterious and fluctuating domain where only sacred and fairy beings are able to move about. This is why gods, and particularly goddesses, often appear in the shape of crows or swans. To be specific, the famous druidesses of the Isle of Sein, who, according to Pomponius Mela, had the power to don animal form, were also reputed to know how "to calm the winds with their spells" (III, 6). For this reason the druids claimed to master the winds and make use of them for very specific purposes.

The epic tales speak often of a "druidic wind." When the Sons of Milhead, after landing for the first time in Ireland, returned to their ships in search of shelter, the druids of the Tuatha de Danann "sang spells behind them that were so effective that they were pushed far away from Ireland."[6] When Fuamnach, Mider's first wife, wished to get rid of Mider's new bride Etaine—who she had already transformed into a puddle of water, and then an insect—she caused "to blow a wind of aggression and druidism."[7] And it was also believed that the druidic wind would sow confusion among a troop of enemy warriors who would no longer recognize their comrades and thus kill each other. Such is the case in *The Siege of Druim Damghaire* where the working magic of the druid Mog Ruith is cause for astonishment.[8] In addition Mog Ruith furnishes an explanation himself: "My god promised me that I would transform them into stones when I had them within my reach, if only I could manage to blow upon them. He sent a druidic breath their way, and they changed into stones."[9]

WATER

The third element, water, seems to have been of considerable importance in druidic practices. Symbolically the water of a spring is a kind of gift from the invisible powers that reign in the center of the Earth. Water is primarily fertile. Brooks, streams, and rivers have the same sacred character, for without them all life would be impossible. Numerous sanctuaries were located at river sources, the Seine in particular, where countless ex-votos have been found. But there were also quite a few others, and all springs, wells, and fountains had to be *loci consecrati*. The Fountain of Barenton is evidence of this, as is that of the ancient city of Glanum in Saint-Rémy of Provence that carries the stamp of the Gauls, Greeks, and Romans. The name Glanum refers to a root word meaning "purity," further supporting that it was a purifying spring, a well of health, similar to that of the god Diancecht.

For water is curative not only because it contains plants, as does the Fountain of Health, but because it cleans and eliminates impurities. Of course in this case the physical and spiritual planes are not separate. The water that purifies the body purifies the soul and vice versa. This notion is widespread and the practice of Christian baptism is but one of its numerous illustrations. Before being coopted by profane medicine, thermal springs were also assumed to act on both planes. But none of this occurred without specific rites, gestures, ambulations, and invocations, which can be rediscovered in all the folk customs that concern healing fountains or the waters of a purifying river. And if we do not come across any ancient Gallic or Celtic ritual, we are in our right to imagine that current practices are probably not so different from those of our remote ancestors.

Moreover, if we reflect on the Cauldron of Bran Vendigeit and on the vat in which Peredur saw thrown the cadavers that were subsequently reborn, we can make some curious observations. There is a strict relationship here with the barbaric rite described by Lucan's scholiast regarding Teutas, specifically the plunging of a man's head into a cauldron until he suffocates. Wouldn't this be considered a water ritual? There are legends that tell of the sacrificial death of the king by drowning in a vat. Such clues should not be overlooked.

To perform a ritual above water, around water, in water, or to enchant water, is to master the mysterious energy contained in the liquid element and to make it serve the will of the one performing the ritual. This is perhaps magic, but overall it is a realization that there are invisible forces in nature that only need to be freed and utilized in accordance with certain methods to arrive at positive results. But whoever says positive also says negative. In several Irish tales the druids often enchanted the waters of this lake or that river so that they vanished and could not serve the druids' enemies. Before the Battle of Mag Tured, the cupbearer of the Tuatha de Danann declared to Lugh that he would cause the lakes of Ireland to disappear from the eyes of the Fomor so that they would find no water, "no matter how great their thirst."[10]

It seems that there was a special ritual to give thirst to an enemy king. In the first Battle of Mag Tured, the king of the Fir Bolg, Eochaid, begins to feel thirsty at the moment the battle takes a turn for the worse, which is undoubtedly the result of the druidic prowess of the Tuatha de Danann. In a curious Irish legend, *The Death of Muirchetach,* in order to get revenge on the king, the heroine, Sin, lures him into a series of magical traps and ends by making the king so incredibly thirsty that he drowns himself in a tub. In the tale *The Destruction of Da Derga's Hostel,* King Conaire is attacked by pirates. As the battle rages, the magicians accompanying the pirates cast a spell of "an unquenchable thirst" on Conaire. The king asks for water, but there is none, so he sends the hero Mac Cecht in search of some. Mac Cecht vainly traverses the whole of Ireland and still finds no water: all the lakes and waterways are dried up. Only one small lake still holds water and Mac Cecht fills a cup with water from it before returning in haste to Conaire. But it is too late, for Conaire is dead: "His great thirst oppressed him and he died of a burning fever, for he had naught to drink." To prevent his enemies from taking possession of the king's power Mac

Cecht cut off the king's head. But first he poured the cup's contents over the king's face at which Conaire's head began to speak: "A brave man, Mac Cecht, an excellent man. . . . He brings a drink, he saves a king. . . . Good would I be to the famous Mac Cecht, if I were but alive, a brave man!"[11] This brings to mind the character Pantagruel who cast salt on his enemies in order to make them thirst. But as everything has its opposite, the numerous legends concerning Christian saints who cause springs to gush from the ground by striking the earth with their staffs, should be recognized as a response to these sorts of legends.

It will be noted that all of these tales are in the domain of fresh water. There is little evidence of any cultural practices concerning the sea. It is as if the Celts, the Irish in particular, were totally unaware of it. These examples are very far from the ceremonies of the "blessing of the sea" type performed by Christian clergy, especially in Britain; however, there is at least a trace of a conjuration ritual of the sea. The Greek author Strabo (67 B.C.–A.D. 23) tells how the Cimbri (who are in fact the Celts) "brandish their weapons at the mounting waves to drive them back" (VII, 2). This ritual is confirmed by Aristotle who, in his *Eudemian Ethics* (III, 1), makes fun of the poor Celts "who take up their arms to march against the waves." By all the evidence, we are dealing with a propitiatory ceremony that the Greeks did not understand and which they attributed to barbarian naiveté.

There is, however, something important here that raises a new problem. How could it be that the sea is not present in the mythology and liturgy of the Celts? We have said that the Celts, contrary to popular opinion, were land lovers (it is the contemporary Celts who, out of necessity, have become sailors, and it is still only a portion of them). Their waves of invasion throughout western Europe occurred on land. They all came from central Europe. Certainly, they crossed over the Channel and the Irish Sea, but that's probably all for we can hardly take literally the numerous tales of navigation to marvelous islands. These are illustrations of the quest in which roaming is reinforced by the notion of immensity and unknown lands.

Enemies also always came from over the sea, the Fomor being the first. The Isle of Avalon and the Isle of Emain Ablach are somewhere in the ocean, but it is the ocean of the Otherworld. This is why Mananann is assumed to reside beyond the sea, on the Isle of Man, or somewhere else. The sole Celtic legend in which the sea plays a primary role is the story of the Town of Ys, a tale that tells of the curse cast on the town as a result of the misdeed of the princess of this town, following which the land, which is lower than the sea, was invaded by the waves. The legend is also known in Wales, and there concerns the Bay of Cardigan. Oddly enough in this version it is not the sea that swallows all, but the water of a fountain, which results from the negligence of its female guardian. The same is true in Ireland where, through the fault of a woman, a magic well overflows and forms Lake Neagh.[12] A strange tale of Upper Brittany, set in Combourg, claims that there is a white stone at the bottom of the Margatte Fountain that prevents it from overflowing.[13] If someone were to rashly remove the stone the entire country would be flooded. Assuredly all of this testifies to a fear of floods.[14]

These are perhaps only echoes of long-ago catastrophes, undoubtedly those of which Ammianus Marcellinus spoke with regard to "foreign islanders come from beyond the seas" who would have contributed to the inhabitation of Gaul. In fact, for Marcellinus, Gaul is a sort of catch-all term that designates all Celtic countries. But then, how can we reconcile this information—that Ammianus Marcellinus reported as coming from Timagenes—with the fact that the Celts are from central Europe?

The first answer is that because the Celts were not very numerous there remained a large proportion of them, if not a majority of the autocthonous population in the Celtic countries, who were first subjugated, then assimilated. A second answer creates a new problem: the Veneti.

Here is how Caesar describes the Veneti: "This people is very much the strongest on the maritime coast. It is they who possess the greatest number of ships, and its fleet engages in trade with the Isle of Britain. It is superior to others by its navigational science and experience. Finally, as the sea is violent and liberally beats upon a coast where there are but few ports, of which they are the masters, almost all those who normally sail in these waters are their serviteurs" (III, 8). These Veneti, who occupied the southern coast of Armorica, almost the entire expanse between the Vilaine and the Odet, were the masters of navigation in the Atlantic, but also in the Channel since they had commercial ties with the Isle of Britain. In any event, this contradicts the earlier assertion that the Celts were land bound. Or else, it implies that the Celts were amenable to the fact that the Veneti occupied themselves with navigation in their stead. If this is the case, it would further support the contention that the Veneti were not Celts, but a Celtically influenced nonindigenous population.

What complicates this matter is that there were Veneti elsewhere who were, by chance, skillful navigators. These are the Veneti of the Adriatic, otherwise known as the Venetians. Regarding them the Greek historian Polybius said, "This ancient nation is hardly distinguishable from the other Gallic peoples by dress and custom, but they speak a different language" (II, 17). But Strabo is more affirmative: "I would be inclined to believe that the Adriatic Veneti are a colony of the Oceanic Veneti" (IV, 4). In addition one cannot help but compare the name of the Veneti with that of the Venedotia from northwest Wales, which in Welsh becomes Gwynedd. And as if by chance, it was those Britons, who for the most part came from the northern area of Wales, that emigrated during the sixth and seventh centuries to the ancient land of the Veneti and formed there the Browaroc'h, or the Vannetais. It so happens that Gwynedd was a strong kingdom in permanent contact with Ireland that was seemingly subject to a Gaelic influence that certain Welsh mythological tales would seem to bear out. This doesn't rule out the possiblity of Gwynedd's reciprocal Welsh influence upon the Irish. And in this case, what do we make of the strange warrior fraternity of the Fiana of Ireland whose king is Finn?

The name of Finn and that of the Fiana are indeed from the same root as that of Gwynedd, Venedotia, and Veneti. The name of Veneti, which has provided the Italian Venezia, the French Vannes (and through reconstruction Vénètes "Veneti"), and the Armorican Breton Gwyned, in fact comes from the ancient Celtic *vindo* that has a meaning of "white, handsome, blond, sacred, of good race." It is known that white was the sacerdotal color reserved for druids as "sacred" personages.

But who were these Veneti, and where did they come from?

The point of departure is the Atlantis of which Plato speaks in the *Critias* and in the fragments of *Timeus* that have been preserved. Atlantis is reputed to have been an island located beyond the Columns of Hercules, inhabited by a highly civilized people who were of an essentially maritime character, and who especially venerated a deity identified with Poseidon. During a catastrophic event, at the time when the Atlanteans were preparing their conquest of the Mediterranean basin in 9500 B.C., the isle of Atlantis disappeared, as Plato describes, "in one single fatal night," as earthquakes and tidal waves ravaged Europe and the shores of the Mediterranean. If the date is moved forward to the end of the Bronze Age—

that is toward the sixth or seventh century—there is nothing impossible about this. In fact, it would corroborate what Ammianus Marcellinus spoke of, quoting Timagenes, with regard to certain components of the Celtic people who had come from faraway isles and been driven out of their land by floods.

But Celtic mythology is rich in these kinds of events, and furthermore, all the invaders of Ireland came from beyond the sea. In addition, the truth of Plato's tale is suspect and many have wondered if he didn't invent Atlantis to illustrate his theses on the grandeur and decadence of civilizations. One detail, however, calls for consideration: the reference to the god Poseidon who, according to Greek mythology, is not only the master of the sea but *also of earthquakes.* The coincidence concerning Poseidon's powers is too perfect: it is either Plato's intention, or the reflection of a higher reality. But it is impossible for us to know which.

If we accept that Atlantis really existed, and that a catastrophe was responsible for its disappearance—which is not impossible whatever the exact circumstances and date may have been—we must also accept that there would have been survivors of this catastrophe, if only those who, according to Plato, were beginning the invasion of the Mediterranean basin. And if Atlantis were located, as in all likelihood it was, in the Atlantic Ocean, it would seem that a certain number of these survivors would have sought refuge on the western coast of Europe. This is where we discover the Veneti, who were not Celts, and who were skillful sailors, rebuilding a kind of maritime empire. For it is probable that if this people had not been vanquished and decimated by Caesar, they would have played a great role in the development of Gaul. The Roman proconsul was not mistaken when in 56 B.C. he engaged in a fierce struggle with them. He knew that by striking down the Veneti he would dismantle Gallic resistance to the Roman occupation.

There is also another piece of information that merits our attention. Citing Timeas, who lived from 346 to 250 B.C., Diodorus Siculus (IV, 56) reports that the Celts of the ocean worshiped the Dioscuri over all other gods. And he asserted that this worship of the Dioscuri had come from the sea. There isn't any trace of the Dioscuri cult in Gaul, save on certain Armorican coins from west of the Loire, a region in which the deity Vintius Pollux (one of the Dioscuri) was worshiped. It should be noted that Vintius is close to the name of the Veneti. In principle this name should designate a Gallic horse deity and it should not be forgotten that Pollux was the mortal member of the Dioscuri. But why a cult to Pollux and not to Castor? It may be related to the fact that the Dioscuri were principally invoked by sailors because they had the reputation of assuring good sailing and preventing ships from becoming lost at sea. The worship of the Dioscuri, like that of Poseidon, was characteristic of a people of navigators. If one considers that the cult of Castor and Pollux—or of two identical twin deities proven to have existed around 300 B.C. on the Atlantic coast west of the Loire—was a maritime cult, why not conclude that we are dealing with the Veneti? Why wouldn't the Veneti, classified by Caesar as being the best navigators of the Atlantic, have had a particular regard for maritime deities or protectors of navigation? If we have no proof in this regard, we at least have some very strong grounds for presumption.

Yes, but Strabo asserted that this cult came from the ocean, a statement that raises more questions than it resolves. While still remaining in the realm of conjecture, it is logical to carry this argument a little further still.

The Veneti of Vannes, the men of Gwynedd, and the Fiana of Ireland could perhaps be survivors of Atlantis who washed up on the shores of western Europe, and the Veneti of the Adriatic could be the survivors of an Atlantean expedition in the Mediterranean. This constitutes only a hypothesis, a simple working hypothesis. But this would explain on one hand the terror the Celts had of the sea and legends of the kind of the town of Ys, and on the other hand the conjuration ritual noted by Aristotle and suggested elsewhere by Strabo (VII, 2). But in no case do I consider the Celts as being the descendants of Atlantis—if it existed. At the present time certain authors, who hide behind the theories Fabre d'Olivet and Edouard Schuré, peremptorily assert that the Celts are Atlanteans and that druidism is the legacy of the ancient religion of Atlantis. This is an absolute untruth[15] and only adds to the misunderstanding of the elements of the question.[16] History, archaeology, and mythology clearly show that Celtic civilization is articulated on basic Indo-European structures, but it would be just as unwise to ignore the contributions from indigenous and other sources that can be discerned in Celtic civilization and druidism. This is why it is possible to envision a hypothesis such as that of the Atlanteans, but only in regard to the Veneti, whose exact identity and origin remain a mystery.

That said, there is a recollection of this conjuration of the sea ritual in a Welsh poem attributed to Taliesin. Although the reference is imprecise, it is possible to see that the magician-king Math, who is from Gwynedd, "had freed the elements." Then "the tempest was unleashed for four nights in the middle of summer. Men fell, the woods were no longer a shelter against the wind from the deep." But the magician Gwyddyon, also a hero of the Gwynedd epic and a character who embodies druidism quite well for the same reasons as does Merlin, held counsel with a certain Aeddon, who in reality should be seen as Amaethon, the "laborer," son of Dôn and brother of Gwyddyon (both moreover are nephews of Math). "And they made a shield of such strength that the sea could not engulf the best troops."[17] All the necessary elements are here: the druidic wind, the druidic power over the elements, the druidic spectacle performed by Gwyddyon, the antagonism between the maternal uncle, Math, whose name is that of the bear, the royal emblem, and his nephew Gwyddyon whose "science" is linked to wood, and to the putting of plant energy to work, the participation of Amaethon, the Laborer. This denotes a state of opposition between land dwellers and sailors, in the context of the land of Gwynedd where the Veneti, the "white ones," the "sacred ones," left their mark. It is not clear just what the shield manufactured by Gwyddyon represented. But these traces of ritual plunge us into an obscure past upon which, at least for the moment, it is difficult to shed any more light.

FIRE

The Greek chronicler Strabo recorded that the druids taught that "the souls of men were immortal, the world also, but that one day, however, only water and fire would reign" (IV, 4). This is the sole eschatological reference that we have concerning the Celts. But it indicates the importance water and fire possessed in the liturgical life as well as in the symbolic thought of the druids.

First off, it is necessary to shake up somewhat everyone's preconcieved notions about the four elements. *Fire is not an element but the transformation of the other three.* It is the manifestation and metamorphosis of the energy contained within an element. The parochial esotericists that abound in our time are very careful not to give any information on this subject when they pompously speak of the "secret fire of the alchemists." There are but three fundamental elements, as there are only three dimensions in our space, and, as we will see, three cardinal points. The druids knew this quite well, especially those who favored the ternary formula—and finally bequeathed the idea of Trinity to the Christians. When a solid burns, it becomes gaseous: earth becomes air thanks to the activity of fire. When a liquid burns, it becomes gaseous, water becomes air thanks to the activity of fire. When a gas burns, it becomes a different gas, whether it is a liquid for example (the hydrogen and oxygen that create water), or a solid: air becomes air, earth, or fire through the activity of fire. For fire is the very principle of action.

Fire seems to have been particularly favored among the Celts, and they are certainly not alone here. All peoples have used fire in their rituals, and continue to do so even when the idea has been secularized (the Olympic flame, the eternal memorial flame, and so on). But what is interesting about this in regard to the Celts is that fire seems to have been understood as the true sign of the transformation of cosmic energy. Thus, when the Tuatha de Danann landed in Ireland, they burned their boats, and in this way they manifested their own metamorphosis. Something had changed, nothing could be as it was before, and yet it was still the same thing. It is significant that their arrival was dated as occurring on May 1, for that is the feast of Beltane.

This Beltane holiday, one of the two poles of the Celtic year, is the feast of Fire and Light, the feast of summer's beginning, placed under the sign of Bel, or Belenos, the "sparkling" or "shining one." The Irish text *The Courtship of Emer* indicates that during this feast the druids lit fires with great spells, and that they made the herds pass between the fires. *The Glossary of Cormac* presents the very same definitions: "'Beltane,' 'fire of Bel,' 'beneficial fire.' It is a fire that the druids made with their magic or their great incantations. To counter epidemics these herds were brought each year to these fires, and the herds were made to pass between these fires."[18] There is no reason to doubt the authenticity of this ritual, in fact it has endured to the present day in such customs as May Day fires, Saint John's Day fires, and other popular manifestations. It was even rehabilitated by Christianity with the Easter Fire.[19] During Lent in Great Britain, Brandon's Day is quite significant; people stroll through the fields, gardens, and forests with lit torches, to ensure a good and plentiful harvest. Saint Patrick, too, knew this very well for according to legend, it was he who lit the Easter Fire several moments before the king's druids lit their pagan fire on the hill of Tara.[20]

The druidic fire required meticulous preparation. In *The Siege of Druim Damghaire*, the druid Mog Ruith tells his assistant to prepare the fire. The assistant "formed it like a churn, with three sides and three corners, but seven entrances although there were but three entrances in the north fire. It was neither set up nor arranged, but the wood had been piled in a heap."[21] The entire nature of the ritual still eludes us, but it seems that the construction of the pyre depended on how it was oriented to various directions, and that this orientation took only three cardinal points into account.

This brings us to another ritual, one for which Caesar has provided testimony. "They have great figures made of willow, that they fill with living men; they set them upon fire and the men within die, enveloped by flames" (VI, 16). Lucan's scholiast on sacrifices to Taranis says almost the identical thing: "A certain number of men are burned in a wooden cage." And Strabo affirms that some Gauls "manufacture a colossus from wood and straw, shut wild and domestic animals, as well as men inside, and burn the whole thing" (IV, 5). Let us remember that the name of the Gallic god Taranis is the result of a metathesis of a theme in *tanar*, which is recognizable in the Germanic Donar, and that this theme contains the root word *tan*, "fire," that is still in use in Armorican Breton today. But these figures or cages of fire need an explanation.

To better understand what we are dealing with here, it is necessary to go back to folk customs concerning Carnival and lepers. The figure of which Caesar spoke is comparable to the grotesque figure of Carnival, who is burned. As for lepers, it is known that they formed small isolated communities, remote from the villages, comprised of huts or cabins. A certain number of lepers performed the job of rope-making by virtue of the fact they lived outside the more built-up areas and had room in which to lay out their ropes. It just so happens that in France the Carnival Fire very often is called "a border fire or a *bordelinière, cabanou,* or *cabanelle* fire. These names designate a small cabin or shed, specifically one that is built within a border zone: the hut of the lepers."[22] The folklorist Van Gennep asked why the pyres of Carnival were called *cabins* when the characteristic of a cabin (which, like the word *cave*, comes from the Latin *cava*, meaning "hollow") is that it is hollow, which is not the case with a pyre. We have just seen in the Irish description of the druidic pyre that it had three sides, three corners, and seven windows, which leads to the conclusion that it was not entirely full.

According to Claude Gaignebet, the solution is furnished by the hut of the leper-ropemaker.

> The pyre was originally constructed in the shape of a cabin, with scraps of hemp, and over the top of a pit dug in the ground. One knows of such underground sites, which are most often in the shape of a bottle. At the bottom a bench allowed one to sit down. Once the lepers or members of an initiatic brotherhood had gone down, the fire would be lit above them. The vapors of the hemp to which they were subjected would allow them to voyage into the beyond.[23]

European hemp, although lacking the potency of Indian hemp, does cause dreams and it had been used for such for a long time in the rural areas that it is quite probable that the druids made use of it.

A folktale from Lower Brittany provides an excellent illustration of this custom. The hero, Yann, at the end of a complicated series of adventures is condemned to be burned by the Breton king in a pyre. His natural father, a magician who assumes the shape of a horse, teaches him what he must do to save himself:

> You don't have to do anything but go see the king and tell him that you wish to make your niche in the pyre. . . . You will also ask him for time to say your prayers. . . . Bring a stool with you to sit on when you have entered *into the pyre.*[24]

Then Yann must coat his body with the contents of a bottle and soak his shirt in it. When this is done, the pyre is set ablaze. Afterward everyone regrets the death of the young man. "It is at this point that Yann leaps from the midst of the flames, all his limbs shivering with the cold."[25] And the spectators saw that he was "more handsome than he had been before."[26] This is a description, of a ritual of regeneration through a marvelous anecdote, integrated into a narrative scheme: the hero emerges from his ordeal more handsome than before.

It should be pointed out that numerous stories, particularly Breton stories, allude to this kind of ritual. It is indeed standard, at least in folktales, to throw someone—not necessarily an evildoer—into an oven. We can also compare these texts that appear to be legendary to a well-known one whose importance will escape no one—a passage from the first Epistle to the Corinthians by Saint Paul. Paul says that one must build with wood, with hay, with straw, with gold, with silver, and with precious stones, but that

> the work of each person will be placed in the light. The Day [of the Lord] will let it be known, for it is by fire that he manifests himself, and fire, precisely, will test the quality of the individual work. He whose construction remains standing will receive salvation, he whose work burns will suffer its loss: he himself will be saved however, but as one is through fire. (III, 12-15)

Is this not a symbolic definition of Purgatory, the concept of which spread throughout Christianity, starting from the speculations of Irish Christians?

In any case, we are introduced to a ritual that appears to have been quite specific to the Celts. The second branch of the *Mabinogion* explains the origin of Bran's Cauldron of Resurrection in this way: one day a red-haired man and his wife were seen emerging from a lake, the man, obviously a being from the Otherworld, bearing a cauldron on his back. The couple established themselves in the country—that is Ireland—but made themselves hated because of their exactions upon the populace. The inhabitants of this country decided to get rid of them, but this proved no easy task. The narrator of the *Mabinogion* says,

> In this predicament, my vassals decided to construct an iron house. When it was ready they had all the smiths in Ireland who possessed tongs and hammers come, and had charcoal piled up to the top of the house. They passed in plenty of food and drink to the man, the woman, and their children. When they were seen to be intoxicated, the charcoal was set alight and the bellows were used on it until everything was white hot. Inside the family took counsel in the middle of the room. The man remained there until the heat became intolerable. He rammed the wall with his shoulder pushing himself outside, followed by his wife. No one but the two of them escaped.[27]

It should be noted that the red-haired man—who has a strong resemblance to the Dagda—could have left at any time as it took no more than a blow from his shoulder to open the door. But he waited until the heat became intolerable, a detail for which there is certainly a good reason. Subsequently the red-haired man and his wife settled in the country of Bran where "they multiplied and grew in every place; everywhere they are, they fortify with the best men and weapons that have ever been seen."[28] By all evidence, this was a rite of regeneration that increased his potency tenfold.

Another version of this theme, Irish this time, exists in the fantastic tale of *The Intoxication of the Ulaid*. After endless disputes, interminable drinking bouts, and wanderings across Ireland, the totally lost and inebriated Ulaid are surprised to find themselves at the fortress of Ailill and Medb, the king and queen of Connaught, their sworn enemies. Ailill and Medb demand advice from their druids and an old man, one of whom responds to them in this way:

> Their coming has been foretold for a long time and thought has been given the matter. Here is what must be made: a house of iron between two houses of wood, with an underground house beneath, a plate of very hard iron on which will be piled faggots and charcoal in such a way that this underground house will be full. It has been predicted that the nobles of Ulster will all gather together one night in the iron house.[29]

Ailill and Medb heed this counsel. The house is constructed and the combustibles piled inside, after which the Ulaid are induced to enter. While food and drink is being distributed among them, the door to the outside is sealed shut and the house is attached to seven stone pillars by seven iron chains. Then "three times fifty smiths were brought who fanned the flames with their bellows. Three circles were made around the house, the fire was lit not only below but even above the house, so that its heat entered the house."[30] Finding themselves trapped, the Ulaid accused Cuchulainn of being responsible for getting them into this predicament. Vexed, Cuchulainn leaps into the air, demolishing the roof, and saves his companions. Full of remorse, King Ailill has them enter an oaken house and provides them with beer and food.

While these two versions agree on the fundamentals, the Irish tale places the fireplace in a cave, whereas the Welsh tale tells of a fire around and above the house-cave. The Irish tale does indicate, however, that a fire was also lit above the house, which is very much the same thing. What is quite remarkable in all this is that the "sacrifices" are placed on the inside of the inferno, as is the case for the hero of the Breton folktale, and this does not contradict the description of the druidic pyre with its seven windows, no more so than does the use indicated by Claude Gaignebet for the leper's cabin. And here is another very interesting thing: the "sacrifices" are given food and drink, and made intoxicated, which further classifies this event as a rite of regeneration. And it is recollections of this very rite that are discovered in the Easter Fire, the fires of Carnival, Brandon's Day, the passage of the animals between two fires on May first, and in the leap of the dancers over fires or embers at the time of the Saint John's Day festival. It is not merely a question of purification through fire, but of regenerating the energy dulled by the sleep of winter, or in other words of *ensuring a surpassing of one's self.*

It is obvious that the sacrifices pointed out by Caesar, Strabo, and in the scholiast of Lucan, fall into the same category. It is certain that the figures or cages that the Greek and Latin witnesses saw set on fire were placed above caves, in which the "sacrifices" waited, probably provided with food and drink to celebrate in some way a banquet of immortality or rebirth. And why wouldn't there be some hemp among the combustibles used, whose fumes, when absorbed by the "sacrificed ones," allowed them to "unhook" and achieve their regenerative journey into the Otherworld? It should be noted in passing that the famous Pantagruelion, the magic herb praised by Rabelais in the *Third Book* is none other than hemp. And also that the Pantagruel of medieval tradition is a demon salt caster, that is to say a "burner," therefore, a master of fire.

Fire rituals appear to be innumerable. And they have survived through the centuries of Christianity, whether in Christian liturgy itself or in folk customs and beliefs. It would take too long to list and classify all of them.[31] The ancient ceremonies of the first of May and the fires of Saint John's Day are sufficiently described and indexed to make it unnecessary to go back over them here. But one very particular remnant of these ceremonies is that of the flaming wheel.

> Once upon a time in the country of Agen, the pagans following an
> ancient custom to celebrate a cult ceremony, assembled together in

Gaul, in a *nemet* (temple). At a given moment, the doors of the sanctuary would open as if by the impetus of an invisible force, and to the eyes of this deluded populace a wheel encircled by flames would appear that, as if precipitated down a slope, would roll to the river at the foot of a hill. Brought back to the temple by a circuitous route and launched anew, it would begin to throw off impotent flames.[32]

This is in regard to a hagiographic text on the life of Saint Vincent of Agen. But an identical ceremony is described in an English poem from the sixteenth century.

The country folk take an old rotten wheel that is no longer in service. They cover it with hay and oakum until it is entirely concealed; then they carry it to some mountaintop. When the night grows dark they set it on fire and start it rolling violently. It is a strange and monstrous spectacle. One would think that the sun had fallen from the sky.[33]

We cannot help but think of the depictions among the Gauls of the god of the wheel, and of the numerous Gallic coins on which the wheel is evident. And we cannot forget the Irish druid Mog Ruith, whose name means "son of the wheel," and who is endowed with the extraordinary power—among others—of mastering fire.

15

THE SACRIFICES

The ritual of fire is explicable only through the idea of sacrifice. All religions practice or have practiced sacrifice, whether real or simulated. The "sacrifice" of the Catholic Mass is a memorization of a bloody ritual by which humanity, in the person of Jesus, surpassed its original mortal state and transcended itself to the divine plane through death and rebirth. Druidic religion also was familiar with and made use of sacrifices. To sacrifice *(sacrumfacere)* is "to make" an object or individual "sacred," to make it pass through an elsewhere, meaning through the divine world, by charging it with all the desires, impulses, and feelings of the community performing the sacrifice. This has nothing whatsoever to do with the ridiculous and degenerate conception present in the majority of daily lived religions in which sacrifice is a negative act. On one hand it has become an act for appeasing some dreadful deity by virtue of offerings, while on the other hand it allows the individual or group to shed its guilt through the "invention" of a scapegoat. Emptied of its metaphysical content, sacrifice is no more than a futile superstition. For this reason contemporary religions tend to eliminate it from their liturgies.

Among the Celts, sacrifices consisted of various offerings: vegetables, best yields of the harvest, tree branches, and flowers. These practices can be rediscovered in popular Christianity. There were also sacrifices of such animals as bulls—mainly rams, but always or almost always, young males. In contrast, one of the rituals surrounding the enthronement of a king as described by Giraldus Cambrensis, includes the sacrifice of a mare after the king has sexually coupled with her.[1] After this, the meat of the animal is boiled, the king bathes in the broth, and eats the mare's flesh. In a ritual of royal election, a man ingests the meat and broth of a white bull before sleeping to see the future king in a dream.[2] The meat of the pig—a sacred animal and the food of the Banquet of Immortality—was also used in rituals, primarily for divination. It seems that dogs were also sacrificed.[3]

Although these types of sacrifices have persisted into our own time under forms that are much more profane, that doesn't alter their ancient sacred character. Hunting today is derived from the authentic ceremony of the death of the stag. Bullfights are extensions of the bull sacrifice; and in rural areas the act of slaughtering a pig is a noteworthy event that brings family or the village community into play, an activity accompanied by ritual gifts, invitations, and feasts.

The question of human sacrifices must also be addressed. In addition to Caesar's writings regarding the willow figures, there are many other testimonies that support the likelihood of the practice of human sacrifice. The Gauls "guard their criminals for a period of five years and then, in honor of their gods, have them impaled and made into burnt offerings" (Diodorus Siculus, V, 31). "At times they kill the victims by shooting them with arrows, or else they crucify them in their sanctuaries" (Strabo, IV, 5). Lucan speaks of "barbarous rituals" and the "sinister custom of sacrifices" (*Pharsalia*, 451). Remember that according to the scholias of the *Pharsalia,* the Gauls suffocated their victims by placing their heads in cauldrons. Others they hung from trees and bled, and still others were burned in wooden cages. And even under Roman rule "there remains traces of a savagery that has otherwise been abolished; even though they no longer bring about such extreme massacres, they still spill blood upon their altars" (Pomponius Mela, III, 2). Irish texts corroborate this Greek and Latin testimony, namely the remarks made regarding Saint Patrick and the first evangelists who set about to suppress these barbarous customs.[4] One may recall what Dio Cassius (LXII, 7) said about Queen Boudicca of Great Britain who sacrificed Roman women to the goddess Andrasta.

The Romans, like the first Christian evangelists, had a vested interest in blackening the picture they painted of the druids and in denouncing practices they deemed contrary to their own. The Romans made a great show of being offended—the same Romans who, while they had abandoned religious human sacrifice a long time before, still practiced similar

customs with gladiatorial combats and the feeding of condemned criminals to wild beasts.[5] Moreover, the Romans often accused the first Christians of sacrificing newborn infants to obtain blood for their practice of
communion, but either they didn't understand the ritual of the Mass, or
were misinformed as to its true nature. This kind of incomprehension and
misreading of the facts very often leads to mistakes and outrageous acts.

For these reasons it is necessary to express some reservations concerning the human sacrifices attributed to the Celts, whether Gauls, Britons, or
Irish. Just as the merciless battles described in the epic legends are symbolic narratives, human sacrifices are mythical realities, that is, sacrifices
through substitution or ritual death. The setting fire to the willow figures
of which Caesar wrote must be scaled down to its proper size. It is simply
a simulation, as it should be in every rite of passage, with apparent death—
and ecstasy—followed by a no less symbolic resurrection. The hanging
from the tree and the suffocation in the cauldron must be of the same
nature. The Gundestrup Cauldron constitutes proof that this rite was a
matter of a regenerative act. The sacrificial death of the king is also a kind
of dramatic game during the course of which the king's rejuvenation
occurs, as well as his inner renewal, for without these his power risks being
diminished to the detriment of the entire collective that he represents. It
can be said without fear that druidism never practiced human sacrifices
other than by substitution, simulation, or symbol.[6] All the accusations
made by the Romans and the first Christians are the results of fully
intentional calumnies, or a lack of precise information.

In contrast, however, there is not a moment's doubt as to the authenticity of the rite of the Severed Heads. But this does not concern a bloody
sacrifice to the extent that it is not a head cut from a living individual, but
one cut off a corpse. Citing Posidonios, Diodorus Siculus and Strabo
report that the Gauls cut the heads off of their fallen enemies and nailed
these trophies over the doors of their houses. Titus Livy says almost the
same thing in regard to the death of the consul Postumius whose cleaned
and gold-plated skull became a sacred vessel. The epics of the Ulster Cycle
make reference to this custom: in King Conchobar's fortress there is a
room reserved for the exhibition of these skulls. This is corroborated by
archaeology as well, for in sanctuaries of central Gaul "skull hooks" have
been discovered, and statuary—namely in the sanctuary of Entremont
near Aix-en-Provence—presents numerous examples of decapitated heads

with their eyes closed. It is also true that in certain situations one would cut off the head of a fallen companion in order to prevent it from falling into the hands of the enemy. Such is the case with Mac Cecht who in *The Destruction of Da Derga's Hostel* cuts off the head of his king, Conaire, and takes it with him.[7] This scenario is repeated for numerous other heroes. After Cuchulainn's death, for example, his enemies cut off his head, but Cuchulainn's companion retrieves it.[8] It seems that possession of the head was the equivalent to total possession of the individual, not only from a physical standpoint but from a psychic and spiritual one as well.[9]

We must not overlook that in the Welsh version of the Grail Quest, (the tale *Peredur*), the Grail is neither a vase, nor a cauldron, but a severed head, bathed in blood and borne on a platter. This speaks to the value of the head not only as a receptacle of life and thought, but also of the mysterious and undoubtedly divine energy that sometimes is manifested by what is called the "Light of Heroes," a ray of light that seems to emanate from the head of the most extraordinary individuals. To view this "Light of Heroes" as the aura, the subtle or astral body, changes nothing as far as what concerns us here. It is a matter of all that links the visible to the invisible world, something infinitely precious that explains both the rite of the Severed Heads and the tenacity shown in the acquisition or conservation of such heads. This is certainly one of the more original and specific features of druidic liturgy.

In this sense the severed heads constitute the sacred treasure. The majority of religions have had this notion of a treasure that is jealously guarded in a sanctuary. It is a sort of down payment on the contract established between gods and humans that must not be confused with the different tithes collected by the priesthood. Here too we find the idea of sacrifice in that every material treasure is transcended and transmuted into spiritual treasure. It is with this perspective that the Celts amassed treasures, principally of gold, that were deposited in sacred lakes or ponds. Strabo speaks of gold hidden in a lake near Toulouse that passed for the gold of Delphi brought back by the Gauls from their expedition to Greece in the second century B.C. Caesar asserts, "It is not often that a man dares, in disdain of religious law, to conceal his own booty at his home or to take from the offerings to the gods; such a crime is punished by a horrible death in the worst torments" (VI, 17). But when the Roman Cepion took Toulouse, he looted the city and used the occasion to lay hands on the sacred treasure. Strabo says that it was fifteen thousand talents, or three tons of gold. And since this brought no good fortune to Cepion, a tradition was soon cobbled together concerning "the cursed gold from Delphi." A sacrilege cannot be committed with impunity, and the Celts were particularly sensitive to this notion, for in druidic thought an object or being graduates to the rank of the divine by means of sacrifice.[10]

16

FESTIVALS AND HOLIDAYS

Built upon a lunar calendar with a leap month every five years, the Celtic year was clearly divided into the two seasons of winter and summer, making its principal axis one that extends from November 1 to May 1. Let me repeat once more that the Celtic calendar, and therefore the druidic festival calendar, has positively no connection with the solstices, contrary to what has been put forth by the waves of neodruids who draw their knowledge and traditions from their own fantasies.[1] In actuality druidic holidays occur forty days after a solstice or an equinox. This is perfectly self-explanatory in that forty days is the period of waiting, incubation, and preparation for the birth of the festival, an event that was considered an "orgy," a crystallization of all the freed energies.

The principal holiday was the first of November, Samhain or Samhuin in Irish, which corresponds to the Gallic term *samnios* from the Coligny Calendar, incontestable documentation of the pagan Celts' calendar year. Samhain (pronounced *cho-ouinn*) etymologically means the "end of summer," or, put another way, the beginning of winter. This is the first day of the new year—or the first night rather, since the Celts reckoned by nights. It may seem surprising that the new year coincided with the beginning of winter but don't forget that druidic belief, as Caesar attested, makes Dis Pater, a nocturnal deity, the origin of beings and things.

This was an important festival that every member of the community was obliged to attend: "Each of the Ulaids who didn't come during the night of Samhain lost his reason, and his tumulus, tomb, and stone were erected the following morning."[2] The festival was comprised of every man and woman in the community. Political, economic, and religious matters were discussed and unending feasts were held, marked by the presence of pork and wine. It is true that the meat of the pig was believed to give immortality, as is shown in the legend of Mananann's pigs, and it is undeniable that wine bestowed intoxication, that is to say a state in which the individual could transcend apparent reality and gain access to the supernatural. Indeed, on this day the community of the living and the community of the dead met one another. The sidh, or the barrows where the gods and heroes live, were opened and the two worlds intersected. The Christian All Saints' Day, a legacy of Samhain, has retained this aspect of the "communion of saints," and in the Anglo-Saxon countries the more or less pagan celebration of Halloween is the ancestor of the feasts and masquerades of the Celtic holiday.

These feasts were reserved for the governing class, the king and the warriors being its essential constituents, yet it is hard to see how the druids could have been excluded. The commoners contented themselves with the festival and with all the various amusements and business transactions it provided. Lawyers also assembled there to address all that concerned the relations between individuals and the community. In some form they constituted a veritable parliament in which affairs of law and politics were debated.

The ritual itself is poorly known, however, we do know that on its eve all the fires of Ireland were extinguished, the sign that the year had died. It would be reborn on the instant that the druids lit a new fire. The Christians have transferred this ritual from the first of November to Easter. But it was always on Samhain that the great mythic events were alleged to occur, such as the battles, expeditions to the Otherworld, conflicts with the Tuatha de Danann, ritual deaths of kings, and the violent deaths of heroes who had broken serious taboos. It was also on Samhain that Mac Oc was conceived and born in a "shrunken time" that is the equivalent of eternity. Indeed, if Samhain is the point at which the divine and the human worlds meet, it is because normal time has been abolished or suspended. It is a neutralized time zone in which Mac Oc takes possession of his father's domain, which he has been given for one night and one day, the length of Samhain and the equivalent of eternity. This idea has been perpetuated in the Christian All Saints' Day, particularly in Armorican

Brittany, despite the contamination of the Day of the Dead that takes place there on November 2. To the Celtic way of thinking, there were neither the living nor the dead, no more than there are either gods or humans. There was *everything*.

In all likelihood it was on this occasion that representations of dramatic reenactments recalling the great primordial myths took place, each re-enactment playing a role in the generalized confrontation of the powers that were present. In addition the festival lasted for three days, which allowed for more activities—and feasts.

Three months after Samhain the festival of Imbolc took place on February 1, most likely under the patronage of the goddess Brigit. The Imbolc festival, transformed by Christians into Candlemass, signified the middle of Winter in that not only was fire exalted, but lustral water also. It was a purification festival, an element retained by Candlemass. But we are very poorly informed as to the exact components of Imbolc as all the pagan references have been obscured by the Christians who were troubled—as might be expected—by the presence of the goddess Brigit, who later reappeared in Christian celebrations under the features of the abbess Bridget of Kildare and whose feast day is February 1. Imbolc seems to present itself as having been of much less importance than Samhain. It didn't concern either the military class or the king and was perhaps a more intimate and local affair.

To the contrary, Beltane, the festival of the first of May, was of considerable importance, it being the other pivotal extreme of the Celtic year. The name means "Bel's fire" and refers to the idea of light and heat, because the festival occurred at the end of winter and the beginning of summer. From this festival derived the particularly abundant fire rites and the sacralization of rites of spring. In a pastoral society like that of the Celts, and particularly the Irish, this was the crucial moment at which the herds could leave their shelters and be put out to pasture in the country. The famous Fiana of King Finn had the habit of spending the six winter months in the houses of Ireland—houses that it was their mission to protect—but on the first of May they would roam throughout the whole of Ireland, living a nomadic life. It was also at Beltane that the mythical invasions of Ireland took place. By all the evidence the Beltane festival served as an opening to life and light, an introduction into the diurnal universe, whereas Samhain marked the entry into the nocturnal world, that which in Brittany is still called *the black months*.

The nature of the Beltane ritual remains very unclear. It was certainly a sacerdotal festival and druids would have to have been in honor there, and without a doubt it included ceremonies, games, assemblies, and feasts. The custom of planting branches in the fields and gardens, and over the stables, a custom that persists into the present day, is a faint remnant of this ritual. The so-called fires of Saint John occurred on this date and the king of Ireland had to be the first person to light the fire. All those who allowed themselves to do so before him would be condemned to death. It is well-known that Saint Patrick did so, with impunity, moreover, and that, as the story has it, this act counted for much in the conversion of the Irish to the new religion. But since the extinction of druidism, May 1 has remained the popular festival of human endeavor, especially economic endeavor. It is certainly not for nothing that the Festival of Work has been placed on this date. In the Germanic countries the night of Beltane is "Walpurgis Night" during which all witches and magicians gather together, implying that on this day—or night rather—the sacerdotal class takes action. But because the druids have disappeared as priests, philosophers, and jurists, they have reappeared in popular memory in the depreciated form of magicians. This partly explains the extremely large number of conjuration rituals that can be noted in folk tradition with regard to May 1: blessings of animals and stables, passage of herds between rows of flames or torches, the magical purification of places where animals are housed, and the castings of various spells to protect the herds from illness and wild animals.

If it is said that on Samhain one entered into a state of "hibernation," then it was on Beltane that a sign of "reawakening" appeared. During the winter, fire is invisible, hidden in the wood, stones, and inert matter. But the energy that fire represents exists in the state of potentiality. At the Beltane festival this energy was manifested and achieved a veritable "epiphany." The flames that sprang forth on the pyre of the hill of Tara, lit by the king of Ireland, under the protection of the druids, were more than a symbol. In the cycle of days and seasons they were the proof that life could be borne from death.

The fourth festival, Lugnasad, took place on August 1. According to tradition, Lugnasad (etymologically the "Festival of Lugh") was established at Tailtiu by the god Lugh himself in memory of his foster mother, the goddess Tailtiu, symbol of Mother Ireland. The festival consisted of various games and especially of plenary assemblies. Above all else, it seems that Lugnasad was a royal festival at which the king presided over horse races and poetic competitions, but one where there were no military games or ritual deaths. At this time of year, the king was supposed to be at the height of his power, which had to be so because this was the beginning of the time of year at which the year's fruits were harvested. It should not be overlooked that all of this transpired under the patronage of a mother goddess who, according to myth, sacrificed her own life in order to assure prosperity to her numerous children. Lugnasad has disappeared from the Christianized calendar, but it survives partially, dispersed into other festivals such as the religious Rogation Days, and the numerous profane harvest festivals. In any event, the summer was not propitious for long festivals and even less so for endless feasts. It was the time of intensive labor, during which preparations were made for the coming of the black months so that they could be safely traversed.

So then, the Celtic festival calendar was structured around four specific time periods, two of which are particularly important: Samhain and Beltane. And as the festivals of Samhain and Beltane concerned and gathered together a considerable number of individuals, it again can be said that druidism was a social religion. The individual attitude had no meaning there unless it had been integrated into the activity of the group. This does not mean to imply that the individual had no autonomy; to the contrary, it seems that druidism favored the idea of free will. But it is a question of justification: individual activity had no meaning and thence was unjustifiable if it didn't enter into the context of the entire society, this society being—at least in its expressed objective—the realization of divine society. The festivals, like the rites, were everybody's business. Those who did not participate excluded themselves from the community. And if for one reason or another a festival was not celebrated (which must have been a very rare occurrence), the equilibrium of society, and thus the world, was threatened. The festivals, like the rites, were operations of a magical or religious kind (or both) that established harmonic relations between beings and objects, humans and gods, and visible and invisible forces.

Hence the necessity of an organized, hierarchically structured liturgy was conceived as the projection—on a human scale—of what transpired on the cosmic level.

17

THE POWER OF THE WORD

Celtic civilization was one of an oral nature. The druids felt that "the religion did not permit them to commit the material of their teachings to writing" (Caesar, VI, 16) but this does not mean that they didn't know how to write. In fact, Caesar adds that "in almost all other matters, and in their public and private accounts, they make use of Greek letters." And in Ireland the druids used ogham script on wood and stone as has been made clear by the authors of numerous stories. But, as they transmitted the doctrine, the tales themselves were not written down. Did this result from the druids' concern for developing the memory, as Caesar thought, or because they wished never to divulge their doctrine? It was for both these reasons, and for a third—oral tradition is a living tradition that, transmitted from generation to generation, is constantly modifying itself and evolving according to what is freshly experienced. It is a kind of living culture, in opposition to writing, which necessarily congeals things and sets them in an immutable fashion. In a way an oral civilization is more supple and free, more susceptible to innovation, than a writing civilization.

Nevertheless, this did not prevent the druids from making use of writing when there was need, mainly for relations with other peoples, but also in particular cases when it was specifically a question of having an effect of long duration. Writing, therefore, had a magical and disturbing role; one could utter an invocation, a curse, an execration, and all manner of "satires" against an individual, and it was always subsequently possible to break the spell, that is to cast a seperate spell that neutralized the first one. But if an execration was written, it took on an absolute and perpetual character. To write a curse against someone on a branch of yew or hazel constituted an extremely serious act that was, in short, quite irreversible. With this in mind, it is easier to understand the druids' ban on writing. The act of writing had to be rare, and, moreover, as it could constitute a danger, it was imperative that the use of it could not be spread to those who would make use of it carelessly.

That said, it was still the Word that mattered most. The dreadful ban known as *geis* is from the same root as the word *guth,* meaning "voice." We will see this root again in the name of the specialized Gallic priest, the *gutuater,* "Father of the Voice," or "he who incants by voice." Georges Dumézil expresses the hypothesis that because they learned so many verses by heart, apprentice druids didn't encumber their memory with the whole of a tale, but only some essential verses. "Not poems that sufficed unto themselves, but articulations and rhythmic references in developments of the prose whose meaning alone was traditional."[1] It is true that the composition of Welsh and Irish tales indicates their authors often embroidered from a starting point of outline types, at times inserting ready-made formulations and portions in verse, indisputably learned by heart, that testify to a model that is at times very archaic. But it is necessary to look at this in greater depth.

INCANTATIONS

It is too often forgotten that in order for them to be effective, certain so-called magic formulas had to be uttered in a certain fashion, according to a certain rhythm, and with a certain cadence. Even today in the country-side there are a large number of those who, if they don't possess the *Great Albert,* at least own the *Little Albert,* or, as it is called in Brittany, the *Agrippa.* These manuals of practical magic are constantly being republished, and, therefore, there are many people who know the formulations and the gestures to perform. But what about the manner in which to say the formulations? No how-to manual can teach that. And this is what constitutes the "secret"—and it is only transmitted by those who know to those they have chosen. In understanding druidism, it is perhaps necessary to reflect on this idea: a formulation, learned by heart and repeated without error, is *nothing* if one does not know how to say it. It is in this that initiation and the transmission of powers resides. This can only be achieved through the spoken word. The voice brings vibrations, frequencies, and many subtleties into play that in no way can be described in writing. It is through vibration that something is transmitted, it is through vibration that those mysterious exchanges, which are the basis of all operational magic are carried out. The word predominates in every ritual—Catholic ceremonies and all others—this is even more apparent when the rules of the ritual are followed.[2] The power of the word comes at this price.

When members of the druid class undertook an incantation, they accompanied their text with music, whether that music was provided by an instrument, such as the harp, or whether they simply employed chanting or song. Furthermore, the incantation would not be effective if it was spoken with no relationship to gestures or particular postures. In *The Battle of Mag Tured,* for instance, Lugh sings a magic song before the Fomor "standing on one leg, with one eye (and a single hand) open while making a turn around the men of Ireland."[3] Here then is where circumambulation intervened, which seems to have been a very precise procedure among the Celts, as it has already been taken account of with the repeated gesture that occurs in the tales of Vercingetorix. Caesar himself does not provide the details, but Plutarch (*Caesar,* 27) describes the scene like this: "Vercingetorix, having taken his most beautiful weapons and adorned his horse . . . described a circle around the seated Caesar and leaping to the ground from his horse, he hurled his weapons . . ." The same version appears in Florus (III, 10) and Dio Cassius (XL, 41). The goal seems to have been to assure a kind of symbolic possession of Caesar, and it is likely that Vercingetorix made his circle going from right to left.

Indeed Celtic orientation takes the rising sun, that is the east, as its base. In front is the east, to the left is the north, the *sinister* side (*sinister* being the Latin word for "left"), to the right is the south, the luminous side, and behind is the west. But in fact there are but three cardinal points visible; the fourth is nonexistent because it cannot be seen and thus is considered as the Otherworld, the invisible world. The north, therefore, is the malefic and obscure direction. Christianity accentuated this tendency making it the diabolical direction.[4] Posidonios asserted that to worship the gods correctly it was necessary to turn to the right.[5] The normal, vital direction follows the path of the sun. When the file Amorgen, the first Gael to disembark in Ireland, left the boat, he made sure to set his right foot on land first before he sang an incantation that constituted a taking possession of Ireland.[6]

When Cuchulainn had to leave for his final combat, his horse turned three times "from the left side toward him," a bad sign. Cuchulainn's driver then made the chariot circle to the right, but that had no effect.[7] When the druid Athirne, "The Troublesome one of Ulster" wished to manifest his bad intentions vis-à-vis the men of Ireland, he began his journey from Connaught on the left side—in other words he left by the west.[8] The logic behind this circumnambulation is clear. The east, in front, was the horizon of birth. The south, on the right, was the normal course of life, for which the west, in back, was the conclusion, the Kingdom of the Dead, the Otherworld that one could not see. But the north on the left is the land of cold and shadow. To go west by way of the north is to break the cosmic harmony. It is to go the wrong way and expose oneself to the worst kinds of ills.

When performed in a way that scrupulously respected vocal and gestural expression, incantation possessed a dreadful power. Before the Battle of Mag Tured, the poet Carpe says: "I will cast the supreme curse upon them. I will satirize them and give them shame to such an extent they will no longer offer resistance to our warriors because of the spells of my art."[9] At the time of his last battle Cuchulainn observed two men fighting one another. A satirist-poet then said to him: "Shame on you if you are unable to separate them!" The spell forced Cuchulainn to obey. He killed both men and took possession of the spear they had been fighting over. But this spear was the magic weapon that had been prepared long before to kill Cuchulainn and, under the influence of a new spell, he was forced to give it up to his enemy.[10] In the tale *Tain Bô Cualngé,* Queen Medb, in order to compel Ferdead to fight against Cuchulainn "sent druids, spellcasters, and magicians to seize him, and sent the three *glam dicin* to cause the three pimples—injury, shame, and fault—upon his face. And if he did not come he would die before nine days passed.[11] The glam dicin was the ultimate curse, the "obligatory shout." We see it again in the most ancient of Arthurian texts, *Culhwch and Olwen,* in which the hero Culhwch seeks to enter the hall where Arthur is presiding over a feast, but the porter tells him that he may not enter unless he is bringing his craft with him. Afraid of not reaching his goal, Culhwch tells the porter that if he doesn't open the door he will bring dishonor to his lord, and give him a bad name: "I will give three mortal shouts at the entrance to this gate such as will be no less audible in Penryn Penwaedd in Cernwy (Cornwall), and in the depths of Dinsol to the north, and in Ysgeit Oervel in Iwerddon (Ireland). Any pregnant women on this isle will miscarry, and the wombs of those who are not pregnant will be overturned so that women will never again bear children."[12] In tenth-century Welsh law, the *diaspad,* that is the "piercing shout," was a legal means of protest, but there is no doubt of its magical and religious nature for it concerns the same kind of compelling incantation.

It should be noted that the power of the spell worked against the reputation of the individual toward whom it was directed: if he didn't obey the magic request, he would incur blame and shame, and it is this shame, often symbolized by an illness or physical deformity, that would lead the recalcitrant person to his death. The incantation was perhaps magical but above all else it was social; it was directed toward human dignity, that dignity of the individual as seen by the society. This was a very original concept that showed the extent to which druidism emphasized the value of the individual and, paradoxically, his freedom of action, for although the spell was obligatory in nature, the individual remained free to choose, with all the risks and perils that choice entailed. This also demonstrates the power of the Word, and through the Word, the power of Breath. One can understand now why the Romans, according to Titus Livy's account, had such fear of the Gallic hordes who invaded Italy while making such extraordinary shouts. These were of the same nature as Culhwch's three shouts.

But an incantation was not created just any which way, for the vocal component and the musical resonance had to be taken into account, as well as a complicated series of gestures that have a very pale and Christianized echo in a text from the medieval manuscript, the Ballymote Book. Before casting a spell, it was necessary to first fast "on the land of the king for whom the poem has been made." The satire should have been composed by "thirty laymen, thirty bishops, and thirty fili." The poet satirist in charge of the operation left with six companions, "titleholders from the six ranks of file," in particular an *ollamh* (meaning very powerful, the highest rank in the fili). The ollamh led the others onto a hill at sunset, "on the frontier of the seven lands" (an obviously symbolic figure). Then, "they turned their backs toward a hawthorn bush that would be on the top of the hill. With the wind blowing from the north, each of them held a slingshot and a branch of hawthorn in his hand and chanted a verse against the king over these two objects. The ollamh sang first and the others after, each in turn. Finally each of them set down his slingshot and branch on the root of the hawthorn bush." But the procedure was dangerous: "If they were in the wrong they were swallowed up by the earth of the hill. On the other hand, if it was the king who was wrong, he was swallowed up by the hill, along with his wife, his son, his horse, his weapons, and his dog."[13] By this account it was no longer small-time magic at work, but a ritual that brought into play latent natural powers that could be awoken. And it was the incantation that awoke these forces. Modern theories on the incredible power of the human mind (we use only a tenth of our brain) and the very real experiments, still concealed by official science, conducted by modern laboratory researches ought to take such rituals into account.

Like all operations of this type, spell casting was not only negative and directed against someone. It was not a question of black or white magic, but a question of a magic that was both black *and* white. A healer could carry disease and a sorcerer could cure, since when all was said and done he was the same person. Thus said a satirist: "I myself will sing your poems and spells, and the series of your elders and your ancestors in your presence, to increase the courage of your fighter."[14]

This in no way contradicts the picture the Greek and Latin authors had on this subject: "They have lyrical poets that they call bards. These poets accompany their songs, that are sometimes hymns and sometimes satires, with instruments similar to lyres" (Posidonios, in Diodorus Siculus, V, 31). Incantations also entered into the divination ceremony.

This divination seems to have been highly honored by the Celts. "In the practice of auguries the Gauls surpass all other nations," said Trogue Pompey (Justin, XXIV, 4), a Gaul of the Voscons people. These divinations were performed by observation of the flight of birds and reading the entrails of victims, as well as by spells and induced dreams. The Glossary of Cormac describes a divination ritual:

> The *file* chews a piece of the flesh of a red pig, a dog, or a cat, which
> he then places on a flat stone behind the door. He offers it to the gods
> on the altar with an incantation, then he invokes his idols [the writer

is a Christian monk] . . . he spells his two palms and he keeps his two palms on his cheeks until he goes to sleep. He is then watched over so that he will not be troubled or disturbed before all is revealed to him.[15]

The ritual is comparable to the ceremonies that precede a shaman's "journey," which also includes a manducation or an ingestion of hallucinogenic substances, a mental preparation, and invocations, all followed by an ecstatic slumber during the course of which the shaman will have the revelation in the Otherworld to which he can go provisionally as a spirit separated from his material body. In Ireland this type of ritual was called the *imbas forosnai* and it had points in common with the bull ceremony that, after the sacrifice of the animal, allowed one the manducation of its flesh and a magic slumber in order to have a vision of the future king.

There is also the *tenim laegda,* the "illumination of the song." To put this into practice, a sacrifice had to be made, an incantation sung, then the individual or object for whom the question is to be asked must be touched by a wand, and, most importantly, he who cast the spell had to place his thumb in his mouth, probably in contact with a "wisdom tooth." This is what Finn Mac Cumail did, according to the different tales in the Leinster Cycle. After having eaten the poet (therefore druid) Finn's "salmon of wisdom," he obtained knowledge: "When he had stuck his thumb in his mouth and sang the illumination of the song, then for whatever questions he had, all was revealed to him."[16] But Finn also knew the custom of the imbas forosnai, and the *dichetal do chenmaid.* This latter procedure, which was an incantation by fingertips, and which included neither sacrifice nor reference to pagan gods, was the only one tolerated by Saint Patrick and so remained in use among Irish Christians. Although information is sparse on this subject, we do know that the procedure "was acquired through great knowledge and application."[17] Nevertheless it was the imbas forosnai that Finn Mac Cumail always practiced, and it was even thanks to it that he was warned of his imminent demise: "He put his thumb under his 'tooth of science' and sang a tenim laegda. It was then revealed to him that the end of his time and life was come upon him."[18] In any case, it can be seen that the techniques of divination were more or less dependent upon each other.

Of course the elements that permitted divination were always obscure and, in order to be understood and expressed, demanded knowledge, hence the intervention of the druids and soothsayers, people capable, through an individual gift, to proceed to an interpretation. The Irish text of the *Baile an Scal* (Prophetic Ecstasy of the Hero) shows us King Conn of the Hundred Battles finding a rock on a mound. When he places his foot upon it, it cries out. He asks his druid: "What did the stone shout, what was its name, from where did it come and to where would it go, and who had brought it to Tara?" The druid requests a delay of fifty-three days to respond. When the appointed time arrives he reveals the history of the Fal Stone and adds: "The number of shouts that the stone has uttered is the number of kings who will be of your race, but it is not I who will name them." At times the elements of the prediction are even stranger, if not downright contradictory. Three druids predict to King Diarmaid that he will die:

> From murder, said the first, and it will be a shirt made from the wool of a single sheep that you will be wearing on the night of your death. By drowning, said the second druid, and it will be beer brewed from a single hop that you will drown in on that night. By burning, said the third, and it will be the lard from an unborn pig that you will have on your plate.[19]

The king vainly remonstrates that all of that is quite unlikely, for everything occurs as foreseen: he is fatally struck down, drowned, and burned alive by the Ulaid.

This brings to mind certain predictions of Merlin the Magician, namely those recounted by Geoffroy of Monmouth in his *Vita Merlini*. Indeed, he predicts in it the death of a child: "The child will die from falling on a rock; he will die in a tree; he will die in a river." Everyone took Merlin for a lunatic. But the child, while pursuing a stag, tripped over a rock and fell into a ravine, where he drowned in a river, his foot, however, caught in the branch of a tree.[20] This incident comes from an ancient tradition concerning an individual by the name of Lailoken, who seems to have been the model for Merlin, a kind of half-mad vagabond who lived among the North Britons around the year A.D. 650 in the countryside of Strathclyde. According to the Latin text of the *Life of Saint Kentigern*, written at the beginning of the twelfth century, Lailoken, who lived in the forest to atone for his sins, declared one day to Saint Kentigern that he, Lailoken, would die from "blows of stones and staffs." Kentigern wished to know more, and Lailoken told him that he would die pierced by a wooden skewer, but also that he would die drowned in water. According to legend, pursued by the king's herdsmen who threw stones at him and struck him with their staffs, Lailoken fell down the steep embankments of a river and drowned, transfixed by a sharp stake placed there by fishermen.[21]

It must be recalled that the Merlin of Geoffroy of Monmouth and of the *Book of Merlin* is an individual who bursts out laughing when asked a question. Then he responds with either enigmas or answers that are, at the very least, quite beside the point. There is a kind of derision in the laughter of Merlin, as if every prophecy shouldn't be regarded as true, or if the vision of the future was senseless folly. It is obvious here that we are in the realm of the irrational, and that, to enter this realm, something must be broken in order to cause a rupture allowing us to access it. Merlin's laughter is a provocation, and the answer to the question put to him must be discovered by the person who poses the question. The seer is only the operator of an action that places the individual in contact with the Otherworld. In this sense, laughter, like the voice, permits the abolition of time. For it is only by abolishing relative time that one can penetrate the secrets of the future, which itself is nothing but a still undefined past. The art of divination was understood by the Celts as being the mastery of time and space, considering them as a single yet multiple absolute.

And if divination had a necessary relationship with vocal incantation, then what can be said about the mysterious procedure that in Ireland is called *geis?* The word is untranslatable. It could be rendered by *taboo* if the connotation of the latter wasn't so strongly linked to the Pacific cultures. It would be better to use the word *ban,* even though that exclusively emphasizes the negative aspect of the concept. Indeed, by nature, the *geisa* (plural of *geis*) has an ambiguous character: the positive value can appear behind the negative aspect and vice versa.

A geis was an incantation pronounced by a druid, a member of the sacerdotal class, a poet, a musician, or, at times, an isolated individual, most often a woman who, afterward, was considered as a prophet, a poetess, a satirist, or a fairy being. In this manner the heroine Deirdre, promised to King Conchobar falls in love with the handsome Noise and offers herself to him. But Noise has no desire to create any trouble for himself with Conchobar and he refuses her. Then Deirdre "pounces on him and grabs him by the ears: 'These will be two ears of shame and mockery,' she says, 'if you do not take me with you.'"[22] Noise cannot do other than obey this terrible injunction that, later on, will be the cause of his death. The same holds true for Grainne, the wife—or fiancée—of Finn Mac Cumail. She set her cap for Diarmaid, a young warrior vassal of Finn's, and Grainne, after having put all the other guests of a banquet to sleep with a magic potion, hurls this challenge at him: "I place you under a geis of danger and destruction, O Diarmaid, if you don't take me with you from this house before Finn and the chiefs of Ireland awaken from their slumber."[23] Against his will Diarmaid takes Grainne with him. They are pursued by Finn and the Fiana, but Diarmaid does not have sexual relations with Grainne until one day when she casts a new geis upon him, a magic provocation that casts his virility in doubt, at which point Diarmaid is forced to have carnal relations with her.[24]

This tale brings to mind the legend of Tristan and Iseult, and sheds new light on the love of these two unfortunate heroes that was recuperated by romantic sensibility. Grainne is the Irish prototype of Iseult the Blonde. She is the woman-sun, the last face of the ancient feminine deity of the sun. If one rereads the legend attentively, particularly the archaistic episodes in prose from the *Book of Tristan,* one will observe that Iseult is in love with Tristan from the moment they first meet. But Tristan remains indifferent, the proof being in that he wins Iseult on behalf of his uncle, King Marc. Hence Iseult's fury when Tristan takes her by boat from Ireland to Marc's kingdom, and also hence the intentional error of Iseult's accomplice, her attendant Branwen, which consists of her giving them the potion that compels them to love one another. Here Tristan is the prisoner of the potion just as Diarmaid was the prisoner of the geis. The potion is naught but the folklorized, Christianized, and guilt-ridden version of the archetypal Irish geis. Henceforth, Tristan, the victim of a magic enchantment, can live for no more than a month without having relations with Iseult, for if he does not he will die.[25]

But Diarmaid, the victim of two geisa for which Grainne, the solar-woman magician, holds responsibility, is also under the influence of previous geisa that are no less dreadful. He should never kill a wild boar, while at the same time he should not hear the baying of hunting dogs on a scent without joining the hunt. And he must never refuse the request of one of his companions. In consideration of this, Finn flushes him from hiding, forces him to transgress his major prohibition by making him kill a wild boar, and thus leads him to his death.[26] What happens to Cuchulainn, the "Dog of Culann" is of the same nature. He must neither kill nor eat a dog. But there arises an occasion when he cannot refuse an invitation to dine. His enemies arrange for him to transgress his first prohibition, after which he immediately breaks all his other prohibitions, one after the other, eventually causing his death.[27] For prohibitions are often quite numerous, and the weakness of the system lies in the fact that one day or another the individual will find himself fatally caught between two conflicting geisa. There is no solution outside of degradation or death. But in any case the degradation, shame before one's social group, inexorably leads to death.

Prohibitions always concerned the kings or certain warriors, but never druids. Caesar informs us that the Aeduen magistrate, the vergobret, who at that time had replaced the king, was bound by prohibitions, one of which was that he was never to go beyond his people's borders. Prohibition-laden Cormac, the son of Conchobar, was never supposed to listen to a certain harp, hunt the birds of the Da Cheo plain, have a rendez-vous with a woman on Senath-Mor, cross over the Shannon with dry feet, to mention only a few of his prohibitions. King Conaire the Great, the hero of the tale *The Destruction of Da Derga's Hostel*, was also well burdened with his own prohibitions.[28]

> It has been forbidden you [from birth] to kill birds. You are not to go southwise around Tara nor northwise around the plain of Brega. You mustn't hunt the wild beasts of Cernae. You mustn't venture out of Tara every ninth night. You are not to sleep in a house where firelight may be seen from within or without after sunset. No theft should be committed under your rule. Finally, you are not to interfere in a quarrel between two of your serviteurs.[29]

Everything went fine for a while. Ireland prospered because its king respected all his geisa. But one day he separated two of his foster brothers who were fighting. He had broken his first prohibition, and he would break all the rest, one after another, leading to his death. It should be deemed that these geisa often appear ridiculous and extremely difficult to obey. The majority of these geisa were presented in symbolic form, while others were fully justified by the precision and moral value that one had every right to expect of a king who governed his realm effectively and with justice. It was perfectly normal that it would be the king who was subject, more than any other person, to the weight and threat of countless taboos. Otherwise he would not have been king.

In any event this proves that the geis had the value of absolute law, on the religious as well as the civil plane. There is nothing astonishing about this since in druidic thought *they were the same thing*. The temporal did not exist without the spiritual and vice versa. The geisa practice was therefore necessary to assure the full functioning of the system; to specifically prohibit something immediately implied a positive value, one that was not named but must be achieved. But here again, despite the obligatory nature of the prohibition, the human being appeared free to make a choice, in full possession of free will, with all of its risks and perils. The Celtic geis has nothing in common with the Greco-Latin *Fatum*. The Fatum was a neutral, blind, anonymous entity that soared over humans and gods, but the geis, through its religious and magical components, concerned the individual, and him alone, in the realization that he operated vis-à-vis himself and the collective group of which he was a part. But it was the human being that governed and guided. This notion is fundamental to understanding druidic thought, and for establishing the essential differences between it and classic Mediterranean thought.

Furthermore an individual, in full awareness, could bind himself by means of a geis when he swore an oath. At that moment the individual was both the spell caster and the object of the spell. The fact of "swearing by the god that my tribe swears by" gave the act its sacred dimension. It was a solemn pledge that took as its witnesses and guarantors the gods—or even natural forces such as the sun, the wind, or the earth. King Logaire, vanquished in battle, had to promise to no longer claim tribute from his vassals and take as guarantors "the sun and the moon, the water and air, the day and the night, the sea and the earth." But Logaire didn't keep his promise and died, "because of the sun, the wind, and all his other guarantors, as well, because no one dared transgress them in those times."[30]

All of this shows the extreme importance that the druids attached to the Word—not to the dead, congealed word, the one that is written and merely preserved, but to the living, spoken, chanted, sung, and shouted

Word. It is somewhat like a musical score: if there are no musicians to interpret it and bring it to life, it is worth nothing. A record, a cassette tape are only props, but if there isn't an *organ* to extract their contents, they are worth nothing. The power of the Word does not exist without the Voice that animates that Word, without a gutuater to invoke the mysterious forces that sleep within and around us. This is the myth of Sleeping Beauty and of the princess of the city of Ys who, swimming beneath the surface of the sea, awaits that bold individual who will come seize her and bring her above to where the sun is shining.

18

TOTEMISM
AND SHAMANISM

The ritual techniques used by the druids refer to traditions that appear quite ancient, but such ritual techniques do not necessarily have an Indo-European legacy. Let me repeat once more that the Celts were only a minority and would had to have commingled with the autochthonous populaces of Western Europe when they first settled there, and so it is impossible not to find remnants of prehistoric societies in druidism. This is evident in the concept of the feminine solar deity, and is probable with regard to the deity who bears the name of Cernunnos. It is possible for everything concerning the role of animals—and plants, as well—in the mythology, at least in those legends where beings in animal form or bearing animal names, make an appearance. It is tempting therefore to speak of totemism.

The question of whether or not Celtic totemism existed has been a controversial one. At the turn of the century, when the influence of Frazer's *Golden Bough* was preponderant, the tendency of scholars was to accept totemism among the Celts because of the numerous animal interventions in epic tales. But currently the trend is to reject totemic elements in the druidic religion. But this rejection appears unjustified. If we believe that the names of people were composed with the help of animals' names by virtue of the symbolic value that the animals confer upon them, there are elements that are difficult to explain except by a certain adherence to totemism.

By definition, totemism is a belief that accepts the existence of animal ancestors from whom an individual or group are alleged to have descended. This belief manifests itself in religion by the worship offered to the animal-ancestor, as well as by different prohibitions, namely those involving food. One cannot consume the flesh of the totemic animal, save, as ethnologists have pointed out, on the day of the ritual feast on which the transgression of the taboo is permissible, if not mandatory. Moreover, it is in this manner that Freud, basing his position on Frazer, tried to explain in *Totem and Taboo* the birth of religions from the guilt that resulted from the murder of the Father, the Original Ancestor, a murder reactualized in the totemic meal.

First of all it must be decided, if, in all the forms of totemism that have been observed, practitioners truly believe in the reality of the animal ancestor. To call oneself "son of the bear" does not necessarily mean that one believes one is the great-grandson of a bear. Ethnologists often have taken literally those things that were only representative images. On the pretext that the fish was a sign of recognition personifying Christ for the first Christians, it would appear that the Christians believed themselves to be descendants of the fish, at least to the unknowing outside observer. But the reality of totemism is more complex in that coded social traditions appear that were transmitted by means of significative signs. Overall, we must avoid stumbling into the pitfall of considering the "primitives" as mentally underdeveloped. The word *primitive* should never be employed save to designate chronological anteriority or cultural otherness. In this sense totemism should be restored to its true meaning: the belief that an individual and a collective group can belong to a lineage whose rallying sign or emblem is, in some way, an animal or plant representation. The motivations behind the totemic plant or animal chosen are of a symbolic or simply sociological order.

In this sense the existence of totemism among the Celts is undeniable. The name of the Gallic Eburovice tribe, built on the word that signifies "yew," is evidence of this. The relationship between Finn Mac Cumail, his family, and the Irish Fiana with the Cervidae (antlered animals) is yet more proof that this very old clan was heir to the prehistoric occupants of Ireland from the era of the reindeer hunters. And in this case the totemic reference to the stag is fully justified by sociology. The same is true for the principal characters of the Ulster epic who are all marked by a relationship with the bull and the dog.

Cuchulainn is the prototype. Originally named Setanta, he received the surname of "Dog of Culann" following the murder of a dog, who was more infernal than real. This bears strong resemblance to an initiation rite. After Cuchulainn kills the Smith's dog, the Smith protests that he no longer has a guard or protector. Setanta, who apparently is in the wrong, makes reparation, and, henceforth, becomes the Smith's guard and protector, or in other words the dog of Culann. Thus it can be said that he chooses his practical name, he joins a brotherhood, a clan. The druid Cathbad who is on the scene ratifies the act by saying that, thereafter, Setanta will bear no other name than that of Cuchulainn.[1] This is a rite of passage, a rite that permits entrance into a clan. But this clan's emblem is the dog, for which Conchobar, the name of the king, the uncle—and father—of the young hero, bears witness.

There is more. The glorious "career" of Cuchulainn transpires entirely between two dog murders. The first one gives him his name and introduces him into the warrior class. The second occurs immediately before the hero's death, after he has been forced, because of a geis, to eat a dog roasted by a sorceress, a daughter of Calatin. "Alas!" said Cuchulainn. "I will never kill a man after this animal. It was a dog that was the object of the first deed I accomplished, and it was prophesied to me that a dog would be the last deed that I do."[2] The fate of the hero Diarmaid, the prototype of Tristan, according to his own testimony, is bound to that of a wild boar. Certain versions of the legend explain that Diarmaid's brother, who was killed accidentally, is metamorphosed into a magic boar, which constitutes the basis of Diarmaid's major prohibition: to never hunt a boar, under pain of death.[3] This magic boar can be found again in Welsh tradition, not only in the tale of *Culhwch and Olwen* in which Arthur and his companions track down the boar Twrch Trwyth, but also in certain *Triads of the British Isles* and in the *Historia Britonnum* of Nennius.[4] The boar is a frequently seen emblem in Gaul; almost all of the rediscovered war insignia are poles topped by a bronze representation of a boar. All the warriors depicted on the plate from the Gundestrup Cauldron that represents the suffocation rite are wearing helmets surmounted by a boar. But it remains unknown whether the boar represents the physical and solitary strength of the warrior, which would make it symbolic, or whether it concerns the mythic animal that is considered the ancestor of the warrior class.

There are other stories, many not very clear, concerning the bond that exists between a human and animal. Thus the young Culhwch is born in the midst of a herd of domesticated swine and the young Pryderi, Rhiannon's son, is stolen at birth, then deposited in a stable in which a foal has just been born.[5, 6] It seems that symbolism is singularly exceeded in these instances and that it is necessary to recognize in them the survival of totemism in mysterious circumstances. It must also be asked why the Irishman Art, son of Conn, who is "bear, son of dog," must take as his wife the daughter of Coinchend Cenfada, which means "heads of dogs," after having won her by triumphing over the worst dangers.[7] The name of King Arthur, which, despite what people would have one think, is not of Latin origin, is derived from *artu* or *arto*, "bear."[8] The name of King Math is also one of the Celtic names for the bear, *matu*.[9] And the name of King Marc is that of the horse, *march*. Is this symbolism? Certainly. The properties attributed to an animal were carried over to the individual who bore the name of that animal. Yet this in no way contradicts the certainly that we are confronted by remnants of totemism, those belonging to a lineage whose rallying sign is the animal in question.

The prohibition of killing the animal whose name one bore was then the rule. This is the case for Cuchulainn, and it is probable that it must have been the same for Arthur with regard to the bear. Indeed, an archaic text, the *Romance of Yder*, presents some curious adventures: Yder (Edern), son of Nudd, whose relations with Queen Guinivere are ambiguous—to the point of sparking the king's jealousy—kills a bear that has gotten into the queen's chamber. The bear either symbolically represents Arthur or else, in this instance, Yder replaces Arthur who cannot be permitted to kill a bear.[10] In any case it is likely that such prohibitions weighed on other individuals with animal names. Finn, whose true name was Demne, could not kill a buck, his son Oisin could not kill a fawn, Arthur could not kill a bear, King Marc a horse. As for food prohibitions, they were complementary.

This does not reduce druidism to a bastardized form of the original totemism. The role of animals as well as plants in Celtic mythology must be taken into consideration, although this great familiarity between man and nature doesn't explain everything. Symbolism always presupposes yet older beliefs since it borrows its signifiers from objects that are allegedly familiar to everyone and, therefore, belong to a remote tradition solidly based in memory. If totemism had been more important, it certainly

185

would have manifested itself in a clan system. Clans, as such, didn't exist in Celtic society. What is sometimes called a clan is only a convenient name for designating a group of families united by common interests, if not a common origin. But from a strictly legal standpoint, clans no longer existed. Consequently, if there are traces of totemism in druidism—and we are seeing that there are—they are left over from a time previous to the arrival of the Celts, and they were not accepted nor integrated into their system. But if a religion officially eliminates all references to beliefs or customs of an earlier religion, these beliefs and customs reappear in new forms, more or less adapted to the current situation but that still testify to their heterogeneous nature.

The importance of plants and animals in Celtic mythology, as well as in druidic rituals, raises other questions. Was there a shamanic component in druidism, or at least elements that can be identified with shamanic practices?

At first view one is tempted to respond in the negative, that druidism constituted a hierarchical religion with Indo-European structures, whereas shamanism has never been anything but a grouping of beliefs and rites spread throughout very different cultures and original populaces. Shamanism is practiced in the Far East among the so-called Asiatic people, much the same as it is in Siberian regions inhabited by Indo-Europeans. In addition it was formerly widespread throughout the northern fringe of Europe, not to mention the Russian steppes and the Caucasus. It is certain that a relationship between shamanism and the Scythian civilization existed. And it is known that Germanic mythology included tales of shamanic feats, namely regarding Odin-Wotan who appears as the preeminent shaman-god. Moreover the links between the Celts and the Scythians no longer require proof, if only in the realm of influences on the plastic arts. In all likelihood, the Scythians transported ideas similar to those found in shamanism, and we know that Sarmatian auxillary troops (who were Scythians) were charged by the Romans along with more or less independent Briton tribes, with the task of monitoring Hadrian's Wall in Great Britain. "The Scythians," says Georges Dumézil, "are called upon to play an important role, that of being providers or transmitters in another field of research: the connections between Japanese mythology and Indo-European ideology."[11] This perhaps takes us a long ways off, but it sheds light upon the existence of a cultural and necessarily religious current in northern Asia and northern Europe that stood in fundamental opposition to that of South Asia and the Mediterranean. It is plausible to call this current, which must have run in an unbroken line from the Pacific to the Atlantic, a "barbarian" current.

It is extremely unlikely that the different peoples included in this current didn't influence each other. We have proof of the presence of Indo-European elements, namely the functional tripartition in Korean mythology and in ancient Japanese mythology, particularly in the tradition of the Ainu, an indigenous people of Japan. This same Indo-European presence is clearly visible in the shamanic beliefs and practices of various peoples. So why shouldn't this current have flowed in the reverse direction? To peremptorily assert, as some have done, that there isn't a trace of shamanism in druidism smacks of burying one's head in the sand. We now possess a deepened knowledge of the shamanic phenomenon, and so it is possible to establish solid comparisons. To dismiss shamanism from druidism is to disdain shamanism as a witchcraft tradition. As Mircea Eliade, the foremost scholar on shamanism, says, shamanism is "the most valuable experience of archaic religions," and that, most of the time, the ritual practices based on profound beliefs and on metaphysical reasoning, "often have the same precision and nobility as the experiences of the great mystics of East and West."[12] The practices are an indispensable support for any religious doctrine, and what would there be to druidism without ritual practices?

The continual reference the Celts made to animals and plants is one of the elements of possible comparison. The link between the shaman and plants is obvious, as obvious as that between the druid and the tree. The shamanic tree of the world is most often the silver birch, the deciduous tree that is best resistant to the cold and that is most often found in the north. In the famous poem *Kat Goddeu,* the hero Gwyddyon, who transforms the Britons into trees, takes the shape of a birch himself. And a good number of the traits of Gwyddyon are reminiscent of a shaman. He is a sacred magician capable not only of awakening the plant forces, but also of metamorphosing human beings into animals, and animals into human beings, such as when he changes Blodeuwedd into an owl, or when he restores Lleu Llaw Gyffes, who has become an eagle, to his human form.[13] It is known that through their incantations and through their ecstatic practices shamans believe they can become animals, whether by incorporating the animal spirit into themselves or by projecting themselves into an animal. The transformation may not occur on the real "material" plane, but it does take effect on a real psychological and mystical plane. The Tuatha de Danann, who are both gods and druids, are capable of performing such transformations. And it is these transformations that undoubtedly are what is found in numerous Celtic texts.

A good example of this is the story of Tuan mac Carill, a very interesting character from Irish tradition. Witness of the five great invasions of Ireland extending back to the time of Partholon, he survives by changing his shape. First a man (more precisely a druid), he later becomes a stag, a boar, a falcon, and a salmon before becoming a man again. The idea of reincarnation has been suggested with respect to this example, but it is not a matter of successive lives, but simply a question of successive metamorphoses of the same body, the same being, endowed with exceptional powers. Tuan mac Carill is the image of primordial man who is still capable of reconstituting, as Mircea Eliade says about the shaman, the golden age of humanity's beginning, at a time when men and animals spoke the same language and did not kill one another. Certainly Tuan's transformations are symbolic, adapted to a system of civilization that is their basis, but they also testify to the realization that the individual is not isolated in the universe but a part of a unity that groups together all the elements and all the energies.[14] In Irish tradition another character by the name of Fintan (his name means "old sacred one," Vindo-Senos, in which we again find the word *finn-gwynn-vindo*) has comparable metamorphoses, but no doubt this concerns a doublet.[15] As for the bard Taliesin he routinely makes such transformations. The *Kat Goddeu,* which is attributed to him, makes mention of these, as do certain of his poems.[16] His legendary history, though gathered later, testifies to the antiquity of the belief in the possibility of metamorphoses.[17] The theme is even recognizable in certain folktales. It is clear that oral tradition has preserved, more than any other tradition, shamanic coloration from the depth of the ages. A story of Upper Brittany thus presents a young hero, a servant of the devil, who, having gained knowledge of some of his master's secrets, performs surprising transformations on objects and himself.[18]

Shamanic elements seem particularly abundant in relation to the figure of Cuchulainn. His famous "contortions" are of same the order as the metamorphoses, except that he is no longer seen as having the shape of an animal, but deforms himself to the degree that he becomes monstrous as a result of what is incontestably warrior rage. "The little boy raised his head above the ground, and placed his hand over his face. Turning purple, he took the shape of a mill from his head to his toes. . . ."[19] He twisted his body beneath his skin; his feet . . . went behind him . . . pulling his nerves from the top of his head, he pushed them behind the nape of his neck in such fashion that each of them made a round bump. Then he distorted his features, his face. His mouth distorted in monstrous fashion. . . ."[20] His hair stuck up above his head like branches of red hawthorn above a hedge. . . . Balefire surged from his head and forehead, as long and large as a warrior's fist."[21] Obviously we are dealing with a trance phenomenon here, and it should be noted that Cuchulainn often takes the form of an enormous, flaming wheel. He exceeds all other warriors when it comes to hurling the wheel. In *Bricriu's Feast* he hurls a wheel over the roof of a house where it buries itself in the ground of the courtyard. In *The Wooing of Emer,* when having to cross the Plain of Misfortune where it is so cold that men freeze solid, Cuchulainn receives a wheel from a warrior who tells him to cross the plain as if he were that wheel. This calls to mind the god of the wheel in Gallo-Roman statuary, as well as the use of flaming wheels indicated in the *Life of Saint Vincent of Agen.* But the wheel, a substitute for thunder, is also a shamanic symbol. Moreover, when he finds himself for his initiation into the military and magical arts at the hands of women witches in Scotland, Cuchulainn has to pass a singular ordeal of crossing a magic bridge: "When one leapt onto the bridge it would shrink to the size of a hair and become as hard and slippery as a fingernail." On other occasions it would become taller than a pole. This is reminiscent of the "Bridge of the Sword" in Chrétien de Troyes's *Chevalier à la Charette* that Lancelot of the Lake must cross to reach the mysterious city of Gorre, a city in the Otherworld, where Meleagant has taken Queen Guinevere. After numerous unsuccessful attempts, Cuchulainn becomes enraged. "He leapt in the air while balancing himself as if he were in the wind, and managed to hold himself on the center of the bridge. And the bridge did not shrink, nor did it become hard, nor did it become slippery beneath him."[22] There can be no doubt as to the initiatic nature of this trial, or about its relationship to shamanic techniques.

Indeed, Mircea Eliade informs us, "shamans, like the dead, must cross a bridge in the course of their journey to the underworld. Like death, ecstasy implies a 'mutation' to which myth gives plastic expression by a 'perilous passage.'" On the other hand, this symbolism of the bridge is dependent upon "the initiatory symbolism of the 'strait gate' or of a 'paradoxical passage.'" And Eliade explains the complex in the following manner: "In *illo tempore*, in the paradisical time of humanity, a bridge connected earth to heaven and people passed from one to the other without encountering any obstacles, because there was not yet *death*." This is why in regard to the Celts, the Samhain festival can be considered a veritable bridge to the dawn of time, symbolically reconstructed for one night and one day. But now, people can no longer "cross the bridge except 'in spirit,' either as dead or in ecstasy . . . this crossing is difficult; it is sown with obstacles and not all souls succeed in traversing it; demons and monsters seeking to devour the soul must be faced, or the bridge becomes as a razoredge when the wicked try to cross it. . . . Only the 'good,' and particularly the initiates, cross the bridge easily . . . for they have under-gone ritual death and resurrection; certain privileged persons, neverthe-less, succeed in passing over it during their lifetime, be it in ecstasy, like the shamans, or by 'force,' like certain heroes, or finally, 'paradoxically,' through 'wisdom' or initiation."[23]

There is no denying the important role shamanism has played in Celtic tradition, in as much as the theme of the bridge, or ford to be crossed, is without a doubt the essential element, in a symbolic form, of the druidic spiritual journey. Everything seems to converge toward this bridge, which serves as the point of contact between the two worlds. One may recall that the Ford of Souls from the Welsh tale *Peredur*, where the white sheep turn black when crossing the ford, and vice versa upon their return, as well as all those battles that take place on bridges or fords in Celtic tales and in the Arthurian romances. In folktales there is also the matter of bridges and fords to cross, and an insistence on the strange nature of the ferryman, a disturbing personality, who is the mediator between both worlds. And there is still more to consider.

Cuchulainn, who metamorphosizes (a deformation) himself and be-comes monstrous, which is to say he passes from a human to a superhu-man, quasi-divine state that is manifested in the symbolism of the story by a physical abnormality. But he subsequently must return to his human shape; he must come back down to earth. And this is not as easy as the ascent. Possessed by battle rage that verges on total ecstasy, the young hero risks disrupting the social group to which he belongs if he doesn't take certain precautions. In the tale of *Cuchulainn's Childhood,* when one sees him returning from battle, King Conchobar gives explicit orders for extinguishing his nephew's battle rage. He starts by making the girls and women of Emain Macha come forward to reveal their naked bodies to the little hero. It is not for nothing that one talks about the "warrior's rest." Battle rage is linked to sexuality, and in the case of Cuchulainn it is a question of transforming his bloodthirsty aggressiveness into sexual desire. When Cuchulainn arrives—don't forget that he is still a little boy, gifted for his age certainly, but still very young—he turns around so as not to see the women's nudity.

> Then he is helped out of the chariot. To calm his anger, three tubs of fresh water are brought to him. He is placed in the first tub and he makes the water so hot that it breaks the staves and the copper hoops of the tub much as one cracks a walnut. In the second tub the water makes bubbles as big as a fist. In the third tub the heat is such that some men can bear it and others cannot. Then the anger of the little boy is diminished.

Following this, Cuchulainn, clothed once again, makes a kind of triumphal parade, and "with his body formed a kind of wheel."[24]

In the tradition of the Nart, a Scythian people, there is a hero by the name of Batradz whose characteristics correspond closely to those of Cuchulainn. Batradz appears to be the Indo-European, Asian version of the hero represented by Cuchulainn in the Celtic, Western version. The character has an extraordinary birth, comparable to that of Cuchulainn. His mother, a woman-frog (Cuchulainn has Dechtire, a woman-bird for a mother), dies while she is pregnant, but the seed of the infant to be born has been sealed beneath the skin on his father's back, and this is how he comes to maturity. His aunt, Satana, prepares the birth and opens the "abcess."

> Like a waterspout, filling everything with flame, the child, a child of molten steel, rushed out the bottom, where seven cauldrons of water were not enough to contain him. "Water, water," he shouted, "so that my steel will strengthen." His aunt Satana ran out with six jugs to draw water from a spring, but she was late returning because the devil

> did not consent to her taking the water unless she gave herself to him.
> . . . Finally she returned and watered the child to whom the Nart
> Syrdon would then give the name: Batradz.[25]

This tale is an obvious parallel to Cuchulainn's story. The Nart are people of central Asia who are in permanent contact with shamanism, even though they are Indo-Europeans themselves. The legend of Batradz is quite ancient and has even been assimilated by neighboring peoples. It belongs to a common fund of traditions that all stress the fiery nature of Batradz-Cuchulainn.

And this "magical heat" is still a shamanic element. "Like the devil in the beliefs of the European peoples, shamans are not merely 'masters over fire'; they can also incarnate the spirit of fire to the point where during séances, they emit flames from their mouths, their noses, and their whole bodies."[26] After having drawn up a quick chart of beliefs of this type, Mircea Eliade says "Often the shamanic ecstasy is not attained until after the shaman is *heated* . . . the exhibition of fakiristic powers at certain moments during the séance springs from the shaman's need to authenticate the 'second state' obtained through ecstasy."[27] But how does one attain this "heated state" that only heroes such as Cuchulainn seem to possess as an innate ability?

> There is every reason to believe that the use of narcotics was encouraged by the quest for "magical heat." The smoke from certain herbs, the "combustion" of certain plants had the virtue of increasing "power." The narcotized person "grows hot"; narcotic intoxication is "burning." . . . Mystical ecstasy being assimilated to a temporary death or to leaving the body, all intoxications that produced the same result were given a place among the techniques of ecstasy.[28]

It certainly appears that this could have been the case for the Celts. We do not have absolute proof that they used hallucinogens, but the knowledge of plants was so important to them, it is unlikely that they weren't aware of the "heating" properties of certain plant types. We can assume with some confidence that they used certain mushrooms such as *Amanita muscaria* whose consumption causes visions and delirious states. And hemp, whose use was widespread in the manufacture of cloth and ropes also would have been known to them. The carnivalesque techniques and willow figures pointed out by Caesar prove that the effects of hemp were not only known, but employed in séances of initiation and "seeing." In any case, there was alcohol, and the Celts had a reputation, even in the writings of the Greek and Latin authors, for being impassioned amateurs of fermented beverages. Drunkenness is a widespread theme in the epics, especially in the Irish tales. Gods and heroes outdid one another with their unquenchable thirst for alcohol, in the form of beer, wine, and mead. A religious festival could not take place without an unbridled drinking bout, and these can still be seen today in numerous, so-called folk customs. The important thing is to *depart,* to *detach* oneself, to forget that the human being is attached to the Earth. Queen Medb of Irish epic legend is literally Drunkenness. And when she bestows upon numerous warriors the "friendship of her thighs," she is only providing sacred intoxication for those she has called upon to perform a mission in the name of the society of which she is sovereign. This explains in large part the Celtic propensity for drunkenness: it constitutes a kind of profane degeneration of an ancestral religious tradition, but it retains all of its characteristics, particularly on the unconscious level, since it permits the "crossing of the bridge."

It remains to be seen whether these techniques of ecstasy that are based on plants or alcohol are extremely ancient. "But closer study of the problem gives the impression that the use of narcotics is, rather, indicative of the decadence of a technique of ecstasy or its extension to 'lower' peoples or social groups. In any case, we have observed that the use of narcotics (tobacco, etc.) is relatively recent in shamanism of the far Northeast."[29] There are indeed "superior" techniques that permit the attainment of an ecstatic state without the absorption of hallucinogenic or heating products; these techniques, like Indian yoga, are directed at awakening the unconscious forces that reside in each of us. It seems that this may be the case with the Celts, as is testified by Cuchulainn's ritual deformations, which denote an absolute and total mastery of the mind over the body, or, for those who refuse to accept the mind-body duality, the visible manifestation of an internal transformation. For this is what ultimately matters: the appearance of an internal heat by virtue of which one can cross over to the other side. The main objective is to return from the Otherworld from which stems the prudence of shamans who never adventure alone into the forbidden regions. At the beginning of their careers they are always accompanied by an older shaman who acts not only as their guide but their protector. Only predestined heroes and seasoned shamans can cross the bridge with impunity and then return. The techniques of crossing over can be extremely varied. Dream is one form, delirium is another. Orgasm is still another, and the works of Wilhelm Reich, disencumbered of their sociopsychological context, reveal the true value of the orgasm. The orgasm unleashes a considerable amount of energy that, once reinvested—and not diluted as is usually the case—can be of aid in the decisive stages of crossing the bridge. Moreover, the orgasm itself, which is a rupture, is a point where the most difficult joinings between the two worlds can be achieved. Isn't the orgasm called the "little death"? Assuredly death is an orgasm from which there is no coming back, and that is because no one knows the techniques that allow one to come back.

These notions are as familiar to the Celtic domain as they are to other Indo-European territories. The divine furor, the "frenzy" that appears in certain Greek heroes, the name of the preeminent shaman-god Odin-Wotan, the fury of that strange Irish figure Fergus (whose name comes from *ferg*, meaning "fury, potency"), Cuchulainn's "internal heat," all come back to the same theme. And it is Indo-European in origin, while still living in the shamanic societies of today, which in principle, are not Indo-European. The druids were organized according to Indo-European structures, but it is possible, maybe probable, that a good number of their beliefs and techniques are akin, in one way or another, to the beliefs and techniques of the ecstasy that characterizes shamanism.

The ritual concerning the choice of the future king—during which a druid, after chewing a piece of pork and drinking heating beverages, goes to sleep and starts dreaming, protected by assistants who surround him—conforms absolutely to the shamanic ritual of the séance during which the shaman achieves his journey to the Otherworld. This is not a question of a coincidence but one of identical nature. And what is to be said about the druid, man of the woods and linked to the plant, who officiates in the heart of the forest in a sacred clearing? In many respects he evokes the shaman who, whether mythically or in reality, has his sacred site, a site from which rises his tree, a tree on which two idols are propped. This description brings to mind a nemeton (sacred clearing). Moreover, when the shaman dies, his tree also allegedly withers and dies, which further reinforces the link between the plant/nature and the priest in shamanism as well as in druidism. Many folktales also echo this kind of symbiosis between the tree and the individual "who knows and sees."[30] As for the women-warriors who initiated young Cuchulainn and had him cross the narrow bridge, they closely resemble women shamans who are particularly numerous and just as effective in the same way as their male counterparts. Finally the ability of shamans to transform themselves and, according to stories, their custom of confronting one another in animal form, are additional similarities when we consider the druids who confronted one another in magical combat.[31] The Battle of the Trees supports this, as do the feats performed by Mog Ruith in *The Siege of Druim Damhgaire*. And the Irish tale of the *Two Pig Keepers* follows a similar line. It concerns the adventures, metamorphoses, and struggles of two magician pig keepers who compete with one another in magical feats to prove their prowess.[32] As for the constant battles of Celtic heroes against monsters, dragons, troubling supernatural beings, and the Fomor (ugly titanlike warriors), these are similar to the ongoing battle that all shamans lead to reconstruct the world in its original state and to reestablish the free passage between heaven and earth by eliminating all those who lie in wait around the Narrow Bridge.

But to become a hero, that is a shaman or a druid, it is necessary to possess exceptional qualities. Such is the case with the Tuatha de Danann, but they are gods who by nature are on a superior level to human beings—although this did not prevent them from being defeated by the latter. This is made clear in the Welsh tradition with Gwyddyon, son of Dôn, who constitutes a fairly complete image of the druid-shaman, as does Merlin the Magician, no matter which version of the legend is used, even those that are most heavily Christian influenced.[33] Merlin is the exemplary model of the being who travels the bridge between the two worlds for his own purposes, and who aids others to cross over as well. This is the meaning behind his interventions with Uther Pendragon and Arthur. But it is also the meaning of the Varuna element in the traditional druid-king couple. The king leads the army, but it is the druid who makes it possible for the army to cross the bridge.[34] As for the companions of King Arthur in the early tale of *Culhwch and Olwen*, they are all characterized by powers that derive from shamanism. Kai, Arthur's foster brother and oldest companion, can remain nine days and nine nights without water, and nine days and nine nights without sleep. He is gifted with another privilege: he can become as tall as the tallest tree in the forest. Last, another shamanlike characteristic given in the *Mabinogion* is that "while the heaviest rain was falling a hand's span about what he held in his hand would remain dry *because his natural heat was so great*. It could even serve as a combustible agent with which his companions could make a fire when they were sorely tested by the cold." This particular feature obviously connects him to Cuchulainn and Bartradz, as well as to all the wolf-men and bear-men of Germanic mythology who, possessed with the fury of Wotan, would go berserk in battle. In any event there is a large gap between this archaic mythological figure and the clumsy, boastful, braggart Kai who is found in the Christianized versions of the Arthur legend. Another companion of Arthur's, Bedwyr (the Béduier of the French romances), is one-armed— like Nuada and Tyr—but his sword is invincible. Still another is Gwalchmai, "May falcon," otherwise known as Gauvain. He has an interesting idiosyncrasy: his strength grows in the morning, reaching its full potential at noon, after which it diminishes. From this it has been concluded that Gauvain is a solar hero, which really tells us very little.

For what Gauvain represents is something entirely different. He is a kind of medium capable of receiving the force of the sun, who then utilizes that force according to his activity. He is not the sun, or a personification of the sun, but a human endowed with certain powers. He literally collects the sun's energy like a solar battery! The myth, therefore, is teaching that any human being—no matter who—should be capable of utilizing natural forces, on the condition that one knows how to collect and use them with discernment. For traditionally Satan also knows how to employ the forces of nature, but only to very destructive ends. The forces of nature, cosmic energies, are necessarily ambivalent, being only what we make of them.

Other companions of Arthur also have specific characteristics. One companion knows all languages, including the language of animals, which makes him a kind of druid-shaman reactualizing the Golden Age, or calling back the memory of this long ago time in which men and animals could understand one another. As for Menw, he could cast an enchantment over his companions "in such a way that no one could see them yet they could see everyone." This is obviously the gift of invisibility that Mananann procured for the Tuatha de Danann after the Battle of Tailtiu. And Menw, whose name means "intelligence" could also cast an enchantment over wild beasts to charm them. Here again we are dealing with a reconstruction of the Golden Age. Menw is therefore the Dagda of the massive club, a master of magic like King Math of the *Mabinogion*. But he is also a charmer of wild beasts like Merlin.[35] Several of Arthur's companions have sometimes become characters in folktales, such as the character who can drink up all the water from a stream or the one who can run quicker than the wind; the one who can carry enormous quantities of weight or the one who can ingest incredible quantities of food, and so on.[36] Folk tradition is in large part an heir to pre-Christian wisdom and is often colored by shamanic beliefs and practices.

It is also necessary to speak of *dream*. Celtic tales owe a great deal to dreaming, without naming it as such, since they refuse the Aristotelian distinction between the real and the imaginary.[37] Whether it occurs naturally, or is induced through the use of suitable techniques, whether provoked by hallucinogenic substances or intoxicating drinks, the dream is as fundamental a concept for druidism as it is for shamanism. The dream rebalances the world, it regenerates individuals, gives them the means to go beyond the human condition and find the paths, that are at times obscure, leading to the bridge to the netherworld. There the dream perhaps no longer suffices, and it may be necessary to possess several effective formulas to put to flight the demons guarding the bridge. But, in any case, the dream allows people to orient themselves toward the desired objective. And on the strictly quotidian plane, the dream, with the possibility that it includes to imagine, is the most sure method for discovering something new. Every invention is the result of a dream. Every invention is the proof that what is not real can, under certain conditions, become real. Such is the goal of shamanism. Such seems to be the goal of druidism. There are too many similarities for the kinship between the two systems to be illusory or superficial. This kinship is profound, and to not recognize it points toward a certain blindness.

19

NEODRUIDISM

Currently there are perhaps a million people throughout the entire world, principally in Europe, America, and Australia, who claim to be druids or affiliated to druidic orders or brotherhoods. This is an important phenomena. These brotherhoods are quite numerous, varied, and often opposed to one another as much by doctrines, rituals, and actual goals as by the social origins of the participants. Rare are those who are purely druidic, some accepting a double-appurtenance to Catholicism, orthodox Christianity, and different Protestant churches. Others in existence smack more of Masonic lodges than of any authentic druidic tradition. The most serious problem in this is that each of these brotherhoods claim to be the holder of the druidic tradition. But it is quite obviously not the same tradition for everyone.

It is an accepted fact that there are no official written texts revealing an authentic druidic tradition; moreover, this is quite convenient, for it allows any person to claim that he or she is the heir of a tradition transmitted orally over the centuries. This being the case we do not feel compelled to believe such individuals. It would be quite pointless to ask those who claim descent from an oral druidic lineage for the least proof of this lineage, in that, by definition, no proof exists. For this reason we can see how the doors are opened to anyone to claim druidic lineage. The dream and dreaming being one of the characteristics of the Celtic mentality, all of this undeniably has a Celtic tone. Still it is necessary to find our bearings.

198

The druidic brotherhoods can be classified into four principal categories. The first is the line of John Toland (1669–1722), an Irish Catholic who founded his druidic order on September 22, 1717.[1] This order is quite an antiestablishment movement, currently known under the name of the Druid Order, whose founder's paganizing tendencies have been tempered by modifications introduced by the Anglicans. One would seek in vain in this order for pure druidism, even if the order still existed as it did in its original form. The influence of the famous poet William Blake, a member of the brotherhood, appears to have been very important on this clearly esoteric druidic branch that also has the allures of a secret society. The second line of druidic brotherhoods, the Ancient Order of Druids, was founded by Henry Hurle in 1781. Hurle, a carpenter, gave this brotherhood a quite visible Masonic coloring, as well as humanitarian preoccupations, particularly those concerning mutualism and social providence. William Blake was also a member of this group. In any case, their ritual seems to have been very much inspired by Scottish Masonry.

The third druidic line is that of Iolo Morganwg, a masonry worker whose real name was Edward Williams and who was born in Glamorgan County, Wales. This inspired, self-taught man was very interested in old Celtic culture, and did much research and published several works on the subject, the authenticity of which is still subject to reservations. It is probable that Iolo Morganwg collected folktales and that he knew medieval Welsh literature quite well, but little more about him is known, other than the fact that he founded the first druidic and bardic Gorsedd (assembly) in London, on June 21, 1792, the day of the summer solstice. This is a good measure of the reliability (or unrelability) of this information if one recalls that the ancient druids had no solstice festival whatsoever, a fact substantiated by all the documents that we have at our disposal. But solstice or no solstice, the movement was launched. The Welsh Gorsedd would become the quasi-official branch of druidism, and it is to this lineage that the currently existing Fraternity of Druids, Bards, and Ovates of Britain is connected. The concerns of this lineage were nationalistic at the onset but have since developed into preoccupations of literary research in Wales and into much more cultural and even scientific concerns in Britain. In any event, the members of this lineage do not consider themselves as priests of an ancient religion. They admit to double or triple membership with other religious groups and consider their "druidism" an eternal quest for Celtic wisdom.

A fourth category brings together countless brotherhoods, fraternities, groups, and sects not necessarily connected to any one of the three previously described lineages. Some brotherhoods are maintained only by the ephemeral will of their founders. Others are tied to different traditions. Each has its own conception of druidism, but most often it appears that these conceptions are the result of syncretism where the most heterogeneous, even to say eclectic elements, are brought together. Some are openly pagan or anxious to take up again with ancient paganism. A special mention must be made of the Celtic Restored Church, which is part of orthodox Christianity, but seeks to rediscover through Celtic Christianity—such as it was lived by the first Breton and Irish communities—harmony between ancient druidism and the new religion. It is known that Saint Patrick ordained priests and even bishops from the Irish fili, and that these latter, keepers of a double tradition, passed it on to their successors. The Celtic Restored Church claims to have proof of that filiation.

Outside the Celtic Church, the ritual of these brotherhoods is only a conjectural reconstruction of what is imagined to have been the druidic ritual. None of these complex and varied rituals could have been those of the druids before the introduction of Christianity, and it is dishonest to claim that they were. To believe otherwise is to be gullible or very badly informed. When an individual is of good faith, it is possible to find what he is seeking in these rituals and that is a positive aspect. But the lack of information, the manifest errors (in particular regarding the dates of the festivals), the tendency toward esotericism that permits all manner of rambling, syncretism, the pernicious influence of the rites and doctrines of the East and Far East, do not allow for any clarity of the existence of modern druidism, nor of the Celtic character itself. This is not a value judgment. Each member of these brotherhoods has his own motives, quests, and spirituality, all which are perfectly respectable and honorable. My only assertion is that these rituals and their corollary doctrines seem to have little in common with what is known historically and scientifically about the druids.

To utter words in a Celtic tongue, and dress in a large white robe is not enough to lay claim to being a real druid.

Earlier I said that druidism is only warranted within the framework of the Celtic society because the druidic system was in some way the conscience of the social organization. It was logical that druidism disappeared at the time that the Celtic-type of society vanished, *since druidism could no longer be lived as religion.* What would have remained are the principles of druidism, for they could not have vanished. And from this comes the impassioned search in neodruidism, in all its guises, to attempt to find out just what druidic thought and druidic ritual was. To achieve this quest, for it is a true quest for the Grail, would be an interesting development, although again it is important that it be conducted with the necessary safeguards.

One thing is certain: without a Celtic society there can be no druidism. Neodruidism is nothing but archaeology.[2]

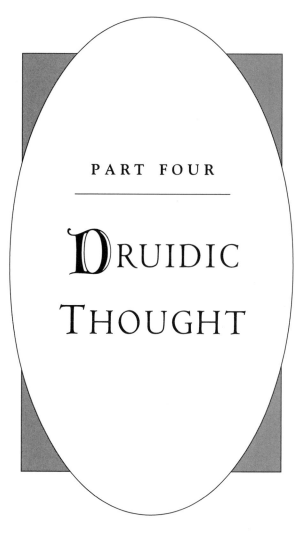

PART FOUR

DRUIDIC
THOUGHT

*I*t must be said that we know even less about the druids' doctrine than we do of their liturgy, and this paucity of information for both springs from the same reasons: the historical disappearance of the druids and the total absence of dogmatic texts. In the attempt to explore this doctrine the sole recourse is to call upon the few rare testimonies of the authors of Greek and Roman antiquity, as well as the interpretation of mythological or heroic sagas. This means it is necessary to interpret them with all the attendant risks. Mistakes always occur when judgments are made on a past era, because the deeds of the past are almost always judged according to modern criteria. Such mistakes are even more common when dealing with a vastly different, if not fundamentally opposed, form of civilization. It should be repeated that to comprehend the Celts, their civilization, their intellectual and spiritual speculations, it is paramount to abandon the Aristotelian system that constitutes Western humanist civilization. Celtism is *another* humanism, *another* fashion of looking at things, of feeling, apprehending reality, conceptualizing the deity. It is *another* way of living, *another* method of reasoning. Not taking these inherent differences into account risks ending up with a completely false picture. Words do not necessarily have the same meaning for a Gaul of Vercingetorix's time and a Frenchman of the twentieth century. Moreover, words in and of themselves mean nothing; they gain value only through having a context. And as long as there is no attempt to define the context, the exact meaning of a word, fact, or concept can never be discovered. Being one of the expressions of what it is to be Celtic, druidism cannot be separated from it, and as the druidic institution is the common denominator of Celtic civilization, to understand druidism is to understand the Celts, and vice versa. But such an undertaking is not easy.

The lack of precise information, the mystery surrounding the druids, their rites, and their beliefs, all have stirred the imagination. Certainly the imagination appears to be, and rightfully so, one of the major elements of Celtic thought. But the Celts had their own imagination that, perhaps again is not the same as our own conception of it at this end of the twentieth century, or at least the imagination as defined by contemporary systems of philosophy. An awareness of this dichotomy already exists in the study of oral folk traditions passed down over the centuries and that include their own rules and their own logic that is hard for modern-day attendants to grasp if these are posed in the terms of a writing civilization. The Greek and Roman contemporaries of the Gauls, who had frequent contacts with them and who were originally from the same cultural and linguistic mold, did not understand the Celts. They definitively classified them as "barbarians." And it is this barbarism that, as compelling as it may be, appears difficult to grasp because it is heterological. It is closer to Heraclitus than to Socrates. It never passed through the "Greek miracle." But the Greek miracle is like any other miracle—we are not compelled to believe it. The human adventure has manifested itself in many different and divergent paths, an adventure that is, without a doubt, unique, but it is also a paradox. But everything is a paradox when one enters the Celtic mentality. And this in no way prevents its structures from being unyielding.

20

A FALSE POLYTHEISM

The commonly accepted theory of the history of religions consists of one governing principle: monotheism appeared slowly and at a late date in human societies, after disengaging itself from polytheism, which itself was constructed, with much trouble, on the ruins of animism and naturalism. This is only a postulate and as a postulate is perfectly undemonstrable. The study of the Hebrew Bible, considered the model for traditional sacred texts, cannot shed any satisfying light here. The Bible is a nationalist saga, in the modern sense of the word, and concerns a nomadic people who had only recently become settled. Next the Bible presents the image of a god who was not unique, since the Hebrews accepted the fact that other peoples had their own gods, but gods specific to the people of these groups, a kind of *teutas,* to speak in Celtic terms, that is an exclusive guardian of the tribe. And if at certain times in their history the Hebrews practiced polytheism it was due to the influence of neighboring peoples. Moreover, their definitive form of monotheism seems to have come about it in the same way, borrowed as it was by Moses from the Egyptian votaries of the Solar Disk. In fact the Hebrews were materialists who did not even believe in the survival of the soul; all they asked was to have a protector god who would assure them the best and longest life possible. Even in the time of Jesus this opinion persisted among the Sadducees. There is nothing in the Bible that can be drawn upon regarding this question of monotheism as being viewed as an evolution of polytheism. It would be better, to ask once and for all, if the fact of worshiping numerous gods was not only a practical means of honoring a unique and unknown deity under the multiple functional aspects attributed to it.

For the gods of polytheism all appeared as the living symbols of a function that was social, dependent upon the way the group lived, and one that translated the group's main concerns. For the Irish there was no god of agriculture, which indicates that the Irish were not farmers, but herders and hunters and had no need for a protector of the harvest—although there was a harvest. Labor upon the earth was reserved for slaves and classless individuals. In a word, the personalized gods did not exist except when the social group under consideration had need for them, meaning the specialized function they represented. This somewhat discredits the very idea of polytheism.

These observations particularly concern druidic religion. The Celtic pantheon that is so numerous and varied, and disconcerting as well, should not give us any illusions. An observer ignorant of Christianity, entering a church, attending a service, seeing the multiple number of saint statues—and their functional specificity—hearing talk about Our Lady of the Good News, Our Lady of the Guard, Our Lady of Aid, would have a tendency to consider Roman Catholicism as a kind of polytheism. And then there is the dogma of the Trinity: a single god in three individuals. Let's be logical—this makes three sacred persons, three personalized deities, three Indo-European *deivos* constituting a single god. If one takes Hegalian dialectical reasoning, which is none other than that of Heraclitus, as a starting point, then God as an absolute is equal to nothing, since he has no awareness of his own existence. God can only have this awareness of being in the face of someone other than himself, or in face of an emanation of himself. The Father is not a father save when confronted by the Son, and vice versa, the Holy Spirit being the dialectical link between the two opposites. In order to manifest, the deity needs to split into its multiple faces—the passage from the absolute to the relative. Under these conditions the gods of the Celtic pantheon are manifestations of the functional multiplicity of an absolute, unknown, incomprehensible, unnamable, and, therefore, infinite god, who is supposed to be the cause of everything.

Certainly the god Lugh, the "Master of All the Arts" appears to correspond to this total deity quite well. But this is an appearance. He is only the "Master of All the Arts," that is to say only active in the world of social realities. He even combats the chaotic forces represented by the Fomor, from whom he himself was issued. He is not the creator at the origin of all, only the animator of all. Though having multiple duties, Lugh does not embody the whole of the sacred; his multiple duties are in reality only a superior function. When Lugh was born from both order (the Tuatha de Danann) and disorder (the Fomor), the world was already established, and Lugh's role was to assume this world in obedience to the overall plan visible in the structures of the Celtic society: to establish or maintain the indispensable equilibrium between coherence and incoherence. This is the meaning of the struggle undertaken by Lugh against his grandfather, Balor. But this is only one episode in a series of adventures that are little more than the dramatic representation of the deity's internal contradictions.

It is not possible, therefore, to believe in the polytheism of the Celts, at least on the society's highest level, the sacerdotal class. That the people may have been able to take the divine depictions literally and worship a multitude of gods is possible, but not certain. The further one removes oneself from an intellectual, abstract doctrine—such as that which is at the disposal of the clergy level—and gets closer to the bottom of the social ladder, the more one will encounter the "faith of the coalman." This is a faith that does not ask itself questions and accepts from the first all images offered to it. But it has not been established that the sacred figures who fill the Celtic epics are necessarily entities. The part narration plays in mythology increases the simplified formulas even more, and in this sense the personalized gods of the era are simplifications a superficial reader might take as experienced realities of the religious life. We should never forget that we only know Celtic mythology through narrative tales of a literary nature, which are adaptations and transpositions of essentially theological assumptions on the level of the story. When one tells us that the gods acted, fought, got drunk, copulated, and even died, we are being given an anthropomorphic image. Considering the famous remark made by Brennos, the Gallic chief of the expedition to Greece, in a temple where he had seen the image of the Greek gods, one can be certain that the druids would never have accepted an anthropomorphic representation of the deity in their doctrine. In truth, if we take Diodorus Siculus (frag. XXII) at his word, that the Celts could have represented their gods in such a way is unlikely. "Brennos started to laugh because the gods were assumed to have human form and they had represented them in wood and stone." This is right to the point: it is both the rejection of anthropomorphic representation in statuary and the impossibility of presuming a human nature for the gods.

So then who are these divine figures coming together, fighting, becoming intoxicated, copulating, and dying in the mythological tales? If one refers back to Brennos's attitude, these cannot be the gods.

In this domain it is always necessary to start off from the base provided by Caesar. This is reliable to the extent that the proconsul, who knew druids and had numerous informers throughout Gaul, always strove to comprehend the workings of his adversaries' thought to better bend them to his will. When Caesar praises himself and "rearranges" historical reality, it is in order to give himself the starring role. When he speaks of the mores of the Gauls, he has no reason whatsoever to misrepresent that reality. And let me repeat once again that Caesar has provided an account of Gallic deities according to social criteria. This is how we have been able to rediscover the three Indo-European functions in the Apollo-Mars-Jupiter triad, a triple function in the single but with three-faced figure of Minerva, and a role that is classless and functionless in Mercury. In short, these Gallic—and therefore Irish—gods are incomprehensible outside of the social function attributed to them. We can conclude from this that the divine figures presented in the mythological sagas are symbolic and pictured projections—necessary for the story—of functional activities that are legal tender in the social group.

It has been observed that in the complexity of epic tales that include vestiges of mythology or that are frankly mythological, there is nothing that brings to mind a cosmogony or a theogony. The birth of the world is never evoked or, if it is, it is a consequence of being Christianized, and has a deliberate intent, repeated many times, of "hooking" Irish tradition to Biblical tradition. If there are elements of cosmogony in these myths, they can only be foreign to the original Celtic tradition. And the same holds true for theogony. The references to a Hebraic filiation that appear at a later date in the texts, and have wreaked havoc since, correspond to this same intent to make it biblical, no matter what it takes.[1] But the origin of the gods is never revealed. They land in Ireland, that's all that is told, and in time they are replaced by other gods who land there as well and take possession of the isle, only to be driven away from it later, as is the case with the Tuatha de Danann.

The reason for all this is that all gods are druids. And if all gods are druids, *all druids are gods.* But they are also men. Certainly these men are quite exceptional and they are described as possessing dreadful and marvelous powers. But the tales concerning them were the best means of providing an account, in a clear and concrete fashion, of the intellectual, spiritual, and magical prowess of the druidic sacerdotal class. Tuan mac Carill, one of the rare figures of this era to metamorphose in a radical fashion (to such an extent that he provides a basis for a belief in a certain form of metempsychosis), is perhaps the best example of this druid-god who traverses the centuries, bearing witness to what he has seen and thus passing along the tradition (which is the role of the druid). And most significantly, during his last incarnation among the Sons of Milhead, the Gaels, he relates all of his adventures to Saint Patrick, is baptized, and dies a good Christian. The conclusion is logical: the druid-god no longer serves a purpose, since a new druid-god has come bearing a message of faith and resurrection. Saint Patrick, witness of Christ, a previously unknown god, replaces all the druids, and, consequently all the gods. This is one of the fundamental reasons why the Irish—never invaded by the Romans, and far from the changes then taking place in Europe—converted so easily and without being forced to the Christian religion.[2]

This observation is not a personal opinion, for an attentive reading of the texts provides complete confirmation. Even the heroes who do not appear as druids, are druids, and thus gods. In the tale *The Courtship of Emer,* Cuchulainn says that the druid Cathbad taught him so that he would be "versed in the arts of the god of druidism."[3] Thus there is a process of initiation that corresponds to a "heroicization," in the objective of knowing the "arts" of the druidic god, that is the primordial druid. And this primordial druid can only be the single and multiple, unnamable god, who is the source of all knowledge and all creation, in that knowledge equals creation. For the Celts the world was nothing other than druidism, and cultural practices were the elements that assured the continual and perpetual creation of the world.

From this point of view it can be understood how, in the druidic doctrine, *God does not exist, he becomes.* And this Becoming encompassed the world for which the druids presented themselves as the regulators. God had need of men. It was an unnamable god of course, one that could not be locked within the anthropomorphic contours of a statue, nor in the chains of a name: for he who possessed a person's name possessed that person. The name of God was ineffable and unpronounceable. It was perhaps written somewhere, but that was of no use, since no one knew how to pronounce it. In the Hebrew legend, Lilith knew it. And this is why Lilith is always lurking in the shadows, under ceaselessly renewed forms. In Celtic legend the druid-god also knows this name, but does not wish to pronounce it. He knows how to do so, but doing so would risk compromising everything. Since God is Becoming, it is necessary that this Becoming be eternal. And the whole of creation participates in this Becoming, in such a way that one can rightfully claim the existence in the druidic doctrine of this large scale ontological concept: *God is to be created.*

Thus there is a gap between this fundamental idea and the pale notion of polytheism, which in large part explains the attitude of the Celtic hero, always ready to carry things through to the end and prepared to do the impossible. This heroism is found again in the saints of Celtic Christianity. To be a hero or a saint is not to submit passively to the decrees of an immutable deity that sits motionless in space. On the contrary, it is to penetrate the great secrets—in other words the sacred master plans—to put these plans into operation and to follow them through to the smallest detail. And this takes strength, truly a boundless violence, energy, and will, the feeling that one can only survive by completely going beyond one's self and the world. And it also requires knowledge. This is what by the druid-god provides and it is up to humans to comprehend its scope.

The universe of the Celtic gods is never static. There can be no respite in the Becoming of God. The practical consequence of this is that nothing is ever definitive as long as God's master plan has not been completely carried out. And it will probably never be. This is humanity's sole chance for survival. If the gods die, humanity will also die. And God will no longer exist. For these reasons the druids are at the root of all decisive workings of Celtic society as the guides who are conscious of applying the divine plan to human society, a plan without which, in spite of everything else, nothing could feed the Becoming of God.

There is a great beauty and serenity in this druidic conception of the deity, but also a constant and permanent appeal to the Being. If the Being was content to be, this would be the void, the vacuum for which certain Oriental philosophical systems are in search. But druidism is at the antipodes of the theory of nonbeing; it is at the antipodes of nondesire, the antipodes of the negation of the desire to live. Through the deeds and gestures of the heroes, gods, and men, the doctrine, such as it appears in all the tales, can be summed up as a relentless desire to live. God is the objective, but God, this unique, unnamable god, ceaselessly retreats before the efforts of humanity. And he will retreat eternally, smiling like the Ogmios described by Lucian of Samosata, and similarly pulling with him, attached by chains that come from his tongue, the herd of humans who are also smiling because they know that their journey will endure for eternity.

21

DRUIDIC MONISM

In the final analysis the druidic god, as has been defined, is the same God as that of the Christians. He is the alpha and the omega, the beginning and end of all things. If the fili, keepers of the druidic doctrine, became Christian priests so easily, it was primarily because, on the major principles, their existing theology was in agreement with the new theology. But it seems the details proving this theological similarity, which would have led to the confusion of their worshipers and presented druidism as having been too close to Christian concepts, were erased from the tradition. It was pre-Christian Greek and Roman authors who displayed their admiration for the exalted nature of the thought in druidic doctrine, comparing it to that of Pythagoras. The first Christians, whether the Fathers of the Church or Irish monks, placed more emphasis on the "superstitions" and "sacrifices" (which they denounced), and pushed the theological arguments off to the side. Consequently, they silently passed over the symbolic elements that would have supported and materialized the true dogma, that of the oneness of the unnamable God.

The sole existing testimony of this doctrine is found with Pliny the Elder. And this is quite confused in that Pliny did not understand the scope of the ritual he described, thus reducing it to a simple magical procedure. His testimony is also the sole truly cosmological allusion that exists concerning the Celts.

Indeed Pliny presents us with

> a sort of egg of which the Greeks don't speak but which is quite well known among the Gauls. During the summer, great numbers of snakes intertwined in a studied embrace to create these objects with the saliva from their mouths and their bodily secretions. This is called a "serpent egg."[1] The druids say that this egg is cast aloft by the hissing of the snakes, and it must be caught in a cloak before it touches the ground. At this moment the thief must flee on horseback, for the serpents will pursue him and will only be stopped by the impediment of a river. This egg is recognizable by the fact that it floats against the current, even when set in gold. The extraordinary skill of the mages [druids] at concealing their frauds is such that they claim it is necessary to only take possession of this egg during a certain phase of the moon, as if it were possible to force this activity of the serpents to coincide with human intention. Indeed, I have seen this egg, which was like a round apple of medium size, with a bony crust like the numerous arms of an octopus. (*Natural History*, XXIX, 52)

Commentators on this text generally think that the serpent's egg described is a "fossilized sea urchin," this identification being based on archaeological discoveries of fossilized sea urchins intentionally placed in numerous Gallic tombs and mounds.[2] A tumulus in Saint-Amand sur Sèvre (Deux Sèvres) even seems to have been specially made to contain a small coffer inside of which a fossilized sea urchin was found. It is likely that the fossilized sea urchin had quite an exceptional value for the Gauls. But with regard to Pliny's text there is something that doesn't quite fit. Pliny was a naturalist, and even though the science of his era was rather rudimentary, one would have to consider him an imbecile in order to claim that he didn't recognize a sea urchin, whether fossilized or not. He described an egg that he affirmed to have personally seen, a description that in no way corresponds to that of a fossilized sea urchin.

It is obvious that Pliny's egg that "floats against the current," even when it is "set in gold," is a marvelous object. It is impossible to not see it as the equivalent to the Cosmic Egg of Hindu tradition, enveloped by the gold embryo, primordial seed of the cosmic light, which is found in the primordial waters, and which is hatched by the unique bird, the swan Hamsa.

What Pliny says regarding "against the current" and a golden setting does not allow for the slightest doubt in this, all the more so since the Gallic egg is quite often represented on Celtic coins. It is seen here as a kind of decorative ornament that accompanies either a horseman, horse, or simple head, and that consists of a vaguely ovoid shape or ball attached to one or more chains. The motif is quite widespread, namely on the coins of the Parisii and those of the Armoricans.[3] But the Celtic version of the myth is quite particular.

Pliny's text is certainly not the description of a ritual, yet it was Pliny who mistook what he described for one. Someone must have recounted a mythological tale to him, the meaning of which he didn't quite grasp, but the essential elements of which he remembered: the entwined serpents (the "knot or nest of vipers"), the egg secreted by the snakes, the theft of the egg by a horseman, the pursuit undertaken by the serpents, and the impossibility for the latter to cross a river. These elements are those of a veritable epic. A horseman—therefore a civilizing hero—comes to take possession of the Cosmic Egg in a land that is the Otherworld, and then flees, pursued by the Otherworld's inhabitants. But these latter cannot cross through certain boundaries. The horseman crosses the border with the egg, which, thanks to the courage of this hero, is now in the possession of the humans.

This epic cannot be truly understood unless it is compared to oral folk traditions that certainly seem to be echoes of the original outline of this tale. First of all it concerns a type of widespread story in which a young man gains entry into the manor of a magician or devil or who becomes the servant of one of these latter. The young man learns their secrets by chance, frees a young girl held prisoner in the manor, and flees with her on horseback while carrying away all the magician's or devil's treasures. The latter pursues them, but they manage to leap a river that their pursuer is incapable of crossing.[4] What Pliny the Elder recounts corresponds closely to this storyline. One must take possession of the serpent egg—the secrets or treasures of the Otherworld—and flee. The inhabitants of the Otherworld, the serpents, hurry to catch the audacious individual who owes his salvation to the rapidity of his flight and because he manages to cross the river. The pursuers cannot leave their own world, but the egg, that is to say the knowledge of a secret, is taken out of their world and into that of the humans.

215

A second comparison can be made with the numerous legends concerning the sirens" the "serpent-women," who come drink at fountains. They have bodies often covered by fire, one of their two eyes is a carbuncle or a precious stone, or else they have magic stones in their tails. When they drink at the fountains they set this stone down, and one can make off with it on the condition that one is fast enough to flee to safety from their pursuit.[5] There is no doubt that the carbuncle or precious stone plays the same role as the serpent egg.[6] The theme is identical. And there are even better examples still. In the Welsh tale of *Peredur,* the hero must defeat a great serpent who hides in a cavern. And "in the tail of the serpent [there is] a stone. The stone has the virtue of granting whoever holds it in one hand, all the gold they can wish for in the other."[7] This is yet another manifestation of the egg of the serpent. It is obviously the Cosmic Egg, in that it can provide a huge amount of gold, the solar symbol of knowledge that provides all the riches that can be desired. But it also represents the Philosopher's Stone of the alchemists, a stone that not only could permit the manufacture of gold, but constitutes the universal secret of creation, the Unity in its complexity, the crystallization of all the ambiguities of the world and all its apparent contradictions.

The Cosmic Egg (or stone) is linked to the serpent, the symbol of knowledge and the infinite mobility of the Spirit. The serpent is that which lurks everywhere, that which slips within the smallest anfractuosity of the Earth. The Serpent biting his tail, the Ourobouros, is the perfect circle, that which represents totality in its primordial unity. In addition, the intermingling of the serpents, the *knot,* is the point of conjunction where all energies converge. And from this conjunction is born the egg (or the Philosopher's Stone); and it is from this egg that everything will come, because it already contains everything.

The symbolism of the egg is obvious. *It is the concentrated Unity.* But it is not the origin. *For there can be no absolute origin.* The egg is secreted by serpents who represent previously deployed energies that, at a certain moment in the history of the universe, ceased their evolution to undertake their involution, their concentration. The egg will be able to free new energies that will deploy in their turn, to recommence their involution and produce another egg, and so on, eternally. This is the scientific Big Bang, the initial explosion, which assumes that after a period of expansion, the universe will one day retract and that everything will start over with another "bang" of the initial cell. This is a cyclical theory of life and the universe, of course, but one that oddly reconnects the pseudoritual described by Pliny to the folktales about the theft of the magician's secrets and treasures, as well as to the plastic representations that largely utilize the spiral motif, which, as is well known, is characteristic of Celtic art. For the spiral is the image of the evolution of the universe, its evolution-involution. This use of spiral, concentric circles, and triskelion motifs by Celtic artists is not gratuitous—every ancient tradition integrates art, daily life, and religion in the same sacred crucible. The egg of the serpent, therefore, is the beginning of a cycle at the same time that it is at the end of the previous cycle. The egg is death but it is also life. It is the most perfect illustration of the fundamental druidic belief that, according to Lucan in the *Pharsalia*, "death is merely the midpoint of a long existence."

In fact it seems as though this could be the very basis of all druidic thought, and, using this as a starting point, it is the justification for the strictly monist position that can be easily gleaned from the entire Celtic tradition. This tradition, such as it is revealed in the mythological and heroic tales, and even in the folktales of Western Europe, necessarily takes support from scientific data. Obviously the "science" of the druids was not similar to that science which characterizes our own era; nor was there anything sophisticated about it in this sense in that it didn't employ perfected technical methods but nevertheless possessed a value that the writers of antiquity did not fail to recognize. The druids "teach many things" (Pomponius Mela) and "also often discuss the stars and their movements, the grandeur of the world and the earth, and on the nature of things" (Caesar); they studied "the science of nature" (Strabo), the "sciences worthy of esteem" (Ammianas Marcelinnas), "calculation and arithmetic" (Hippolytus), and "the laws of nature, what the Greeks call physiology" (Cicero). It is through extremely thorough observations of natural phenomena, through the constant meditation on the problems posed by life and its unfolding, by the realization that the human beings are dependent upon all that surrounds them—and that they can act upon that environment—that the druids attained a very high scientific degree of the knowledge of nature. "The Gauls have found the harmony between their biorhythms and their kind of life."[8]

And it is effectively the spiral that best represents this druidic thought, especially when tripled in the form of the triskelion. If it is true that the druids, through their mastery of the Word—that is by the reasoned use of vibratory phenomena—were capable of acting upon the human psyche, then one must recognize that they discovered certain notions related to ondulatory mechanics and that they were not far from conceiving that everything in the universe, spirit, or matter, was vibrational energy.[9] Just because they didn't resolve the world in equations (which hasn't been proven, by the way), or that they didn't formulate the famous DNA that serves as the cornerstone for the scientific edifice of the future, doesn't mean they had no awareness of the matter. It is indeed known that "the DNA molecule is capable of transmitting a frequency signal at a distance, of a given amplitude and intensity. We could say that the spiral vibrates and that the vibration is transmitted to one region or another at a distance away from the site of the reception of the signal that then begins to manufacture a specific product (messenger DNA and proteins)."[10] Now this DNA has been programmed, in principle, since Adam who contained within him all of future humanity. This program is fixed once and for all, but—and it is here that the problem becomes gripping—*it is open,* that is it retains all possibilities of modification, or in other words, mutation. It is a capital idea to the extent that it certainly seems that the metaphysical thought of the Celts finds itself engaged in this same process of comprehending life, only explaining and justifying itself through a perpetual evolution of a becoming that commingles creator and created simultaneously.

The spiral is the most clear-cut emblem of the Celtic metaphysic. But it can be a general emblem, encompassing in its symbolic signification the entirety of the speculative progress undertaken by the druids. Without a doubt something of this remains in the famous children's game Snakes and Ladders, the image of the quest, but also one of the inner cosmos from which human individuality evolves with its slow ascension toward the center, and with its retreats, prolonged waits, and wanderings.[11] And in the realm of art, considered not a prop but an essential vocabulary of speculative thought, the spiral was the preeminent Celtic motif, reinforced by its tripling into the triskelion. Now the triad, whether it appears in art or mythology, is among the Celts "a manifestation of multiplicity as an idea that is subordinate to the unity."[12] Everything is paradoxical. The destiny of things and beings is fixed from the first, but it is susceptible to modification. The profound unity of beings and things, of subject and object, is an imperious given, but this unity, however, is multiple.

Seen through what the authors of classical antiquity have recorded, through Welsh and Irish tales, the Arthurian romances, and traditional folktales (its continuations), druidic thought is characterized by a total refusal of duality under any of its forms. On a similiar plane, that of morality, no clear distinction can be noted between good and evil. Sin is unknown in the druidic tradition. There is only fault when an individual fails to accomplish what he should accomplish, when he is incapable of moving beyond himself. But this idea of fault refers more to the establishment of an individual's weakness rather than the transgression of a norm classified and established beforehand. There can be no list of capital, mortal, or venal sins, not in druidic morality. There is only that which allows one to achieve one's own destiny or the destiny of the community, and that which prevents one from achieving this end. Obstacles, therefore, exist outside of the individual. Or else the individual has an insufficient awareness of the difficulty and is not sufficiently prepared or lacks essential pieces of information. The individual can also be mistaken as to the road that should be taken, but this is always because of a lack of clairvoyance. Any individual worthy of being considered such should become an authentic druid, one who is "all seeing," and one who is "all knowing." Thus there is no negative attitude. To the contrary, it is a perpetual encouragement toward action and to perfection. It is in fact the definition of morality, which, according to various religious ascendencies—particularly that of Christianity—has become a stock list of what shouldn't be done, a negation of action through passive acceptance of the law. In this sense the prohibitions, the geisa, are never negative. They make do with expressing the limits beyond which an individual strays at his own risk, for the geisa concerns an individual and not the collectivity. There is no reference to an abstract and definitive standard.

This absence of a borderline between good and evil is expressive of the Celtic view of the relativity of things. An action can be good or bad according to the fashion in which it is conducted and not with respect to a scale of objective, absolute values. And if we shift the idea to the metaphysical plane, it can be established that at this place, too, there is neither an absolute good or an absolute evil. The Celts never imagined a god of good waging war on the god of evil, or vice versa. The struggle of the Tuatha de Danann against the Fomor represents the realization of order against disorder, nothing more. There are no moral implications

219

whatsoever. The gods of Celtic mythology are neither good nor evil. They simply are. And as all these gods represent functions attributed to the absolute and abstruse deity, it is necessary to accept that this great supreme God is not conceived of as good or evil either. In reality this God is both, since the idea of evil cannot exist without the idea of good, and vice versa. By the same token, life is impossible without death, and death without life; day cannot exist without night, as the night cannot exist without day. And God, the great unnamable god, does not exist without his internal contradictions, in this case, his creation. The egg of the serpent admirably expresses this druidic vision of the Whole.

This explains numerous kinds of behavior imputed to the Celts: the scorn of death, the lust for life, a certain cheekiness, a constant state of communion with nature (an idea Christianity has almost suffocated by making man the king of creation), a serene amorality, a metaphysical serenity, a blind confidence in human freedom, as well as an obvious refusal to consider the real as an absolute. For beyond the real there is something else, and the Aristotelian distinction between the real and the unreal cannot be formulated. The same holds true for what is called "the truth," something Christianity has always wished to preach as being unique, singular, and theirs alone. For the Celts there is no absolute, revealed truth, since truth is nothing but the result of a judgment made in the mind at a given historical moment. Consequently there is no dichotomy between the true and the false. Each of these two terms make themselves known according to the circumstances.

Druidic thought is perhaps the lone known example of an attempted philosophical system to which monism was integral.

22

Mind and Matter

A particularly important consequence results from this sort of monist state of mind: the fundamental distinction between mind and matter does not exist. The supporters of pure spiritualism who advocate the primacy of the mind as the creator of matter are as ridiculous as the upholders of the materialist doctrine who desperately seek to prove that the mind emerges from matter. To the Celtic way of thinking this is a moot point because mind is matter and matter is mind. The apparent duality is only the result of the world's relativity. Mind that doesn't butt up against matter doesn't think and so it doesn't know that it exists. This is the same problem as that of the unnamable and absolute God. Mind is only a functional appearance of the totality of *being,* matter being but another functional appearance that unfolds from the bifurcation or bursting of the original self. In druidic doctrine emphasis is placed upon the action. Now action is manifested energy, and all is energy, matter like mind. The two terms play their specific roles irrevocably linked to one another. The body, therefore, is considered as a provisional manifestation of the mind, thereby affirming its existence, and the mind is ready to manifest the body through other means when it deems it expedient. Also one can imagine other lives, and even other forms of life.

But in the relative world, which is the real world, matter is equal to Chaos if it is allowed to develop in an anarchic fashion. This movement from matter to Chaos is expressed in the myth of the Fomor, or equivalent myths, such as ones that feature monsters, dragons, or any of those beings called malefic when they are measured on the yardstick of Judeo-Roman-Christian morality. When Lugh kills his grandfather, Balor, he affirms the predominance of developed mind over raw and brutal matter. Lugh organizes the chaotic matter of the forces *whose grandson he is,* and by that affirms he is *one in his duality.* The main objective here lies in becoming aware of the infinite power of the mind, and in this only heroes are capable of drawing on the best part of that power, which, incidentally, is what makes them heroes. And it is why the first saints of Celtic Christianity are heroes. Since the creation of the primordial Cosmic Egg the universe has not ceased to evolve, and the mind has slowly extricated itself from its own dross, which suffocates it and prevents it from reflecting, from acting. Mind can succeed to the utmost degree and even participate in the transformation of the universe. For the responsibility of the universe falls back onto all of the individuals who exist within that universe. In sociological language this would be translated by the term *autogestion.* But for any autogestion to be effective it is first necessary to be conscious of the unity of the "all" in its apparent diversity.

Only then can mind direct the universe, and itself, since it forms part of that universe. Each element lacking, each weakness, each error, are all so many brakes on universal evolutionary momentum. Obviously this presupposes a notion that isn't given much heed these days: *responsibility.* Blinded by scientific determinism—which has reached the point of replacing the religious fatalism of the past—put to sleep by the laws of heredity and the recognition of the role of the unconscious in the life of the psyche, we no longer take into account the fact that all freedom is nonexistent without responsibility. To be free assumes not only full awareness of the causes and effects of one's actions, but also the total acceptance of them. This is as valid on the plane of morality as it is on that of daily life and on the metaphysical plane.

This is what the Celts seem to have understood. Despite the elimination of any notion of sin, they did not eliminate the idea of responsibility. Though they expected neither punishment nor reward in the Otherworld, each individual did assume, however, the responsibility of his actions and accepted the consequences. The same was true on the judicial plane. The law of compensations was not a punishment, but rather a just contribution toward the reestablishment of social—thus universal—equilibrium that had been compromised by a disturbing action. All of this can be found again in the doctrine that Pelagius (a Briton who converted to Christianity and who then became a theologian and moralist) attempted to spread in the Church, thus colliding with the Mediterranean doctrines of human weakness and sin that were bitterly defended by Saint Augustine. Pelagius's essential proposition was that the human being possessed absolute free will. Men and women were capable by their own volition of being saved or damned, of turning to or away from God, and of bearing the consequences of this choice. With this particular point the Pelagian doctrine leads to the negation of divine grace and also places the role of the Church in doubt. The Church reacted vigorously against this Pelagian "heresy," eliminating it almost completely, although it seems to have been easily accepted by the Britons and the Irish.[1] This is quite significant in that Pelagian thought comes in large part from the druidic heritage.

But such favor being accorded to mind is not a negation of matter, nor even relegation of it to an inferior rank, quite the contrary. The manner in which druids acted toward matter, arranging it according to their will, mastering the elements and using them, is proof of their belief that the mind could do nothing without the matter that was its complement. Among the Celts the body was never neglected, nor was it denied. The Celts were not "disembodied" and no trace of the medieval Christian-style asceticism can be observed in their history. To be a druid did not mean the renunciation of the flesh as in the Christianity inherited from Saint Paul and Saint Augustine. We should not forget that Paul and Augustine, before sinking into disembodiment, were joyous and lived life to the full. Their renunciation of the flesh came at the time when sated and repulsed—truly disgusted—by their lifestyles they no longer found charm or pleasure in the manner in which they had been living. Under such circumstances it is easy to preach abstinence and asceticism. The worst partisans of moralism are generally those suffering from liver complaints, impotency, or syphilis, and who cannot accept that others are doing what they can no longer do. But such moralism didn't exist among the druids, since there was no morality, at least in the prevailing negative sense of the word that has reigned since the time of the Fathers of the Church.

An active participation thus exists fully and entirely between the body and, in a general fashion, the material and the life of the mind and spirit. Human evolution, parallel and concomitant to that of the universe, occurs through the common exploitation of mind and body. To be a hero is to be intelligent, all-seeing, useful, and effective, but also requires being quite physically handsome, well-bearing, capable of tolerating the stresses of combat as well as those of drunkenness, and, as is said in the old texts, of seeing "a meeting with a woman" through to its conclusion. When the Dagda, following the feast forced on him by the Fomor, is incapable of copulating with the woman he meets, the woman ridicules and violently reproaches him for it. Bad news for the spiritualists of all stripes who imagine that humanity must be castrated in order to achieve the ultimate objective. After all, Abelard was only a great philosopher before being castrated. The second half of his life was but a series of repeats, even if some viewed in him a sort of sexual transcendency. In this regard the character of Rabelais's, Gargantua presents himself as the model of the Celtic hero, while Friar John of the Hashes is the model for the druid. The Gallic tradition is not a futile term with respect to Rabelais.

In fact, in druidic thought this question did not arise. If a being had a body it was here to be used and there was no thought whatsoever denying its use. The main thing was to know *how* to make use of it. All evidence suggests that in the evocation and utilization of thought the druids had evolved to a high degree. Certainly this is revealed in the symbolic images that appear in the "miracles" they performed, most often described as having an eye for striking the imagination and for bearing witness to this power. But from their speeches, words, and gestures, the druids were essentially there to maintain and perpetuate a creation that began *in illo tempore,* (the beginning time) and which had to be pursued *in saecula saeculorum* (age of ages). They never performed gratuitous miracles nor did they perform them simply on demand. In the early days of Christianity there were jousts between druids and Christian clerics. The clerics demanded the druids provide proof of their power by performing miracles. The druids refused. And why shouldn't they have, since peforming miracles would only have been done to satisfy the disdainful curiosity of clerics full of their new faith? The power of the mind manifests itself at times through inaction, which is itself a form of activity. The real miracle is that concerning intelligence, since all matter is, in the final analysis, the realization of thought. And when the triple-faced Brigit disappeared from the druidic universe, one saw the appearance of Saint Bridget, abbess of Kildare, "the Church of the Oaks," where it is said the nuns and monks maintained the eternal fire of ancient times.

Because fire, which is not an element, but rather something that transcends the three forms of matter by *mutating* and *permutating* them, is the most exact symbol of the spiritual energy, energy without which nothing would exist. But fire is not God; it is only the Word of God, the word that creates eternally and that balances the universe, the word for which the druids were the keepers.

It is with this that druidic religion finds its justification. If God is unknown, abstruse, and unnamable, it is because he is all. But the Word of God represents the energy of this "all" in full action. Human beings, therefore, must know this word in order to conform to it and to act according to divine plans, the *sine qua non* for the existence of the universe. Hence the need for knowledge: the human being cannot remain indifferent before that which in appearance surpasses him, but in reality concerns him, since he forms part of the whole. And if, properly speaking, the druidic god is not a Providence in the Christian sense of the term, neither is he indifferent to the individual case since every individual case echoes upon the whole. In such conditions human beings can pray; their prayers will be an attempt to place themselves in union with the universal whole, and what they desire can be realized if it is in accordance with the divine plan. Oral prayer, which is ritual invocation, will have that much more potency if it is uttered by a greater number of people, since the individualized energies will combine in one single spiritual energy whose effectiveness will in this way be the result of a universal harmony. The majority of the great religions have never claimed anything else. Christianity is foremost in those that place such insistence on the power of collective prayer.[2] Thus the ritual practices organized by the druids, if they were performed sincerely and with all the energy of the individuals assembled, influenced the Becoming of God, since this divine Becoming was that of the universe. For Celts who believed in druidic principles the great unnamable god was realized each moment of relative time thanks to individual and collective actions. But nothing, neither being or object, was outside of this Becoming. The proof of this belief can be found in the numerous descriptions that show the being passing through all the elements, all forms, and all states.[3] The foundation of druidic thought is *the universal harmony of beings and things* in a perpetual realization.

Of course, everything isn't for the best in the best of all possible worlds. Obscure forces enter into play and place the world in peril. In the religion of the ancient Germans these were the giants, ever ready to invade Asgard, the abode of the deities who assured universal equilibrium; hence the necessity of Valhalla, or Valhöll, the battlement composed of the warriors destined to forbid passage to the giants. In the mind of the ancient Iranians, there was Ahriman, the principle of darkness, against which struggled Ahura-Mazda, the principle of light. This Iranian conception influenced the Judeo-Christian tradition in an indelible fashion, making Ahriman the model of Satan, the negator of God. But the symbolic sense of the opposition between Ahura-Mazda and Ahriman is only superficially understood. From a simple image that gives an account of the vital subject-object dynamic, source of all existence in the realm of relativity, this opposition has become dualism, Manicheism, opening into and even beyond Catharism—a Christian theology void of all ontological reality—to a secular morality of good and evil that is incomprehensible because it has been shorn of its roots. This opposition in druidic thought was not taken at its face value, in that each thing, each being, had a double aspect and resolved its internal contradictions in a realization of the totality.

But the problem of the imperfections of the world persists. The so-called dark forces are the phantasmic projections of the irresolution of being. Placed before higher realities, human beings do not always know how to act or react. They are not fully participating in the universal activity from which stems the deficiencies, deviations, dead ends, the metaphysical—and immoral—evil. If all beings knew, that is if they could maximize the use of their thoughts, the balance of the universe would never be threatened. But the universe being what it is, human thought is not yet capable of fully assuming its reality. The druidic religion showed people the path to take in order to attain the degree of understanding at which false oppositions would be revealed for what they were, a dialectical quarrel. From such an understanding comes the necessity of affirming the all-powerful nature of the mind or spirit, the necessity for the ritual that in symbolic terms induces the human being to always go beyond the horizon. In a word the real is an illusory barrier that through laziness or ignorance the human being imagines is in front of him.

But there is no barrier. The horizon does not exist.

23

THE OTHERWORLD

This spiritual course that consists of surpassing the real in order to discover what lies behind it, clearly a very surrealist attitude, can only be followed if one objectifies that which does lie behind. Every human action motivated by a cause—in this instance life—presupposes a goal. And even if one doesn't end at a fixed goal, one does reach a result, a consequence, that can be either near or far in relation to the projected goal. This is a syntactical rule, but overall it is a philosophical reality.

For the Celts the projected, objectified goal was what we call the Otherworld. It bears very little resemblance to the Christian Beyond, or to those vague zones of nonconsciousness that the Greeks and Romans imagined through their rationalist materialism. "According to you [the druids], the shades do not win through to the quiet abode of Hades and the pale, sunless kingdoms of Dis; the same spirit governs another body in another world" (Lucan, *Pharsalia*, 450–51). "Souls do not die but pass after the death of the body into another" (Caesar, VI, 14). The belief in the soul's immortality disconcerted the Greeks and Romans who themselves had no such belief. Caesar, a cunning strategist, deemed it a shrewd move by the druids, "suitable for exciting courage while suppressing the fear of death" (VI, 14). Pomponius Mela says the same thing: "Souls are immortal and there is another life among the dead, this makes them more courageous in war" (III, 3). But even if it did astonish them, all the authors of classical antiquity without exception testified to this druidic dogma of immortality of the soul and a rebirth *elsewhere*. Valerius Maximus found this belief foolish, but

227

admired its similarity to the opinion held by Pythagoras (II, 6). In any case it does not conform at all to classical Mediterranean thought or even to the mentality of a certain number of Jews of that time for whom the Messiah would be only a terrestrial king and the righter of wrongs.

It remains to be determined how the Celts *saw* this "elsewhere." For it certainly concerned the Otherworld. It has been thought, through the literal interpretation of Caesar's words ("from one body to another"), that the Celts believed in the doctrine of the transmigration of souls. All the authors are quite clear about this: the promised rebirth took place elsewhere and there was no trace in Celtic tradition of metempsychosis, transmigration of souls, or reincarnation into this earthly world. The examples often put forth, such as those of Tuan mac Carill, Fintan, and even Taliesin, are but isolated cases drawn from myth; the figures in question are representatives of the perpetual transformation of beings and objects. There is nothing in Celtic tradition that closely, or remotely resembles the Hindu and Buddhist doctrines concerning cycles of reincarnation. Every assertion to the contrary, and every attempt to incorporate druidic thought into Eastern thought by a vague and perfectly hazy "return to the source" are only gratuitous intellectual speculations that result from an absolute misunderstanding of documents that are quite precise and totally unambiguous.

Elsewhere *is* the Otherworld. Descriptions of it can be found almost everywhere throughout Welsh and Irish epic tales, and even in the Arthurian romances. The folktales of western Europe also include details about this afterlife location. It is not a sinister site—at least not before Roman Christianity introduced into it, along with the culpability of human actions, the idea of a diabolical hell as a place of punishment for sinners. Eternal punishment is unknown in druidic doctrines. Hell in the Christian sense of the term is incongruous to druidic thought.

The Otherworld is the intemporal and a nonspatial place where the world imagined by the divine plan is realized. The three functions necessary for the establishment of the divine society on Earth no longer exist since in the Otherworld this divine society exists in its perfected state. No more functions means no more classes. Work no longer exists either since work is the suffering that is necessary for reaching the Beyond, but in the Otherworld the Beyond is already in effect. There is no more old age since time no longer exists, at least in its relative sense. There is no more death either because death has been transcended. Thus appear the sumptuous images of the Isle of Avalon, or Emain Ablach, that *Insula Pomorum* (the Fortunate Isle) of legend. This isle is also called the Fortunate Isle because

> all plant life here is naturally occurring. It is not necessary for the inhabitants to cultivate anything. All forms of cultivation are absent, save those carried out by Nature herself. All the harvests here are rich and the forests are full of grapes and apples. Everything grows as if it were grass. People live for one hundred years or more here. Nine sisters govern there following natural law and teach the knowledge of that law to those who came there from our world. Of these nine sisters one surpasses all the others in both beauty and power. Morgan is her name and she teaches the use of each plant and how to cure illness.[1]

Another description describes the isle as follows:

> There is a faraway isle that stands on four pedastals; about it are shining the horses of the sea in a beautiful race with the white-capped waves. An enchantment to the eyes, glorious extends the plain upon which armies joust. . . . Beautiful land throughout the centuries of the world, where many flowers bloom. An old tree is there with flowers on which the birds call out the hours. . . . Unknown is wailing or treachery in this well-cultivated land; here there is nothing crude or brutal, only a sweet music that strikes the ear. There is no sickness, grief, sorrow, weakness, or death there, this is the sign of Emain; rare is a similar wonder. The beauty of a marvelous land, whose aspects are pleasing, unequaled are its mists. . . . Riches and treasures of every color lie within the serene earth, a cool beauty, who listens to the sweet music while drinking the best wine.[2]

And still more description:

> I arrived to find splendid sport, a wonderful place, though all was customary. . . . A tree at the doorway to the court, fair its harmony; a tree of silver before the setting sun, its brightness like that of gold. Threescore trees there whose crowns are meetings that do not meet.

> Each tree bears ripe fruit for three hundred men. . . . A vat of
> intoxicating mead was being distributed to the household. It is there
> yet, its state unchanging—it is always full.[3]

Directing themselves toward this marvelous island are pagan heroes such as Bran, son of Febal and Cuchulainn, barely Christianized figures such as Maelduin, or King Arthur (after the battle in which he was fatally wounded), as well as saints of Celtic Christianity such as Brendan "in search of paradise."[4, 5] But Greek authors also have testified to a belief in marvelous islands located somewhere in the direction of the setting sun, which means behind a person, if using Celtic orientation as a reference. Indeed Plutarch says that a certain Ogygius island is located "five days sailing west of Britain." And furthermore there are three additional islands: "Chronos was imprisoned on one of these by Zeus, according to the fables told by the barbarians. As his son was his guard, he lived on the one that was furthest away." It seems that humans can land upon this isle: "They are allowed to leave once they have worshiped the god for thirteen years. But the majority prefer to remain, some because they have become accustomed to it, others because they have an abundance of everything, with no pain and no work, and they busy themselves with sacrifices and ceremonies or by studying their letters and philosophy."[6] This is reminiscent of the Voyage of Bran: after a stay on Emain Ablach, Bran and his companions are seized by nostalgia for Ireland. They are permitted to leave on condition that they do not set foot on land once they have arrived within sight of their land. Once they reach Ireland they realize two hundred years have elapsed since they left, although it felt but a couple of weeks. Furthermore, one of them sets foot on land and turns into ash.[7] This is a well-known motif in numerous tales from the Middle Ages, as well as in stories from oral folk tradition today.[8]

This pleasant sojourn in the Otherworld is characterized by an absence of time that consequently causes the elimination of old age, sickness, war, and death. Food and drink are available in an inexhaustible supply, symbolized by the apple, as well as by wine or mead. It is also the "land of women," whose queen is a sacred woman—Morgan—who welcomes, feeds, gives drink, and fills with sensual pleasure. For the erotic aspect is far from absent in these evocations of paradise. There are no more social classes, therefore no more warriors, save when they joust; and naturally there are no more druids, in that all the inhabitants of the Otherworld who have all attained a high degree of wisdom have become druid-gods. In fact it is the third function that is most exalted and the one that encompasses the other two by surpassing them. In this place, to use the Baudelarian phrase, "There is nothing but luxury, serenity, and sensual pleasure." Abundance can be added to this description. The Dagda's cauldron—in other words the Grail—is the container for all riches. The more that is taken from it, the more full it becomes. And thus the contradictions of the world find themselves reabsorbed.

This Otherworld is not always located on islands at the ends of the Earth. It also can be localized in the mounds, the sidh, whose name properly means "peace." But the landscape is the same: a vast plain where horses run and herds graze, where ex-warriors joust, where marvelous orchards produce apples in all seasons, where there is always celestial music and tranquil weather, wealth and beauty, fairylike women, and sacred beverages. And this land is located right next to humans, right under their feet, in the universe of the mounds, beyond normal sight. Those who are not in the know see nothing but cold and dank underground structures. Those who don't know are those who have been incapable of going beyond the seemingly real to observe the "surreal" universe opening before their blind eyes.

One question does arise, however: Is this marvelous universe eternal? The eternal existence of such an Otherworld would be in complete opposition to the metaphysical conceptions of the druids who understood everything as only movement, who believed everything is in a state of perpetual transformation, and if nothing dies, neither does anything remain stable.

> According to Demetrios, among the isles surrounding Britain, several are deserted and scattered, and several take their names from some hero or demon. Sailing through these regions by order of the king, Demetrios landed on the closest of these desert islands. It did not have many inhabitants, in the eyes of the Britains these inhabitants were sacred and protected from any harm on their part. At the moment he landed a great disturbance made itself known in the air, accompanied by numerous marvels in the sky. The wind blew with great noise and lightning struck in several places. Then calm

reestablished itself. The islanders told him that the eclipse of some higher being had just occured. They added that just as a lamp does not produce anything irritating when lit, but can cause noxious problems when extinguished,[9] the great souls are bountiful and never cause evil as long as they live, but that they cause winds and hail, like today, at the time they are extinguished or when they *frequently* perish. Often they can also cause pestilential emanations in the air. It is in these isles, Demetrios again says, that the sleeping Chronos is held prisoner, guarded by Briarias.[10]

It should be noted that Chronos, which means "time," is sleeping. It also should be noted that there is a question of frequent deaths. It is not clear from the text whether this is a question of the repeated death of one "higher soul," or the frequent nature of the event. Regardless, the higher souls *are extinguished* in this Celtic Otherworld. But where do they go since there is no death in the earthly sense of the word?

The answer: elsewhere, always elsewhere. The Otherworld is only transitory, and as Lucan says in *Pharsalia,* more than ever "death is the midpoint of a long existence." In the cycle of time, worlds can be infinite and individuals can pass from one to another, and the Otherworld described by the Celts is but one among infinite worlds. But the gates of this Otherworld are never shut and there is no irrevocable state. The druidic opinion is that the perpetual movement of evolution is a periodic movement, ruled by frequencies. In fact, energy is frequency that accords perfectly with the most recent scientific theories. This conception of frequency is illustrated in the Celtic tales by the ease with which characters pass from one world to another, whether they are living or dead. On Samhain night, the world of the sidh is open to the one who desires to enter it. The inhabitants of the sidh often mingle among the humans, and numerous humans—on the condition that they are heroes, that is "initiates"—make sojourns into the sidh, even if only in dream, much like the shaman. There is no shortage of these "expeditions to the Otherworld," these "ocean voyages toward the land of fairies," or toward Paradise, in Irish and Welsh tales, Arthurian romances, and folktales. Furthermore, there is a significant myth, the *Ford of Souls,* that tells the story of the white sheep who turn black, and vice versa, while crossing from one bank or side of a palisade to the other. There can be little doubt that the Celtic conception of the Otherworld makes it a kind of waiting platform to which individuals are drawn and from which they can either return to this world or move toward an elsewhere.

Every human being, therefore, is summoned by essence, nature, and function to make the journey through the Otherworld. Hereby two speculations of Celtic belief are made explicit: it is preferable to know the path that leads to the Otherworld, even if it necessarily entails one's death; it is possible for certain sages to accomplish the journey during their lifetime without passing through death. Thereby appears a theme that has had immense literary success but that is only a rite of initiation: the Quest.

24

THE QUEST

The Otherworld is difficult to enter. First of all it is invisible to most human eyes, which are blinded by the apparent reality of things. Second, human beings don't possess the gift of the Tuatha de Danann, that of seeing without being seen. Finally, we are hindered from entering the Otherworld because the path leading there is as dangerous and as full of snares as the shamanic bridge. Residing in these ideas is the essence of druidic teaching, which provides everyone with guidance on how to follow the difficult path that leads to the Otherworld, it being well understood that the paths are many and varied, perfectly individual and even singular. The experience of the collective all is never the experience of one individual multiplied by that of the others. The experience concerns only one single individual, since in this world of relativity the individual is completely isolated and totally autonomous. Thus the individual liberty of each is safeguarded, and any teaching worthy of the name must take this into account or run the risk of being ineffective. It certainly seems that druidism—in contrast to Christianity, which seeks to teach a universal truth to which no choice is given but to conform—attempted, like certain Eastern philosophical systems, to prepare individuals for their particular path in the unfolding of their quest.

To reach a result it is necessary to amass obstacles over which the person claiming initiation must triumph. The first obstacle that must be overcome is the vague and unfocused nature, the very nonexistence of a precise location, or at least the off-putting or dangerous aura that surrounds the entrance to the Otherworld. Folktales are quite successful in describing the disturbing and hellish atmosphere that spills out from these border zones: the dwindling or bramble covered paths; the sinister, dark manors and fortresses protected by walls or grills that indicate dilapidation or abandonment, but which are in actuality stealthily inhabited by fantastic beings. Sometimes there is a river or flood to cross, as in the Arthurian romances in which giants or hostile figures prevent access to fords or bridges. The bridges themselves are narrow and dangerous and wild beasts lurk in the forests. In the Celtic tales access to the Otherworld is more direct and less burdened with guilt-inspiring fantasies. What Christianity has not changed is the original universe that is still without sin. What prevents the Celtic hero from entering the Otherworld is his lack of valor, wisdom, or courage, and the prohibitions are much more internalized.

In truth the method necessary to cross the border zones is not obvious. Human beings live in an imperfect world, in the strictest sense of the word, which is to say incomplete, hence the suffering, sickness, grief, violence, and destitution that are the representations of minds hesitating before the choice of which path to take. In some ways similar to the philosophy of the Stoics, this is a question of reducing the importance of these internal hindrances. Vanquishing this suffering, grief, violence, or destitution is the first step toward liberation of the soul. This does not occur without struggle, however, generally translated as heroic combat between warriors. But it is also necessary to vanquish one's own despair, one's own hesitations. And it can happen that one doesn't see the gate to the Otherworld; it is only visible from time to time or when one seeks it through one's inner vision, the only kind of vision that matters in the quest. The human beings who undertake a quest must correct all the imperfections of the world through their own actions. The solution is perhaps that which is presented when they successfully eliminate the "monsters" that embody these imperfections and which are obstacles en route to the universal dynamic. This is why, according to druidic thought, every human being is "commissioned" to accomplish something. The druidic attitude is not a passive one like that of the Eastern teachings that are satisfied to denounce *maya*, that is the illusion of the world, by advocating renunciation as the sole source of harmony and joy. The druidic attitude is turned toward action: each human being has a role to play perfecting the world, in completing it, and this achievement can only be realized by an individual action at the heart of a collective action.[1]

This raises another question: Did the druids believe in a universal soul like the Indo-European Hindus or in a personalized and specific individual soul? Taking into consideration their conception of a God who is the Whole, a whole of which human beings are active components in its Becoming, it is tempting to answer that they believed in a collective universal soul. The authors of classical antiquity have affirmed that according to the Celts "souls were immortal" and they also made reference to the Pythagorean system that exalted the individual soul. Moreover, if the Celts were so easily converted to Christianity it was because Christianity presented them with a doctrine of individual salvation. It is not possible to reconcile druidic thought with Buddhist thought for they are two completely opposite registers, two parallel conceptions. This belief in the individual soul is expressed by the obvious pains taken in all Celtic tales, or those that were originally Celtic, to describe individual activity, the personal course, the responsibility of the individual, and, as a consequence, his free will. As in the Pelagian doctrine, individuals are entirely free to assume their destinies and choose their own paths. It is a choice they make themselves, hence exemplifying the importance of the individual quest as a source of knowledge and as an attempt to attain perfection. The essential element to note here is an individual's heroic surpassing of him- or herself.

This is to say that action prevails over all else—the exact opposite of the Eastern system. The Celtic hero *lives in the world* and *acts upon it,* with the desire to *change the world* in a manner that makes it conform to the divine plan. The Celtic kingdom is of this world, as well as of the other. In these conditions it would be futile to wait passively in an attitude of resignation for the situation to become its opposite in an Otherworld of justice and reparation. Every effort must be made during an individual's human life to command respect for justice. The druids were also legislators and judges who looked after the implementation of divine justice. What was least tolerated by the druids was injustice. They wished to see the perfection of the Otherworld realized in this world, which is, perhaps, the only means of escaping death.

But in order to install perfection in this world it is necessary to know how to present the perfection of the Otherworld for this is the justification of the quest. Each individual, recognized as autonomous, free, and endowed with specific talents, has the duty of attempting the quest and returning to tell what he has seen. All the "questers" will not have seen the same thing, and so the individual experience will enrich the group. The best illustration of this kind, of course, is the Knights of the Round Table, a conception inherited in large part from the druids. Each knight achieves a solitary and singular quest toward a single goal, the Grail for example. But when the knight returns to the court to recount what he has seen one feels very strongly that the responsibility of the group is engaged in the individual action of one of its members.

Therein lies the paradox. But druidic thought is paradoxical because it pertains to a heterology. It is a dialectical thought. God is the Whole. God, therefore, is the multiform grouping of all individual actions. There is unity within the multiple and a multiplicity within the unit. This is the spot where Celtic logic digs a ditch in front of Mediterranean logic. Druidic logic is neither collectivist nor individualistic; it is both simultaneously, since it refuses all dualism. It has been said that this is an irrational kind of thinking, but this makes no sense as the irrational does not exist, or rather it is simply a mental structure not based on the same references as those of the predominant and everyday rationalism of any given civilization. The Greeks and Romans did not understand the Celts, but they did often admire them. Their failure to understand the Celts was normal. The Celts themselves certainly did not understand the Greek and Roman thought process. In any event, it is proof of the infinite variety of the human mind, which, when confronted by the realities of existence and fate, succeeds in finding explanations, justifications, and solutions. The concept of one single universal tradition is a decoy. If such a tradition came from a unique revelation in primitive times—from the Golden Age, for example—traces of it could be found. But outside of the tendency toward syncretism, which scrambles data instead of clarifying it, it is difficult to discern a "dark and profound unity" in human thought. Furthermore, this unity of human thought would be an impoverishment of human thought. Because God and the world are in a state of perpetual Becoming, it is up to each individual and each collectivity to bring something to it. That convergences will occur is a certainty. That there may be mistakes, reversals, oversights, and misunderstandings is obvious. The human spirit seeks itself in seeking the "Grail," whatever that may be. This is the meaning of the *quest*, a word that means "search."

And the quest is mandatory. No one can hide from it without drawing shame upon oneself vis-à-vis the collectivity. According to druidic doctrine this magical and sacred shame is the most terrible thing that can befall an individual. Blaise Pascal was saying nothing other than this in his famous "argument of the wager": every human being is *engaged* in the game of life, he has to wager. The quest is a wager. And it is better to wager an infinity of winnings.

In the beautiful Irish tale *The Voyage of Art, Son of Conn,* the young hero, after playing a chess game with his father's concubine—who is not worthy of the son—is obliged to depart in search of a young girl he should wed.[2] But he doesn't know where to find the young girl in question, and no one else seems to know either.[3] He cannot ignore his duty and undertakes this desperate quest for a bride, traveling from island to island, adventure to adventure, and danger to danger. In the end he wins the woman destined to be his, but it would never have happened without his wanderings and sufferings. And when he returns with his newfound wife the people of Ireland welcome him back with great displays of joy and happiness because the success of his enterprises reflects positively upon the entire population. Individual happiness is also the happiness of the collectivity. Furthermore, from this impossible quest the hero has brought back not only a wife, but all the riches he found in his travels beyond in that Otherworld, that elsewhere, a place that is undoubtedly little different from our world.

To dream, that it all might have been . . . perhaps. But there are dreams that provide a more faithful account of higher realities than the quotidian vision of a universe in perpetual transformation. The druids were all-seeing and of the opinion that any individual could attain this high degree of inner vision. They placed their confidence in human beings, claiming there was no impossibility that could not be overcome because human beings, in the image of the druid-gods and the unnamable god, possess an infinite power, the extent of which they didn't always understand or know how to make use of.

In this sense druidism is a humanist belief. But it is a sacred humanism. The monist conception of the druids is such that there is no distinction made between the sacred and the profane. The human being is sacred. It is because he has forgotten this idea that the universe is in the grip of dark forces. Druidism, therefore, presents itself as a perfectly coherent, perfectly organized, perfectly human and divine system for going the furthest possible way toward the discovery of the shores of the marvelous island where, finally, contradictions are revealed for what they are, merely the sterile games of a thought that doubts itself. It is a generous attempt at the reconciliation of individuals with themselves.

It is important to acknowledge that druidism is definitively dead—dead as an institution and as a religion since it can only exist within a sociocultural context for which it forms the hierarchical structure and from which it emanates. But the druidic message has not disappeared entirely. It is up to us to find it beneath the deceptive arboresence of the fairylike gardens that enchanters have caused to bloom in the deserts. The laughter of Merlin can lead us astray. But perhaps it is through leading us astray that it allows us to discover the sinuous path that leads toward the sidh.[4]

CONCLUSION

The harder one tries to penetrate to the interior of druidism the greater one's impression that it is sealing itself off. The lack of reliable documents compels us to remain on the outside of the subject, and though this position can serve as guarantee of a certain objectivity and provide a certain bird's-eye view, it can become quite uncomfortable when it concerns comprehending the deeper meaning of the doctrine that the druids, in their shadowy retreats within the Celtic forests, took twenty years to teach their students. The objective vision one can gain, thereby, is necessarily incomplete. And it is obviously distorted by the tendency to rationalize according to Mediterranean humanist criteria.

This is to say that this study on druidism is but an approach to the subject, patiently constructed from the most representative elements of what druidism may have been at the time of Celtic independence in Gaul, as well as in Ireland and Britain. What would druidism have become if the Romans hadn't invaded Gaul, then Britain? There is no way to know. But the example of Ireland, which didn't experience Roman occupation, proves that druidism would have disappeared anyway, melting into the early Christianity that was still vibrant with the message of Christ's resurrection. This is not a hypothesis but a reality: druidism was diluted into the Christianity of those earlier times.

The best explanation for why this took place resides in the kinship that had to have existed between druidism and the evangelical message. This could not have been merely a kinship of appearance but a similarity of vision, that being the immortality of the soul and the resurrection. In some manner Jesus supplied the proof for the druids' assertions. Everything else, meaning the quarrels between druids and Christian missionaries, were only rivalries for influence and the struggles to retain the best positions in the society. At the moment the two traditions found agreement on the essential positions, a synthesis, not a syncretism, was created. This is what must have occurred, even though the druidic contribution has been denied, contested, and deliberately pushed aside. But by traveling back through time via the speculations of Celtic Christianity as it was lived in Ireland and Breton communities, it is possible to arrive at an understanding of what the religion of the druids might have been. A religious tradition, especially when its hold was quite strong—as was the case with druidism—never totally disappears. In this regard, what happened June 27, 1970 in Brittany, during a Christian ceremony in the heart of the Restored Celtic Church that was connected to the orthodoxy, is profoundly significant. One of the members of this Celtic church, wishing to leave, appealed to his superior Archbishop Iltud for, if not an apostolic benediction, an initiatic filiation. The archbishop accepted and said in a preliminary notice: "My intention is to give X all the initiatic lineages of which I am the holder and particularly those of the lineages that passed over into the churches since the time of my predecessors the druids, for example, at the moment of the consecration of the druids to the rank of bishops."[1] It is in fact known that Saint Patrick and his first disciples baptized, ordained, and consecrated numerous members of the druidic sacerdotal caste. One can draw whatever conclusions one wishes from this but it is a certainty that very often one looks for druids where none are to be found and brushes by them elsewhere without ever knowing it. Let's take this even further and say that there are heirs to the druids that do not even know they are the trustees of an initiatic lineage.

That said, and erasing all the mistruths that have been spread about the subject, it is possible to have an idea about the whole of druidism. It was undeniably a religion of Indo-European origin, parallel to the religions of India, Greece, Rome, and Germany. But like every religion anchored in a given country confronted with the beliefs of the aboriginal populace, druidism has been charged with elements that don't belong to its Indo-European base. If the very structure of the sacerdotal hierarchy and the trifunctional distribution that characterizes its pantheon are undeniably of Indo-European essence, then there are numerous beliefs and rites that don't seem to share the same origin. Hence the specificity of druidism, as well as the references to earlier religions such as the megalithic cults and the solar cults of the Nordic Bronze Age. For in any case, druidism has a Nordic coloring compared to Mediterranean religions. It appears closer to Germanic religion, and even the Finno-Ugrian religions, than that of the religion of classical Greece or republican Rome. It is even within this "Nordic" perspective, concerning the immense Asiatic-European plain that stretches from the Atlantic to the Pacific, that druidism has beliefs and practices similar to those of shamanism. The heritage of the Scythians, the intermediaries between East and West by way of the North, makes itself felt here. The Greeks of antiquity were perhaps not mistaken when they commingled the Celts and the Germans together under the vague category of Hyperboreans. And while this may not be a complete truth, it is, nonetheless, a significiant indication of what that truth would be.

What can still perhaps be placed in evidence is the social nature of druidism. Never was there a religion that formed so much of a piece of the social group, assuring the latter its balance and reason to exist, and realizing the druid-king couple, it seems, to perfection. The king could not exist without the druid, nor the druid without the king. It is proof of the fundamental monism that characterizes druidic thought: the definitive rejection of the false problem of duality; a dialectical vision of the universe, unity and multiplicity of the Deity; a certain tendency toward a pure monotheism, God being single and multiple in his manifestations.

Which is to say that druidism was not satisfied with simply assembling and putting in order certain, more or less magical, ritual practices. Druidism possessed a spiritual range that the Greeks and Romans admired without understanding, but to the existence of which they have assuredly provided testimony. Druidism was certainly one of the greatest and most exalting adventures of the human spirit, attempting to reconcile the unreconcilable, the individual and the collective, creator and created, good and evil, day and night, past and future, and life and death; reasoning according to heterological terms and boldly speculating on the *Becoming* that is a perpetual movement within an annulled time.

Certainly it is impossible to go very far in the exegesis. Through its obscurities, often intended by the druids themselves who little cared that their doctrine might spread no matter where and no matter how, druidism excites the imagination. There is a confused sense that it may have contained the seeds of a western tradition perfectly adapted to the peoples of Europe. Those people desperately seeking to rediscover their spiritual roots in northwest European culture are often reduced to turning toward the East. But the East, too, has its mirages, and in any case, the East has its own logic that is not strictly our own, and Christianity, which is also Eastern, has distorted the normal play of Western evolution.

More than ever the question that arises in this time of challenges and mutations is this: Who are we? Druidism would have been able to provide us with an answer. Is it too late?

It is up to each of us to achieve our quest and provide our own answer.

Notes

Foreword

1. Alésia is the site in the Côte-d'Or region of France where Vercingetorix, leader of the Gaulish coalition against Rome, surrendered to Julius Caesar (translator's note).
2. See Jacques Ellul, *La subversion du Christianisme* (Paris: Le Seuil, 1983).
3. See J. Markale, *Vercingétorix* (Paris: Hachette, 1981).
4. *Encyclopédie des Sciences religieuses.*

PART ONE: THE DRUIDS

1. See J. Markale, *Le Christianisme celtique et ses survivances populaires* (Paris: Éditions Imago, 1983).

1. The Druids' Name

1. This, unfortunately, is the case with those who persist in asserting that the *Barzaz-Breiz* by Hersart de la Villemarqué, especially the so-called historical songs at the beginning, are of authentic popular tradition. On one hand, it is known now through internal study of the Breton texts that these songs "miraculously rediscovered" in the Breton cultural memory were composed first in French and then clumsily translated into Breton. On the other hand, Villemarqué was quite talented and full of noble intentions. He wished to give Brittany the equivalent of what was found in the medieval manuscripts of Wales and Ireland. This is why, perhaps in starting from popular songs, he embroidered, arranged, and developed that which appealed most strongly to him, copying in passing all that he knew of the Welsh bards. The first song of the *Barzaz-Breiz* is presented by Villemarqué as a dialogue between a child and a druid. And the author did create here a kind of catechism of druidic wisdom. Villemarqué, a great poet, can be forgiven everything, but what can be said of those who strove to gloss over the hoax (to which Villemarqué, moreover, confessed at the end of his life in a letter to his detractor Francois-Marie Luzel) against all logic? The supposed dialogue between the child and the druid, which Villemarqué entitled *Ar Rannou,* "The Series," is a trituration of an authentic popular song, *Gosperou ar*

244

Raned, "The Vespers of the Frogs," a sort of mnemonic litany frequently encountered in popular tradition for which we have several Breton examples. There is obviously no question of any kind of "druid" here, and if the word was to be found here, it would have had to have been added. This isn't to imply that the "Vespers of the Frogs" doesn't contain some echoes of a druidic tradition, even though this influence is highly dubious. It simply means that it is difficult, if not impossible, to rediscover the druids in a popular song. And what to say about the word play between *Rannou* and *Raned?* Was Villemarqué really so innocent?

2. There have been even more radical examples in this domain: in the desire to avoid the Jewish origin of Jesus, Christ has been turned into a Celt, not such a stretch in that he was a Galileen, therefore, Galatian or Gaulish (the two terms being variations of the same word). Rabelais made a great mockery of this type of etymology, in particular with Gargantua ("que grand tu as," "what a big one you've got," the "gosier," ["gullet"] being implied) and the Beauce ("que beau ce," "what a handsome thing").

3. J. Zwicker, *Fontes Historiae Religionis Celticae,* I, 50.

4. J. Markale, *L'Épopée celtique en Bretagne,* 2nd Edition (Paris: Payot, 1975), 59–76.

2. The Druidic Hierarchy

1. I have greatly expanded on this in my *Christianisme celtique* (Paris: Éditions Imago, 1983), 28–48.

2. For more on this subject see my *Vercingétorix* (Paris: Hachette, 1984), 160–61 and 184–88.

3. Quoted by Guyonvarc'h-Le Roux, *Les Druides,* 58–59.

4. This is the opinion of Joseph Loth. The main arguments are as follows: frontiers of the Carnutes, the Senones, the Aeduens, and the Bituriges; at equal distance from Lake Constance, the race of the Seine, the Mouths of the Rhine, and from the Garonne Valley; at the center of a triangle rich in Gallic archaeological discoveries, notably Neuvy-en-Sulia; the basilica of Saint Benoît that contains Roman capitals of Celtic inspiration, a Benedictine abbey on the site of a Celtic sanctuary and remnants of three sacrificial pyres. But Caesar, who knew this area, would certainly have mentioned it by name if it was truly the great sanctuary in the land of the Carnutes.

5. This is at the intersection of numerous Roman roads, therefore, also Gallic paths renewed by the Romans (Paris-Blois, Chartres-Bourges and Poitiers, Orleans-Tours). Prehistoric, Gallic, and Roman ruins. There is a curious stone with symbolic drawings (currently in the Blois Museum) that could be an *omphallos.*

6. Let us recall that the Celtic people are divided by language into two main groups: the Goidelic or Gaelic group which in our time consists of Irish, Manx, and Scottish Gaelic; and the Britannic group, which includes Gallic, Cornish, and Armorican Breton. The Britannic language is distinguished particularly by the transformation of the Indo-European *kw* into *p* (for example *pemp* in Breton and *pymp* in Gallic means "five") whereas the more archaic Gaelic has kept its *kw* (for example the Irish *coic* means "five").

7. To such an extent that it is possible to say that the Vannetais dialect of Armorican Breton, which is very different from the other three dialects of the peninsula, is a descendent of Gallic modified by the influence of insular British from the time of the British immigration into Armorica (this hypothesis of François Falc'hun is interesting but controversial).

3. The Druids and Society

1. See my *Vercingétorix,* 58–65 as well as my *King of the Celts: Arthurian Legends and Celtic Tradition,* (Rochester, Vt: Inner Traditions, 1994), 222–42.

2. It is this complex totality that I analyzed and commented upon in the first part of my *Christianisme celtique et ses survivances populaires*. There is no need to go over it again here.

3. Truth obliges me to say that, especially in regard to the well-to-do classes, the Gauls hardly hesitated to adopt the new order. The Romanization of Gaul is certainly the result of a military conquest and a defeat (Alésia), but it was pursued gently with the agreement of the interested parties themselves, at least those who had the right to speak for them. There are a great many nationalistic clichés to be corrected concerning this subject.

4. See *Le Christianisme celtique*.

5. Guyonvarc'h, *Ogam*, XII, 497, trans.

6. *Oratio*, XLIX.

7. Caesar, VII, 33.

8. One can benefit from a reading of the excellent book by Jean Hani, *La Royauté sacrée* (Paris: Éditions Trédaniel, 1984) that, despite several debatable hypotheses, presents an almost complete historical synthesis of the matter.

9. In particular the *geisa* (prohibitions) of a magical nature that surrounded the king can be rediscovered, in regard to certain Gallic magistrates at the time of the Gallic War who were the successors of the kings (in particular the obligation not to go beyond the borders of the kingdom, or the city).

10. Everything rested on the following affirmation: the Pope, inspired directly by God, advises; the emperor who, having taken these counsels into consideration, decides. This theoretically perfect concept was never applied, notably because the temporal ambitions of the papacy were exposed. This was the famous quarrel between the Sacerdoce and the Empire. In the purely Celtic framework it is impossible for the druid to become king, save for quite special circumstances, and, since he enjoys privileged status, he has no need to satisfy temporal ambitions.

11. G. Dumézil, *Les Dieux des Germains* (Paris: P. U. F, 1959), 61.

12. Ibid, 59.

13. Certain individuals of our time would do well to think about this before declaring *urbi et orbi*, that they are druids, in defiance, moreover, of all reference however unserious these may be.

14. See J. Markale's *Merlin* (Rochester, Vt: Inner Traditions, 1995).

15. J. Markale, *Le Christianisme celtique*, 44–45.

16. "The Siege of Druim Damhgaire," *Revue Celtique*, XLIII, 82.

17. Caesar, II, 5.

18. J. Markale, *L'Épopée celtique d'Irlande*, 2 ed. (Paris: Payot, 1978), 139–40.

19. *Ogam*, XI, 325.

20. *Ogam*, XV, 153.

21. Caesar, VI, 14.

22. The most striking examples are those concerning the "Gallic Wars," that is the Gallic expeditions in northern Italy that ended with the capture of Rome in 387 B.C., then the later quarrels between the Romans and the Gauls. One episode is quite famous: the death of the consul Postumius and a number of his legionnaires who were killed by the falling trees of a Gallic forest. This specifically concerns a historicized transcription of a fundamental Celtic myth, the "Battle of the Trees" that was the subject of a very obscure poem by the Welsh bard Taliesin. See the chapter "Rome and Celtic Epic" in my book *The Celts* (Rochester, Vt: Inner Traditions, 1993).

23. This is in regard to a ritual of conjuring the sea that the philosopher mocked because he didn't grasp its meaning.

24. With all the risks of confusion that such a lack of understanding entails. Thus, on the basis of a real expedition of the Gauls on the Hellenic peninsula, and by superimposition with historical memories dating from the Persian War, Greek authors such as Diodorus Siculus and Pausanias have depicted a capture of Delphi that probably never occurred. See the chapter "Delphi and Celtic Adventure" in my book *The Celts*. As for the famous belief attributed to the Gauls that they feared but one thing, the fall of the sky upon their heads, this results from the literal interpretation of a very arrogant response to Alexander the Great from some Galatian mercenaries.

25. J. Markale, *L'Épopée celtique d'Irlande*, 61–64.

PART TWO: THE BEGINNING TIMES

1. One can read Jacques Ellul, *La subversion du Christianisme* (Paris: Le Seuil, 1984) for further information. The author, an ardent Calvinist, shows how on the one hand the Christian message was subversive with regard to Mediterranean thought, but on the other hand how this message was recuperated and detoured from its original sense.

2. J. Markale, *Le Christianisme celtique*.

4. Where Did Druidism come From?

1. This is the popular French comic strip, "Astérix of Gaul"(translator's note).

2. Fabre d'Olivet, *Histoire philosophique du genre humaine*, Vol. 1.

3. *Revue Celtique*, 1879, 47.

4. Its complete title is *Les grands Initiés, esquisse de l'histoire secrète des religions*. It looks at Rama, Krishna, Hermes, Moses, Orpheus, Pythagoras, Plato, and Jesus. The work went almost unnoticed at first, but it has enjoyed great popularity and has been constantly reprinted since after the first World War.

5. Another one of his works, *The Celtic Soul and the Genius of France Through the Ages*, is quite revealing. The same goes for the title of the book written about him by a certain Jean Bornis: *An Alsatian Celt, the Life and Thought of Édouard Schuré*. It should be noted that Schuré sought through every possible means to integrate himself into the anthroposophy of Rudolf Steiner, who seemed very suspicious of this character. This did not prevent Schuré from translating Steiner and publishing a book of essays based on Steiner's conferences.

6. Schuré claims that whites have been slaves of blacks for centuries, but not just any blacks, of course, these were an elite race located in Abyssinia and Nubia and not "degenerate Negroes" (*Les Grands Initiés*, 6). In the same manner, he manifests a veritable racist attitude against women who he claimed were responsible for the heresies against the archaic true religion.

7. Schuré lived in the context of the Dreyfus Affair. He was not alone among the writers of his time to think this way. He availed himself of Fabre d'Olivet's explanation for why Hebrew writing goes from right to left: the Semites learned writing from blacks who, living in the southern hemisphere, looked to the South Pole to write, their hand pointed toward the left, the east, source of all life, whereas the Nordic whites did the same but while facing the North Pole. This obstinate desire to claim Semitic civilization as a "negro" legacy is not gratuitous. They certainly refrained from telling us why the Chinese write from top to bottom. If one follows the logic of Fabre d'Olivet and Schuré, one could well imagine they were the heirs to an extraterrestrial civilization.

8. Schuré, by presenting himself as an "Alsatian Celt," foreshadows the doctrines of recent and troubling memory. Again it should be stated that he was not the only one of his time

to be blinded by the European scientism of the century. Strange things can be read in lesser texts of the end of the nineteenth century, as in a "Journey Among the Magicians and Sorcerers of Corrèze" an account of what took place in 1898–1899. One learns in fact that the Limousin populace is encumbered by "foreigners" who have characteristics such as "coarse, straight, black hair, dark, narrow eyes, and yellowish skin." We are not too far here from "swarthy people" hunts. These individuals are Liguroïdes "in whom nature has preserved the cruel, bestial, and rapacious nature of their ancestors." And in the middle of radical, republican France, no less! But we can be reassured: "quite luckily, living next to these Liguroïdes and Berbers of perverse instincts, are the descendants of superior races, Gaels, Arabs, Phoenicians." The author of this stupefying hodgepodge, a certain Gaston Vuillier, was visibly not a very gifted anthropologist, but his prose is very revealing of a state of mind. After the druidomaniacs of the beginning of the nineteenth century, after the "Gallic" nationalism revived by Henri Martin and supported by Napoleon III, after the exaltation of Vercingetorix (a Gallic, therefore French, but non-Christian, therefore secular hero), over Joan of Arc, the emphasis has been placed upon the Celts. Henri Gaidoz, d'Arbois de Jubainville, Joseph Loth, and all the Celtifiers of the *Revue Celtique* tried in vain to bring the debate back to its proper dimension, which is essentially cultural, Celtism fueled political, racial, and other quarrels as well as speculations of a spiritual nature. This was also the era that saw the creation in Brittany of the college of druids, bards, and ovates, modeled on the one in Wales.

9. Even better than this has been said since. In a stupefying book entitled *The Face of Druidism* (Visage du Druidisme, Paris: Dervy-Livres, 1977), the late André Savoret, who claimed to be a druid himself and at times signed his writings Ab Galwys (Ab mean "son" in Welsh, and Galwys, a nonexistent word in any Celtic language, but one that according to Savoret, meant "Gauls"), tells us—without naming him although the context is too specific to leave room for any doubt—that Jesus Christ was busy following the teachings of the Brahmans, *then the druids* during the years before his public life. We are even entitled to a description of Lutece of that era, but the author clearly seems to have forgotten that Gaul had already been Romanized for at least seventy years, and that the druids were forbidden to teach. It is true that the unfortunate Savoret became tangled up in bogs worse than those in which the warriors of Camulogene decoyed the legionnaires of Labienus in 52 B.C. In the midst of this delirious pile of rubbish, in which he passes off the claims of Fabre d'Olivet and Édouard Schuré as his own, notably those concerning Ram, he makes reference to the Coligny calendar and shows us Ram quitting Gaul for India, after having taken the pains to establish the mistletoe drink as a "magic potion" and especially after having resolved "to give the feast of the Winter Solstice (Prianni Giamon on the Gallic calendar of Coligny) a burst of pomp and significance without precedent" (p. 33). A burst of laughter is more like it. In the first place there has never been a Celtic feast on the solstice, and in the second place, if Savoret had carefully studied the so-called Coligny calendar or one of it reproductions *right side up*, he may have perceived that the feast of Giamon, far from being the winter solstice, corresponds exactly with the first of May, the feast of Beltaine, exaltation of the coming summer. Luckily, on the same page, the author reminds the reader that he is neither a "linguist" or a "philologist" and if the "nonspecialization spares him from certain blinders, it makes him vulnerable to critics."

10. In English tradition of Breton origin, the monument of Stonehenge is also called the Choir of Giants (Chorea Gigantum), but it is said that it was Merlin who transported the stones from Ireland to this spot by magic, which could give grounds to the existence of the worship of an archaic deity who was incorporated into the character of

Merlin. One thing is certain: particular stones of Stonehenge come from the county of Pembroke in Wales, which is to say quite a distance away. The testimony of Diodorus is troubling. Diodorus lived from 63 B.C. to A.D. 19, and his informer Pytheas preceded him by a century, which means the testimony concerns a still archaic era that has no connection with the Roman conquest. This Apollonian cult of Stonehenge thus appears to have already been archaic in a traditional Celtic context, and little but a pre-Celtic substratum can be assumed, which does nothing to resolve the problem posed by its integration into the druidic religion.

11. This was a cult characterized by the abundance of chariots or solar barks, and by the exaltation of gold or copper solar disks. For more on this subject see Régis Boyer, *La Religion des anciens Scandinaves*, (Paris: Payot, 1981).

12. J. Markale, *Le Christianisme celtique*, 88–89.

13. See Georges Dottin, *L'Épopée irlandaise* (Paris: les Presses d'Aujourd'hui, 1980), 17, as well as Ch. J. Guyonvarc'h, trans., *Textes mythologiques irlandais*, Vol 1 (Rennes: 1980), 61.

14. See Jürgen Spanuth, *Le Secret de l'Atlantide* (Paris: Éditions Copernic, 1977).

15. In 1969 I touched on this problem in *The Celts*, 37–64, in regard to the Cimbri and the Teutones, Celticized peoples, but not Celts, limiting myself to pointing out that the Tuatha de Danann seemed to me as the mythical expression that corresponded to these enigmatic populations. This was only a hypothesis. I held it without being able to supply the slightest bit of convincing evidence in its favor. The confusion of the Greeks regarding the Cimmerians who are sometimes called the Cimbri, sometimes the Celts, and also Hyperboreans, is not accidental. It is however quite remarkable that the art of the Celts is akin to the art of the Steppes, and that the Scythians were, for the authors of antiquity, a convenient designation encompassing the barbarian populaces of the great plains of Russia, central Europe, and northern Europe. This confusion has been maintained by Latin historians, Tacitus in particular. It should be noted as well that the numerous Belgian peoples on the banks of the Rhine have passed for a long time as Germans or Gauls intermarried with Germans, even though they certainly constitute the most purely Celtic populace of Gaul, the last to have crossed the Rhine around 100 B.C.

16. The military technical terms of ancient German appear to have been borrowed from Celtic. The German word *volk* (people) comes from a Celtic root that can be found in the name of the Volcae Tectosages of Toulouse. As for the generic name of the Germans, Deutsch, it comes from the same root as the Irish *tuath*, "people, tribe" and the Breton *tud*, "folk." It is the name of the Tuatha de Danann.

17. Guyonvarc'h-Le Roux, *Les Druides*, 389.

5. Gods and Men

1. Guy Rachet, "La Gaule Celtique, des origines à 50 avant J.C." In *Histoire de la France*, Robert Philippe, ed. (Paris: 1975), 146.

2. Ibid., 147.

3. Étienne Renardet, *Vie et croyances des Gaulois avant la conquête romaine* (Paris: Picard, 1975), 138.

4. Georges Dumézil, *Mythes et Dieux des Germains* (Paris: 1939), 8.

6. The God Above the Gods

1. These statues are in need of an explanation. Jan de Vrie's contention (*La Religion des Celts*, Paris: Payot, 1963, 207) is unsupportable. Jan de Vries claims that these were statues depicting Mercury, and not crude pillars as the majority of archaeologists and

historians maintain. In fact the Celts never made anthropomorphic representations before their contact with Mediterranean culture. The sole anthropomorphic representations are those that date from after the period of Romanization or those that have been discovered in those regions where a Greek influence existed among the independant Gauls, such as in Provence (see namely the Severed Heads of Entremont at the Museum of Aix-en-Provence). There is also the famous incident recounted by Diodorus Siculus (frag. XXII) in which the Gaul Brennos bursts into laughter on entering a Greek temple because he saw the gods there represented in human form. Both examples constitute irrefutable proof that this was not a practice of the Celts. There is another example in Lucan's *Pharsalia* (III, V, 412) in which the author insists on the raw state of the *crude* statues. And, like Caesar, he uses the word *simulacra*, and not *statuae* or *signa*. With all due deference to Jan de Vries, who bases his contention on one single example to prove the contrary, the primary meaning of *simulacra* is "in the place of." The word designates all symbolic representation fixed in wood or stone but has no artistic connotation. Salomon Reinarch even claims (*Revue Celtique*, XIII, 189–99) that these are simple menhirs that Caesar mistook for crossroad Hermes, which isn't impossible, given the countless number of megalithic monuments that there were and still are on Gallic soil.

2. Guyonvarc'h, *Textes mythologiques irlandais*, I, 51.

3. Ibid.

4. This character can also be found in Welsh tradition. The tale of *Culhwch and Olwen,* which is the first Arthurian literary text, describes the father of the young Olwen, Yspaddaden Penkawr (Big Head) in almost exactly the same manner. He, too, is one-eyed and he, too, has a pernicious eye of which it takes two men to lift the eyelid with a fork (J. Loth, *Les Mabinogion,* Paris: les Presses d'Aujourd'hui, 1979, 119). The figures Balor and Yspaddaden Penkawr are certainly cyclopes, but essentially they are Titans, and the final combat that brings them in opposition to their grandsons, or to their future offspring, makes them the equivalents of the original Greek Chronos, also a Titan, who ate his children, the very same who later dethroned and emasculated him.

5. "If the depths of our minds harbor strange powers capable of augmenting those on the surface, or fighting victoriously against them, there is every reason to capture them first, then, if need be, submit them to the control of our reason" (Surrealist Manifesto, 1924). It is obvious that the Tuatha could represent the conscious mind and the Fomor the unconscious mind, supporting the idea that ancient societies, without knowing in any way the hypotheses and laws of psychoanalysis, knew perfectly well the mechanism of unconscious activity upon the conscious mind.

6. *Textes mythologiques irlandais*, I, 51. Two similar scenes can be found in the Welsh tale of *Culhwch and Olwen.* When the young hero Culhwch asks to enter the room where King Arthur is presiding over a feast, the porter, the dreadful Glewlwyt of the Strong Grasp, answers him: "Only allowed entry are the sons of a king of a known kingdom or an artist who brings his art" (J. Loth, *Mabinogion,* 102). Later on, Culhwch and Arthur's companions are seeking to enter the castle of Gwrnach. There they receive a similar answer from the porter: "It is only to the artist bringing his art that this door will be opened this night" (*Mabinogion,* 130). Kay, Arthur's foster brother and his oldest companion, immediately finds his vocation as a sword polisher. He is allowed to enter, but then he must submit to a practical test and demonstrate that he knows how to polish a sword. It seems that this custom concerning initiatic trials, known both among the Welsh and the Irish, could be at the origin of the formation of a certain kind of chivalry such as that shown by the Knights of the Round Table.

7. Ibid., 52.

8. Ibid.

9. It is in this way that Odin-Wotan finds himself replaced for a certain period of time as king of the gods. According to Saxo Grammaticus (*Gesta Danorum* 3, IV, 9–13), Odin, suspected or accused of *ergi* (the passive homosexual practice considered as shameful) was forced into exile, while his wife, Frigg, was given to a lover, Ullr, who had to take over the royal duties until Odin's return. "This fable is difficult to interpret: does it reflect a naturalist myth, more or less solar or telluric, attached to a deity whose seasonal and periodic absence would be inscribed in the annual cycle?" (Regis Boyer, *La religion des anciens Scandinaves,* Paris: Payot, 1981, 162). Let us not forget that Nuada has already been compelled to abandon his kingship for a certain time because of his weakness. The identical myth appears in the Grail Quest where the mutilated Fisher King can no longer perform his duties.

10. The Irish game of chess, *fidchell,* is probably not quite the same as the one with which we are familiar, but the principle behind it is identical. It is a struggle between two opposing sides in which the king, an essential but fairly inactive piece, is the stake of the activity. In fact, the king in chess is the very image of the Celtic type of king (J. Markale, *King of the Celts,* 158–59, 170, 204–05). The majority of epic Irish tales accord a great place to chess, which is always played by royal individuals. The same holds true in the Arthurian romances. But it is perhaps in the quest of Perceval (and of Peredur) toward the kingdom of the Grail, that the theme appears most often—in magic or marvelous contexts—causing the initiactic character of the game of chess to emerge. See also J. Markale, *Le Graal* (Paris: Éditions Retz, 1982).

11. The Land of Promise is the mysterious country where the Tuatha de Danann reside, but only after the Battle of Tailtiu in which they were beaten and replaced on Irish soil by the Sons of Milhead. It therefore is one of the names for the Otherworld.

12. Guyonvarc'h, *Textes mythologiques irlandais,* I, 66–67.

13. Ibid, 67.

14. At the time of the conquest there were distinctions made between Narbonnais Gaul, which had been Romanized for a long while, Aquitaine Gaul, which had very little Celtic influence, south of the Garonne, Celtic Gaul, between the Garonne and the Seine, and Belgian Gaul, between the Seine and the Rhine. See J. Markale *Vercingétorix* (Paris: Hachette, 1982), 29–52.

15. "Mercurius lingua Gallorum Teutates dicitur" (Zwicker, *Fontes Religionis Celticae,* I, 51, 18). But another of these same scholias assimilates Teutates to Mars. It speaks to the misgivings of the commentators of antiquity.

16. Guyonvarc'h, "Second Battle of Mag Tured," *Textes mythologiques irlandais,* I, 47.

17. This lance or spear is also "flaming." It reappears in the different stories of the Grail Quest, namely in the texts of the Robert de Boron tradition. There has been an attempt to make it the spear of the centurion Longinius, under the pretext that it is presented, in the Grail retinue, with a drop of blood, which is used by Perceval-Parzival to cure the Fisher King. But it is also the mysterious spear that Balin, the knight with two swords, takes possession of to stike the "dolorous blow" to the Fisher King, a blow that will end the barrenness of the Grail kingdom, and consequently the Quest itself. According to the tale of *The Death of Tuirenn's Children* (*Ogam,* XVI, 224), the power of this spear was so destructive that its tip had to be stuck within a cauldron for fear that the city in which it was located would catch fire. This remark prompts a good deal of reflection as to the presence of the spear, with its drop of blood, in the Grail retinue. See J. Markale, *Le Graal,* 200–205. In the *Book of Conquests,* it is the spear of Assal that never misses its mark and returns to the hand of the one who has hurled it when he speaks the word *ibar*

(yew) and *athibar* (yew).

18. See J. Markale, *Les Grandes Bardes Gallois* (Paris: Picolleec, 1981), 70, 74–81, and 90–91; J. Markale, *L'Épopée celtique en Bretagne* (Paris: Payot, 1975), 60–76; J. Loth, *Les Mabinogion*, 59–81; J. Markale, *The Celts*, 243–51. It shouldn't be forgotten that Gwyddyon is one of the children of the goddess Dôn who is the strict equivalent of the Irish goddess Dana. But British mythology has been more mistreated and altered than the Irish by Welsh transcribers of the Middle Ages, and it is much more difficult to recognize these connections. Nevertheless the relationship between Lugh and Gwyddyon is certain.

7. The Physician and the Sun

1. J. Markale, *The Celts*, 46–47.
2. Guyonvarc'h, "Second Battle of Mag Tured," *Textes mythologiques irlandais*, I, 54.
3. Ibid., 49.
4. Ibid.
5. Ibid.
6. Ibid.
7. Miraculously brought back to life as one can see.
8. Guyonvarc'h, *Textes mythologiques irlandais*, I, 55.
9. Ibid., 56.
10. J. Loth, *Mabinogion*, 30.
11. Ibid., 38.
12. The famous silver cauldron kept at the Copenhagen Museum that consists of an astonishing illustration of Celtic mythology, mainly from the Welsh tradition.
13. This scene is reproduced on the cover of the second edition of my *Épopée celtique en Bretagne* (Paris: Payot, 1975).
14. Zwicker, *Fontes Religionis Celticae*, I, 51, 13.
15. J. Loth, *Mabinogian*, 221–22.
16. The tales about Perceval contain a certain number of anecdotes on this theme. See in particular J. Markale, *Le Graal*, 231–33.
17. See also the short story on this included in my *Contes populaires de toute la France* (Paris: Stock, 1980), 155–57.
18. See also J. Markale, *L'Épopée celtique en Bretagne*, 168–69, and especially, J. Markale, *Merlin: Priest of Nature* (Rochester, Vt: Inner Traditions, 1995), 122–31.
19. J. Loth, *Mabinogion*, 132–35.
20. This is a German adaptation of a lost Anglo-Norman text that itself must come from a Breton or Welsh model. Archaic details are evident in the tale's framework and in any case it is much earlier than Chrétien de Troyes's *Chevalier à la Charette*, the first French text to present Lancelot, as the same story is not involved in any way whatsoever. To the contrary, this original Lancelot served as the basis for the prose tale of Lancelot but with numeorous modifications and an integration into the Arthurian cycle that is not done in the German version. See also J. Markale, *La tradition celtique en Bretagne amoricaine* (Paris: Payot, 1984), 109–32.
21. In particular in "The Story of Etain" and "Diarmaid and Grainne" (see J. Markale, *L'Épopée celtique d'Irlande*, 43–55 and 159–60). In "The Story of Etain" and another story, "The Food of the House of Two Goblets," the Mac Oc fraudulently takes possession of his putative father's realm by virtue of a remarkably reasoned philosophical argument on time and eternity. See Ch. J. Guyonvarc'h, *Textes mythologiques irlandais*, I, 242–43 and 257–59.

22. At Bourbonne-les-Bains there is a dedication to Apollo Maponos.

23. He is even divided into two as Balin had a brother Balaan who, incidentally, he would engage in battle without recognizing. The two brothers killed each other.

24. The central stone of the monument, which is called *the altar,* is in fact struck by the first rays of the rising sun on the day of the summer solstice. These rays pass through a series of "triliths" to reach this point. Let us again repeat that there was no Celtic festival on the solstices.

25. Guy Rachet, *La Gaule celtique des origines à 50 av. J.C.,* 148.

26. Guyonvarc'h, *Textes mythologiques irlandais,* I, 14.

27. Paul-Marie Duval, *Les Dieux de la Gaule* (Paris: Payot, 1976), 83.

28. This is the same theory that I put forth in detail in my study of *Siegfried ou l'Or du Rhin* (Paris: Éditions Retz, 1984). I maintain, with the aid of numerous supporting documents, that the indivudual who mistakenly was dubbed the solar hero is in reality a "culture hero," a "civilizing hero" who has no power of his own if he doesn't regenerate constantly from the woman-sun, the true possessor of sovereignty. This necesarily leads to a new interpretation of not only the Siegfried legend, but also those of Tristan and Irish heroes such as Cuchulanin and Finn mac Cumail. It also provides proof that neither among the Germans nor the Celts is there a solar god or sun represented under the form of a god. To the contrary, the image of an ancient feminine solar deity persists, even in historicized form, in epic tales.

29. This has led to numerous folktales utilizing the same theme. See in particular a typical Breton story in J. Markale, *La Tradition celtique,* 186–91.

30. See the chapter on "Iseult, or the Lady of the Orchard" in J. Markale's *Women of the Celts* (Rochester, Vt.: Inner Traditions, 1986), 201–43.

31. J. Markale, *L'Épopée celtique en Bretagne,* 168–69 and 210–15.

32. G. Dottin, "The Courtship of Finnabair," in *L'Épopée irlandaise,* 75–90.

33. His importance is reinforced again by the fact that it appears he was invoked even within Christianity. A manuscript in the Gaelic language from the Abbey of Saint Gall, founded by Saint Colomban, in fact presents a magical incantation against wounds in which Diancecht gets on well with the Savior. See J. Markale, *Le Christianisme celtique,* 145.

34. The same process can be seen with the Greeks. The ancient Artemis, of Scythian origin and undeniably solar, became the Diana-Artemis hunting in the night forest by the light of the moon, which is why light became her symbol. In any case Artemis is not the goddess-moon. That is the role of the terrifying Hecate or the historicized Helen. But her solar components have been doled out to other figures, in particular to the Hyperborean Apollo who has been made into her brother. In fact it is possible that the mother of Apollo and Artemis, Latona-Leto, is the true face of the ancient goddess-sun. As for Apollo, not only is his priestess and confidante a woman, the Pythian Oracle at Delphi, but he is Chief of the Muses; he leads the Muses, which proves his ties with femininity.

8. The Warrior Deity

1. J. Markale, *L'Épopée celtique d'Irlande,* 139–41.

2. This was the opinion of J. Vendreys, *La Religion des Celts* in *Mana,* 2nd series, III, 255, that bases itself on a comparison between Nodens and the Gothic *nuta,* "fishermen." A. Brown, *The Origin of the Grail Legend,* 1943, 145ff, notes that in Chrétien de Troyes *Perceval,* the Fisher King who first appears in the form of a *notonier* is without a doubt Nuada-Nodens. Is there a play on words here between this name of nodens and the Latin *nauta* that became "naute" in French? Chrétien and the authors of the Arthurian tales were in the

habit of doing so. In the later versions of the legend, King Méhaigné is only a double of the Fisher King, which invalidates the reserve shown by Jan de Vries in *La Religion des Celtes* (Paris: Payot, 1963), 110. There are a good many additional arguments in favor of the identification of Nuada-Nodens with the Fisher King, even when the latter is the Anfortas of Wolfram von Eschenbach. See J. Markale's *Le Graal* 225–30 and 261–63.

3. Mac Neill, *Duanaire Finn*, XLIII.
4. Second version of "The Second Battle of Mag Tured," *Textes mythologiques irlandais*, I, 60.
5. *Discourses*, Hercules, 1–7. This is an interesting, polygraphic writer who despite his materialist tendencies has left us important testimony about the beliefs, rituals, and mythology of antiquity, namely in his "Dialogues of the Dead" in which he has the philosophers Diogenes and Menippus intercede, and in his "True History," a parody of the Odyssey and the Argonauts. He mustn't be confused with Lucan, the Latin poet of Spanish origin who is the author of the *Pharsalia*, an epic in honor of Julius Caesar that contains very valuble bits of information concerning the Celts and druidism.
6. *The Works of Lucian of Samosata*, Vol. III, *Hercules*, 1–7, H. W. and F. G. Fowler, trans. (London: Oxford University Press, 1905).
7. *Anraicept ne necés*, cited by Guyonvarc'h-Le Roux, *Les Druides*, 253.
8. Ibid.
9. Ibid.
10. Françoise Le Roux, "Le dieu celtique aux liens," *Ogam*, XII 209–34. There is much more that can be said about the relationship between Ogma-Ogmios and Hercules. In fact, numerous authors of Greek and Roman antiquity (Diodorus Siculus, Denys of Heliocarnassus, Parthenios of Nicea, etc.) mention an adventure of Hercules that is totally unknown in Greek tradition, but resolutely localized in Gaul. Hercules, passing through the Celtic region, is supposed to have founded Alésia (we are not told which one, as there are several), married the daughter of the king, and had a son by the name of Galatus. It is this Galatus who would have given his name to the Galatians, that is the Gauls (the two terms are identical). This legend that makes Hercules the founding ancestor of the Gauls is quite strange. Which Hercules are we dealing with exactly? It is probable that the name of Hercules replaced that of a Gallic hero of "herculean" characteristics. The same thing must have occurred with Ogmios, the Greek name masking an indigenous name and spreading in that guise throughout the Celtic world until reaching Ireland, where it became Ogma.

9. The Father of All

1. Guyonvarc'h, *Textes mythologiques irlandais*.
2. J. Markale, *L'Épopée celtique d'Irlande*, 119.
3. Guyonvarc'h, *Ogam*, XIII, trans.
4. J. Loth, *Mabinogian*, 169.
5. Guyonvarc'h, *Textes mythologiques irlandais*, I, 58–59.
6. G. Dottin, *L'Épopée irlandaise*, 17.
7. J. Markale, *L'Épopée celtique en Bretagne*, 94–100.
8. J. Markale, *Le Graal*, 186–99 (the chapter on "The Cup and the Cauldron").
9. Guyonvarc'h, *Textes mythologiques irlandais*, I, 53.
10. Ibid.
11. Ibid., 54.
12. Guyonvarc'h, *Textes mythologiques irlandais*, I, 242–43.

13. J. Loth, *Mabinogian*, 35.
14. Ibid., 39–42. See also J. Markale, *L'Épopée celtique en Bretagne*, 51–53.
15. See the chapter "Delphi and Celtic Adventure" in my book *The Celts*.
16. J. Markale, *Women of the Celts*, 86–92 and 141–42.
17. J. Markale, *Le Graal*, 225–30.
18. See *Arthur, King of the Celts*, 49–50 and *Merlin*, 31–34.
19. J. Markale, *L'Épopée celtique en Bretagne*, 237. This Gwrgant, during the course of a maritime expedition, meets a group of ships whose leader is none other than a certain Partholwn, in who it is easy to recognize the Partholon of Irish tradition, the first invader of postdiluvian Ireland. Geoffroy's *Historia* is contemporaneous with the composing of the *Book of Conquests*. Rabelais, who knew both French folk maritime tradition and the erudite texts of the Middle Ages, remembered Gwrgant's maritime expedition and used part of it in Pantagruel's navigation in the *Fourth Book*.
20. In certain academic milieux much ill has been said about Henri Dontenville, mainly criticism for his lack of scientific rigor and accusations of wild interpretations. Certainly precision is glaringly absent in the works of Henri Dontenville who often takes his desires for realities and appearences for absolute truths. Yet it must be recognized that he devoted himself to a wonderful job of clearing what was still virgin territory, causing here and there the appearance of valuable observations, mainly in regard to Gargantua and Melusine. Henri Dontenville's great merit, in the wake of Paul Sébillot's purely ethnographical works, was to ask precise questions concerning characters that had been definitively classed as "belonging to folklore," and also to have sparked the creation of a remarkable Society of French Mythology whose patient and impartial activity is rich in elements of knowledge and reflection.
21. It didn't occur to Paul Sébillot no more than it did to Henri Dontenville or Claude Gaignebet, despite the fact all three were convinced of Gargantua's Celtic origin.
22. See "King Konomor" in my *La Tradition celtique en Bretagne armoricaine*, 22–26. I myself proceeded to lead a narrow inquiry into this tale collected in my native land. The "evil lord of Camors, or Kamorh," who we are concerned with here is never named, but it can only concern Konomor, that certain traditions attribute as eponymous of Kamorh. In the south of the Camors Forest the story concerns an "evil lord of Lanvaux." I only have heard fragments of the legend, and no one could explain the name of Gergan to me. On the other hand his job as a salt seller has been attributed to the contraband trade that went on at one time in the region from the salt pans in Carnac. The salt vendor, therefore, is a dropout, an outlaw who comes to the aid of a woman being pursued by her husband, who, therefore, is an outlaw herself. No one has identified the wife of the lord of Camors or Lanvaux with Saint Trifine, the legend of whom is known not far from there, and who is actually the wife of Konomor. But in the official, hagiographic legend, she is saved by Saint Gildas. Finally, no one has mentioned anything at all to me about Gargantua, and Rabelais is totally unknown here.
23. P. M. Duvall, *Les Dieux de la Gaule*, 74.
24. Ibid.
25. Text and trans. by M. L. Sjoestedt, *Revue Celtique*, XLIII.
26. As are all the Celtic sacrifices, incidentally. It was the Romans, then the Christians who insisted on the bloody nature of these sacrifices, whether because they did not understand the exact ritual or whether they wished to systematically blacken the reputation of the druidic religion all the better to ban it.
27. André Varagnac, *Revue de Folklore français*, XII, 20.
28. French idiom for "getting rid of the dead wood" (translator's note).

10. The Three-Faced Goddess

1. Guyonvarc'h, *Textes mythologiques irlandais*, I, 269.
2. Ibid., 270.
3. Ibid.
4. This brings to mind the curious novel *She* by H. Rider Haggard, whose heroine—a very beautiful and mysterious woman (she served Pierre Benoît as inspiration for the character of Antinea in his book *Atlantide*) who is gifted with longevity and lives in a subterranean palace—in order to please a young lover with whom she is smitten—wishes to regenerate herself in a spring of fire that bursts from the earth. But the ritual is unsuccessful: she withers and falls into ashes, thereby showing her true age and dying for good.
5. This legend shouldn't be taken at its face value. The Boyne River *is not* Boinn. The Irish knew this quite well and it would be insulting to think that they believed that the river was the goddess. The same holds true for all the peoples who supposedly have deified their waterways or mountains. They weren't that naive or imbecilic. The fables show only the symbolic relationships between visible things and abstract concepts. Boinn disappeared as the "white cow," as a symbol of fecundity. There remains as evidence of this a river of life and, therefore, of the fecundity humanity has at its disposal. The same idea exists in Roman Catholicism, but it has not been understood for centuries. Jesus has disappeared, but the Eucharist is the evidence of his passage that is perpetuated in the spirit under real but symbolic appearances.
6. Guyonvarc'h, *Textes mytholgiques irlandais,* I, 241–81. There is a summary and commentary of this in my *L'Épopée celtique d'Irlande*, 43–55.
7. Starting with a hypothesis of Arthur Brown who saw the possibility of explaining the name of Vivian by an evolution of Be Finn, pronounced "befionn." I have dealt with this problem in detail in *Merlin*, 81–87.
8. Guyonvarc'h, *Textes mythologiques irlandais*, I, 257–66.
9. J. Markale, *Mélusine*, 132–72.
10. Guyonvarc'h, *Textes mythologiques irlandais*, I, 53.
11. Ibid., 57.
12. Ibid., 59.
13. Ibid., 60.
14. J. Markale, *L'Épopée celtique d'Irlande*, 58–59.
15. J. Loth, *Mabinogion*, 1–23 and 43–57. See also my *Women of the Celts,* 86–93 and 141–42.
16. Guyonvarc'h, *Textes mythologiques irlandais*, I, 56.
17. See my *Siegfried ou l'Or du Rhin,* namely 115–20.
18. J. Markale, *L'Épopée celtique d'Irlande*, 81–85.
19. Ibid., 143–44.
20. J. Markale, *Contes occitans* (Paris: Stock, 1981), 161–72.
21. J. Markale, *Le Christianisme celtique*, 144.

11. In the Depths of the Sanctuary

1. J. Markale, *L'Épopée celtique en Bretagne*, 149–51.
2. Mainly in Edern (Finistère). Saint Korneli or Cornely of Carnac should also be noted. Always represented in the company of a cow, this saint was the protector of horned beasts and seems to have replaced an indgenous horned deity.
3. See the episode "The Hunt of the White Deer" in Chrétien de Troyes's *Erec,* the stag hunts in the different versions of the Grail Quest, and the vision of "The White Stag with

the Golden Necklace" in which the stag represents Jesus. Also see my book *Le Graal,* 231–34.

4. Not to mention the famous "baphomet" of the Templars.

5. J. Loth, *Mabinogion,* 50–60.

6. This is the basis on which I developed my argument in *Women of the Celts.* I returned to it in *King of the Celts,* 148–59, in the more precise framework of the Arthurian epic.

7. J. Markale, *Women of the Celts,* 93–103.

8. Ibid., 111–17.

9. The etymology is subject to controversy. According to Ch. J. Guyonvarc'h, Eochaid would derive from *ivo-katus,* "that which fights with yew," an implicit allusion to the double role of the yew wood as support for ogamic writing and as a material used for the manufacture of weapons (*Les Druides,* 384).

10. *Women of the Celts,* 86–93.

11. The Isle of Man does not form part of the United Kingdom but enjoys a special status that harmoniously combines the ancient customs of the Celts and the Vikings. The Manx dialect, or Manxish, recently restored to honor, is a kind of Gaelic that is just a little different from the Irish and the Erse of the Scottish Highlands.

12. Guyonvarc'h, "The Food of the House of Two Goblets," *Textes mythologiques irlandais,* I, 259.

13. Ibid., 258. Emain Ablach is an exact equivalent of the Isle of Avalon.

14. J. Markale, *La Tradition celtique en Bretagne amoricaine,* 143–44.

15. G. Dottin, *L'Épopée irlandaise,* 117–41.

16. Guyonvarc'h, *Textes mythologiques irlandaise,* I, 203–32.

17. G. Dottin, *L'Épopée irlandaise,* 35–46.

18. J. Loth, *Mabinogion,* 43–57.

19. J. Markale, *L'Épopée celtique en Bretagne,* 266–67.

20. Guyonvarc'h, *Textes mythologiques irlandais,* I, 241–81.

21. J. Markale, *L'Épopée celtique d'Irlande,* 43–55.

22. There are other deities in the so-called Celtic pantheon that are more or less classifiable. The Fomor Balor is a kind of Chronos, the hero Curoi mac Daire is perhaps the image of an ancient proteiform god and has points in common with the Green Knight of Arthurian romances. Cuchulainn is a kind of Hercules, but whose heroic aspect prevails over the divine aspect. There comes a point in the Celtic epic at which the borders between divine and heroic functions can no longer be distinguished. It is probable that the two originally were commingled. The same problem occurs in the Welsh tradition: Pwyll, Bran, and his sister Branwen are sacred figures, so, like their uncle Math, are Arianrhod, Amaethon, and Gwyddyon, the children of Dôn. They are the equivalents of the Tuatha de Danann since Dôn and Dana are identical. Moreover, Govannon, son of Dôn is clearly Goibniu. Another son of Dôn, Gilvaethwy, the accomplice of the ill deeds of Gwyddyon in the fourth branch of the *Mabinogion,* is seen again in the Arthurian romances under the name of Girflet, son of Do. Arthur himself, beneath his apparent historical reality and triumphant Christianity has retained divine aspects, and numerous Arthurian characters are often literary "avatars" of ancient Celtic gods. I have developed this theme further in *King of the Celts* in the chapter on "The Arthurian Myth," 135–83.

PART THREE: INITIATIONS AND RITUALS

1. For everything concerning theater and the sacred, I refer the reader to my two essays, "Concerning Ambiguous Liturgies," in the review *Question de* 52: 32–45, and "Funny Games," in the review *Corps Ecrit* 10: 167–74.

2. Ancestors are always naive with regard to the time in which one is speaking. If you think about it, our more or less remote descendents will certainly have a tendency to see superstitions in those beliefs we hold currently as certainties. That said, we only know of certain druidic beliefs and rituals thanks to the Fathers of the Church who were delighted to cover the vain superstitions of the pagans in opprobrium.

12. The Druidic Sanctuary

1. It must not be forgotten that the dolmens and covered aisles were all topped by an artificial mound, made of earth *(tumulus)* or a blend of earth and stones *(galgal)* and the entrances were not visible. Only the menhirs, ley lines, and cromlechs were in the open air. But over the course of the centuries peasants have salvaged the earth from numerous mounds, thus denuding the monuments (and using them on occasion as quarries).
2. This is the opinion of Jan de Vries, *La Religion des Celtes*, 200–206. In any event the author blends everything together without taking chronology into account and without perceiving that public druidic worship did not exist after the conquest. It would also be good to think that a sanctuary—of whatever kind—deserved a priest, and that this individual would have had to live nearby. It is not customary to confuse the presbytery with the church.
3. Guyonvarc'h-Le Roux, *Les Druides*, 217.
4. This fountain, in contrast to others, was never Christianized, which is surprising to say the least. See my *Merlin*, 113–31, the chapters "The Sacred Clearing" and "The Sanctuary and the Spring."

13. Mistletoe and Plant Ritual

1. Mistletoe for the New Year, trans.
2. Images of Epinal were popular nineteenth-century prints showing idealized scenes of heroic events, well-known characters, and daily life in France and abroad (translator's note).
3. Guyonvarc'h-Le Roux, *Les Druides*. Among these authors the word magic has no pejorative connotations.
4. This is the case with numerous "savants" of the end of the nineteenth century, such as Alexandre Bertrand, author of *La Religion des Gaulois*, a work written from lectures he had given his students. This poor wretch, tangled up in a scientific rationalism marked by a simplistic anticlericalism that was quite characteristic of the time, totally missed the point of his subject while maintaining an air of knowing more about it than anyone else. His work in fact is an indignant denunciation of druidic superstition, but the arguments he develops and the conclusions that he draws are stupefying. This case is obviously opposite than that of Édouard Schuré and his disciples, but it is just as excessive and irrelevant.
5. It is paradoxical to see growing numbers of doctors discretely supporting certain healers and hypnotists, and recognizing by that the effectiveness of traditional "practices" that in all logic should not be seen as contradicting official medicine but completing it.
6. G. Dottin, *L'Épopée irlandaise*, 37.
7. Cited in Guyonvarc'h, *Les Druides*, 158.
8. A medieval tale of Armorican Brittany, with hagiographic tendencies, recounts a similar story, but the apple is replaced by the fairy's veil. See my *La Tradition celtique en Bretagne armoricaine*, 30–32.

9. Guyonvarc'h, *Textes mythologiques irlandaise*, I, 152.

10. J. Markale, *Les grandes Bardes gallois*, 74–81.

11. Cited by Guyonvarc'h in *Ogam*, XIII, 512–13.

12. Guyonvarc'h, *Textes mythologiques irlandais*, I, 74.

13. J. Markale, *The Celts*, 65–90, the chapter on "Rome and Celtic Epic." This text was written in 1958 and published for the first time in 1960 in the review the *Cahiers du Sud*, no. 355.

14. J. Markale, *Les grands Bardes gallois*, 78–79.

15. J. Loth, *Mabinogion*, 73.

16. Ibid.

17. J. Markale, *Women of the Celts*, 147–72, the chapter on "The Rebellion of the Flower-Daughter."

18. J. Markale, *Les grands Bardes gallois*, 90–91.

19. J. Loth, *Mabinogion*, 62–63.

20. R. Steiner, *Unsere atlantischen Vorfahren* (Berlin: 1918), 14.

21. Éditions Triades, Paris.

22. Éditions Anthroposophiques Romandes, Geneva.

23. Association Olivier de Serres, Issigeac (Dordogne).

14. The Four Elements

1. Taliesin, J. Markale, *Les grands Bardes gallois*, 74.

2. J. Markale, *Les grands Bardes gallois*, 29–30 and 48–57.

3. Ibid., 100. This concerns Uryen Rheged, chief of the North Britains of the fifth century A.D. This historical figure has become a hero of legend, just as did his son Owein, the Yvain of Chrétien de Troyes.

4. J. Markale, *Le Christianisme celtique*, 140–43.

5. Guyonvarc'h, *Textes mythologiques irlandais*, I, 68.

6. Ibid., 16.

7. Ibid., 245.

8. *Revue Celtique*, XLIII, 28.

9. Ibid., 114.

10. Guyonvarc'h, *Textes mythologiques irlandaise*, I, 53.

11. J. Markale, *L'Épopée celtique d'Irlande*, 182–83.

12. I have provided a long explanation on the theme of the Town of Ys in the chapter "The Submerged Town or the Celtic Myth of Origin" in *The Celts*, 21–36; and in the chapter "The Submerged Princess," in *Women of the Celts*, 43–84. *See also* "The Inundation of Loch Neagh," in *L'Épopée celtique d'Irlande*, 39–43, and "The Saga of Gradlon the Great," in *La Tradition celtique en Bretagne amoricaine*, 60–108.

13. J. Markale, *Contes populaires de toute les Bretagne* (Rennes: 1977), 48–50.

14. It mustn't be forgotten that in the Breton language, the word *mor*, "sea," is masculine. More accurately it is not the Sea, but the old Ocean, a terrible male entity against whom one must constantly struggle.

15. There are many others. One author goes so far as to assert that extraterrestrials are responsible for druidism, and goes on to say that I understood nothing of the entire question because I didn't have the "vision." I prefer to not understand anything and remain honest. All these various forms of make-believe rest on delerious fantasies and unverifiable analogies (mainly word plays) resemblances between names belonging to

various language groups (Carnac and Karnac, for example), a total disdain for the fundamental texts, which are only known through hearsay, and always from third- or fourth-hand citations, the whole characterized by a systematic lack of references and an appeal to public gullibility. Prophets and gurus are multiplying when it comes to Celts and druidism.

16. On another level the problem of René Guénon, who serves as a master thinker for numerous sincere spiritual seekers, needs to be addressed. Each time Guénon makes reference to the Celts in his voluminous work, he mixes everything together and, especially, he piles misfact upon misfact due to a lack of information. This casts a certain shadow on other facets of his work. Why don't esoteric writers ever cite their sources? It's quite simple: *because it is a secret and they do not have the right to say it.* I know full well that this is the armature of esoterism, but there are all the same limits that have to be respected on pain of falling into an abuse of trust.

17. J. Markale, *Les grands Bardes gallois,* 110.

18. W. Stokes, *Three Irish Glossaries,* 6.

19. J. Markale, *Le Christianisme celtique,* 195–203.

20. Ibid., 33–34.

21. *Revue celtique,* XLIII, 109.

22. Claude Gaignebet, *Le Carnaval* (Paris: Payot, 1974), 74.

23. Ibid. The Irish text, which Claude Gaignebet was unfamiliar with when he composed this work, reinforces the author's arguments.

24. J. Markale, *La Tradition celtique en Bretagne armoricaine,* 166.

25. Ibid., 67.

26. Ibid.

27. J. Loth, *Mabinogion,* 30–31.

28. Ibid.

29. Guyonvarc'h, *Ogam,* XIII, trans. See my summary and commentary in *L'Épopée celtique d'Irlande,* 114–22.

30. Ibid.

31. See Paul Sebillot, *Le Folklore de la France,* reprinted in several volumes by Éditions Imago, Paris. One will find there a prodigious quantity of valuble information.

32. *Bulletin de la Faculté des Lettres de Poitiers,* 1892.

33. Ibid.

15. The Sacrifices

1. A Welsh chronicler of the late twelfth century who recorded useful information on the beliefs and customs of the Celts in Ireland and Great Britain, and of their survivals in his time. See also my *Women of the Celts,* 90.

2. "The Illness of Cuchulainn," *Ogam,* X, 294.

3. In killing the Smith's dog the hero Cuchulainn performed an authentic sacrifice that would weigh heavy on his destiny. See my *L'Épopée celtique d'Irlande,* 81–82.

4. J. Markale, *Le Christianisme celtique,* 141.

5. See Rolans Auguet, *Les Fêtes romaines* (Paris: Flammarion, 1970).

6. In the Irish tale *Bricriu's Feast,* Cuchulainn is obliged to cut off the head of the giant Uath on condition that he (Cuchulainn) returns one year later to have his own head cut off by Uath. Cuchulainn cuts of Uath's head who goes on as if nothing were amiss. The following year Uath is satisfied with laying his ax on Cuchulainn's neck. This is the well-

known adventure of Gawain and the Green Knight in the Arthurian romances. The example is significant. See also my *L'Épopée celtique d'Irlande*, 112–13.

7. J. Markale, *L'Épopée celtique, d'Irlande*, 183.

8. Ibid., 136.

9. There is a more detailed study of the ritual of the "Severed Head" in my book *Le Graal*, 205–12. See also, with regard to plastic art of this theme, François Salviat's *Entremont antique* (Aix-en-Provence: 1973).

10. For the sake of completeness it would be necessary to mention the folk customs that still persist almost everywhere, even in the context of Christianity, particularly the act of tossing a coin in a fountain, whether the latter has been Christianized or not.

16. Festivals and Holidays

1. Not a single ancient text mentions any Celtic holiday around the time of the winter and summer soltices. Saint John's Day, which is Christian, has recuperated certain first of May rituals and owes its structure to a pre-Celtic religion. The Christmas holiday is Christian, but of Roman origin (the Saturnalia and the worship of Mithra). It is absolute nonsense to perform Celtic rites on the solstices. It is true that these rites—the origin of which the practitioners are incapable of explaining—have become grotesque caricatures or folkloric manifestations.

2. Guyonvarc'h, "The Birth of Conchobar," *Ogam*, XI, 61, trans.

17. The Power of the Word

1. *Revue de l'Histoire des Religions*, CXXII, 132.

2. This currently is no longer the case. The Roman Catholic liturgy was built upon Latin and goes back quite far into the past. It not only consists of a group of words, but also of rhythms and articulations of great precision that are manifested in recitation, chant, and song. To set the Latin text to other musics and other rhythms is a misinterpretation. To put them into other words, for example their translation into official or vernacular living languages, is absolute nonsense.

3. Guyonvarc'h, *Textes mythologiques irlandais*, I, 56.

4. The representations of the devil, or legends concerning the devil, are always located on the north entrance of cathedrals or churches. In the Middle Ages, and even later, men were placed to the right in the nave, and women, who were allegedly "diabolical" beings, were placed on the left.

5. Atheneus, XXIII.

6. Guyonvarc'h, "The Book of Conquests," *Textes mythologiques irlandais*, I, 15. This ritual of the right foot endures in folk customs: someone who is in a bad mood or who has had a rotten day has "gotten up by his left foot." The same connotation has been maintained for a long time in politics: the left is troubling and the right is reassuring.

7. "The Death of Cuchulainn," *Ogam*, XVIII, 346.

8. "Talland Etair," *Revue Celtique*, VIII, 48.

9. *Textes mythologiques irlandais*, I, 56.

10. J. Markale, *L'Épopée celtique d'Irlande*, 135.

11. Guyonvarc'h, *Les Druides*, 172, trans.

12. J. Loth, *Mabinogion*, 103.

13. *Revue celtique*, XII, 119–21.

14. W. Stokes, *Three Irish Glossaries*, 25.

15. Ibid.
16. J. Markale, *L'Épopée celtique d'Irlande,* 146.
17. *Ancient Laws of Ireland,* I, 44.
18. O'Grady, "The Death of Finn," *Silva Gadelica.* See also my *L'Épopée celtique d'Irlande,* 165–68.
19. Cited by Guyonvarc'h-Le Roux, *Les Druides,* 206.
20. J. Markale, *Merlin,* 3–4.
21. Ibid., 62.
22. J. Markale, *L'Épopée celtique d'Irlande,* 65.
23. Ibid., 155 and 160–61.
24. See the chapter "Iseult or the Lady of the Orchard" in my *Women of the Celts,* 201–43.
25. Tristan is a moon-man who cannot live without receiving the light of the sun, that is without having periods of contact with the woman-sun. For more on this subject see my *Siegfried ou l'Or du Rhin* (Paris: Éditions Retz, 1984), particularly the chapter concerning the woman-sun.
26. J. Markale, *L'Épopée celtique d'Irlande,* 162–63.
27. Ibid., 134–37.
28. *Revue Celtique,* XXI, 152.
29. J. Markale, *L'Épopée celtique d'Irlande,* 177.
30. *Revue Celtique,* VI, 165.

18. Totemism and Shamanism

1. G. Dottin, *L'Épopée irlandaise,* 108–10.
2. *Ogam,* XIV, 498.
3. J. Markale, *L'Épopée celtique d'Irlande,* 154.
4. J. Loth, *Mabinogion,* 139–44. See also my *King of the Celts,* 285–90.
5. J. Loth, *Mabinogion,* 99.
6. Ibid., 16–20.
7. J. Markale, *L'Épopée celtique d'Irlande,* 184–91.
8. J. Markale, *King of the Celts,* 120–21 and 180–81.
9. Ibid., 162–64 and 176–81.
10. Ibid.
11. Georges Dumézil, *Romans de Scythie et d'alentour* (Paris: Payot, 1978), 13.
12. Mircea Eliade, *Shamanism,* 2 ed. (Princeton: Bollingen/Princeton, 1972), xix.
13. J. Loth, *Mabinogion,* 78–79.
14. Guyonvarc'h, *Textes mythologiques irlandais,* I, 145–56.
15. Ibid., 157–66.
16. J. Markale, *Les grands Bardes gallois,* 72–81 and 115–16.
17. J. Markale, *L'Épopée celtique en Bretagne,* 94–100.
18. J. Markale, *Contes populaires de toutes les Bretagne,* 23–36.
19. J. Markale, *L'Épopée celtique d'Irlande,* 85.
20. Ibid., 100–101.
21. Ibid., 134.
22. Ibid., 91–92.
23. Mircea Eliade, *Shamanism,* 482–83.
24. J. Markale, *L'Épopée celtique d'Irlande,* 87–88.
25. G. Dumézil, *Romans de Scythie et d'alentour,* 84–86.

26. M. Eliade, *Shamanism*, 474.
27. Ibid., 476.
28. Ibid., 477.
29. Ibid.
30. J. Markale, *La Tradition celtique en Bretagne armoricaine*, 250–54.
31. Mircea Eliade, *Shamanism*, 509.
32. J. Markale, *L'Épopée celtique d'Irlande*, 34–38.
33. For more on this subject see my book *Merlin*, 150–51.
34. J. Loth, *Mabinogion*, 35. In the Second Branch of the Welsh *Mabinogion* the hero Bran himself serves as a bridge for his army, therefore, proving that he is not only king but druid, thus a shaman.
35. See also the tale of *Culhwch and Olwen* in J. Loth, *Mabinogion*, 99–145 and the commentary on these characters in my *King of the Celts*, 185–89.
36. See J. Markale, *La Tradition celtique en Bretagne amoricaine*, 273–81.
37. As for me, I refuse to speak here of *cartesianism*. The French are not Cartesians, as is repeated endlessly, but Aristotolians—not by nature but through academic apprenticeship. This is unfair to Descartes who understood full well that the sole reality was the mind and that the sole demonstrable reality was that of thought. This seems, to me, to be quite far from the vulgar realism that only believes what it can see.

19. Neodruidism

1. Certain are officially established organizations (of the 1901 law type), others are study groups, assemblies with no legal status.
2. For everything concerning neodruidism and the currently existing brotherhoods I refer you to Michel Raoult's work, *Les Druides, les sociétes initiatiques contemporaines* (Monaco: Éditions du Rocher, 1983). This is a very clear historical presentation of the problem, followed by a concise and well-documented survey. Essential information concerning all the listed druidic orders can be found here, as well as a general idea of their doctrines and rituals. The author takes no personal position and his book offers every assurance of being objective.

PART FOUR: DRUIDIC THOUGHT

20. A False Polytheism

1. In particular, the esoteric or allegedly esoteric speculations on the "Stone of Jacob," that if brought from Palestine and placed on Tara would have been the Fal Stone. This Fal Stone, then transported to the Isle of Iona, would become the famous Stone of Scone that served at the coronations of Scottish kings. The *stone of coronation* currently in London, therefore, would be this Stone of Jacob. Another wild legend makes the Isle of Iona, seat of the renowned monastery of Saint Columcil, one of the high places of Celto-Hebraic syncretism, because the name of Iona would be that of Saint John (the Baptist), otherwise known as Jokanaan. Of course, this is really quite simple. All you have to do is think about it.
2. For the whole picture of this subject, I refer the reader to my work on *Le Christianisme celtique*.
3. Cited by Guyonvarc'h-Le Roux, *Les Druides*, 328. In his commentary he suggests: "Every god had total competence in his functional and theological domain. By definition he,

therefore, is a druid. As for the human druid, he is a god for at least two reasons: primarily because he descends in a direct line, *in principio*, from the primordial druids . . . ; secondly because his abilities and knowledge make him an intermediary between gods and men. The druid of the ancient Celts is truly an "earthly god" in so much as he is a temporary embodiment of a divine function, just like the Catholic priest who, when he pronounces the sacramental words of consecration, is himself Jesus Christ at that moment.

21. Druidic Monism

1. Translated as "wind egg" by some due to the numerous variations in the various manuscripts available of Pliny's text, (translator's note).
2. See "The Egg of the Serpent," *Ogam*, XX, 495–504, and J. Gricourt, "The Ovum anguinum in Gaul and Persia," *Ogam*, VI, 227–32, as well as Guyonvarc'h-Le Roux, *Les Druides*, 321–23.
3. Numerous examples can be seen in Lancelot Lengyel's *L'Art gaulois dans les médailles* (Paris: 1954).
4. A good example of this kind of tale is the "Saga of Koadalan" (J. Markale, *La Tradition celtique en Bretagne armoricaine*, 160–85), but the hero is only half successful at making use of the secret with which he has returned. Indeed he attempts to acquire immortality, but after a death and a symbolic dismemberment, fails. See also "The Young Girl in White" (J. Markale, *Contes populaires de toutes les Bretagne*, 36–47) and the "Black Mountain" (J. Markale, *Contes occitans*, 223–35).
5. Paul Sébillot, "The Fresh Waters," *Le Folklore de la France*, vol. IV (Paris: Éditions Imago, 1983) 43–44.
6. J. Markale, *Mélusine*, 96–99. This siren of folk legend is one of Melusine's images.
7. J. Loth, *Mabinogion*, 220.
8. Étienne Renardet, *Vie et croyances des Gaulois avant la conquête romaine* (Paris: Picard, 1975), 184.
9. For example, the movement of objects at a distance without direct material contact, or even the possibility of moving oneself without physically moving (the gift of ubiquity so dear to Merlin the Magician), and all the phenomena that, for want of understanding, are classified as "magical" or "hysterical."
10. Étienne Guillé and Christine Hardy, *L'Alchimie de la Vie, biologie et tradition* (Monaco: Éditions du Rocher, 1983), 51.
11. All "childish" games are the more or less remote reminiscences of rituals or religious or metaphysical speculations, including the innocent hopscotch played by young girls, or the most harmless seeming counting rhymes.
12. Guyonvarc'h-Le Roux, *Les Druides*, 326.

22. Mind and Matter

1. J. Markale, *Le Chrisitinisme celtique*, 99–111.
2. The Catholic Mass is constructed on the same principle. The psychic energy of all the faithful echoes on the priest who, at the moment of the consecration of the Eucharist, becomes God, the Totality, in order to pronounce the sacramental words of absolute transcendence. This is why saying the Mass while facing the faithful is an aberration from the strict point of view of the ritual. In order to be effective, the individual psychic forces should converge toward the backbone and the nape of the priest to "fill" that latter and manifest through his words and gestures.

3. In particular, the poems attributed to the bard Taliesin, which seem to be reminiscences of the druidic doctrine that passed over into the ranks of literary or poetic motifs during the course of the Middle Ages.

23. The Otherworld

1. Geoffroy of Monmouth, *Vita Merlini*. See also my *L'Épopée celtique en Bretagne*, 120.
2. Georges Dottin, "The Voyage of Bran," *L'Épopée irlandaise*, 37–41.
3. Jeffrey Gantz, "The Wasting Sickness of Cú Chulaind and the Only Jealousy of Emer," *Early Irish Myths and Sagas* (London: Penguin, 1981), 167–68.
4. J. Markale, *L'Épopée celtique d'Irlande*, 196–202.
5. Bénédeit, *Le Voyage de Saint-Brendan*. (Paris: 10/18,1984), trans., Ian Short.
6. Plutarch, *On the Surface of the Moon*, 26.
7. G. Dottin, *L'Épopée irlandaise*, 35–46.
8. See "The Hunt of the White Swine," in my *La Tradition celtique en Bretagen armoricaine*, 52–59, as well as the Armorican tale "The Forgotten Time," in my *Contes populaires de toutes les Bretagnes*, 258–63.
9. Smoke and odor, for example.
10. Plutarch, *On the End of the Oracles*, 18.

24. The Quest

1. It goes without saying that contemporary neodruidic speculations on the wanderings of the human being through the circles of existence, Abred, the world of human actions, Gwenved, "the white world," the paradisical circle, and Keugant, the empty circle where the sacred dwells, are completely devoid of any foundation. The origin of this hierarchical setting goes back no further than Iolo Morganwg, the founder of Welsh neodruidism at the end of the eighteenth century. One would be at great pains to discover the slightest allusion to Abred, Gwenved, and Keugant in the Welsh and Irish texts of the Middle Ages. Iolo Morganwg is an odd character who, like Villemarqué later in Brittany, was convinced he was working toward a renaissance of druidism and wished to make it coherent and comprehensible for an intellectual elite on whom Christianity and esoteric societies had made their mark.
2. J. Markale, *L'Épopée celtique d'Irlande*, 184–91.
3. J. Loth, *Mabinogion*, 99–145. The same detail can be seen in the Welsh tale of *Culhwch and Olwen*, the earliest dated Arthurian literary text and one that contains numerous references to the more ancient Celtic mythology.
4. Among the snares set by the "enchanters" the famous *Triads of the British Isles* must be singled out, which numerous contemporary "druids" have made their bible and their gospel. Certain of these Triads, which are purely mythological and anecdotal, can be found in the Welsh manuscript *The Red Book of Hengest* that dates from the fourteenth century (this manuscript also contains the *Mabinogion*). Others, equally mythological but already altered, can be found in the collection *Myvirian Archaeology of Wales,* a collection of different (more or less) lost Welsh texts established by Owen Jones, Owen Pughe, and Edward Williams (Iolo Morganwg) in 1801–1808. These triads were translated into French at the end of the second volume of Joseph Loth's *Mabinogion* (Paris: Fontemoing, 1913), and edited and translated into English in 1961 by Rachel Bromwich under the title *Trioedd Yns Prydein* in Cardiff. *These are the only Triads whose authenticity can be guaranteed*, but none of them concern the theology or metaphysics of the druids. On the other

hand, Edward Williams, otherwise known as Iolo Morganwg, established a series of theological and metaphysical Triads published later in 1829, under the title *Cyfrynach Beirdd Yns Prydain,* then translated into French by Adolphe Pictet under the title *Le Mystère des Bardes de l'Ile de Bretagne.* They were translated into Breton in 1931 by Yves Berthou-Kaledvoulc'h, under the title *Sous le chêne des Druides,* with a French translation by the poet Philéas Lebesgue (Paris: Éditions Heugel). These so-called traditional triads are the result of a stupefying syncretism of Catholic, Methodist, and Presbyterian Christianity; Scottish Freemasonry, unverifiable folk beliefs, simplistic notions borrowed from Buddhism and Hindusim (what was known of these around 1800), and speculations of the "esoteric" variety that were in vogue at that time. There is absolutely no serious basis, nor any reference to an ancient druidic tradition in any of these Triads. It is the purely pre-Romantic intellectual reconstitution of a druidic wisdom that had long since disappeared. Iolo Morganwg wished to make it the catechism of his neodruidism.

Conclusion

1. Michel Raoult, *Les druides, les sociétés intiatiques celtiques contemporaines* (Monaco: Éditions Rocher, 1983), 198.

INDEX

Battle of Cnucha, 82
Battle of Mag Tured
  casualties of, 71
  Dagda, as spy, 92–93
  magic in, 143, 145, 171
  preparations for, 64–65, 84,
    90, 92–93
  victory banquet, 91–92
  warriors of, 87, 108
The Battle of Mag Tured, 26,
    31, 51, 52, 61, 73, 134
Battle of Tailtiu, 110, 117, 196
The Battle of the Trees, 134, 143
Bay of Cardigan, 147
Be Finn, 106
Bedwyr, sword of, 196
Befinn, fairy woman, 80
Bel-air, 75
Belenos, 75, 77, 79, 80, 152
Belenus, cognomen, 74–75, 76
Belgian migration, 20
Beli the Great, 75
Belisama, 77, 103, 107
Belle-île en Mer, 21
Bellovaci lands, 29
Bel-Orient, 75
Beltane festival, 53–54, 55, 75,
    152, 166–67
Bible, 206
Biturige tribe, 128
Blake, William, 199
Blodeuwedd, 135, 136, 187
Bodbh, 104, 108–09
Boii tribe, 124
Boinn, 94, 104–7, 119
Bolg men, 56
Book of Conquests, 53, 56, 76, 78
Book of Merlin, 177
Book of Tristan, 178
Borvo, cognomen, 74
Boudicca, Queen, 108, 109, 160
Bran, son of Febal, 118, 133,
    230
Bran Vendigeit's cauldron, 71,
    92, 94, 115, 118, 145
Brandon's Day, 152, 157
Bréganz, tablets of, 87
Brennos, Gallic chief, 94, 208
Briciu's Feast, 189
Brigit, triple, 109
  Christianization of, 166, 224
  daughter of Dagda, 93–94
  other names for, 77, 94,
    104–07, 119

Bri-Leith, sidh of, 118
Britain, x
  Apollonian cult, 49
  Aylburton, Lydney Park, 83
  Bath, town of, 77, 79, 104
  Boudicca, temples, 126
  druid schools, 21, 50
  Gauls in, 3, 20, 82
  "popular wisdom," 24
brithem, judicial druid, 10
Brittany, x
  etymology, 13, 128
  fountains/wells, 79
  language, branches of, 4
  medicinal waters, 105
  see also Armorican Brittany
Bronze Age, 54
  legacies of, 77–78, 79, 80
  monuments of, 43, 49–50,
    124
  solar worship, 49, 76, 242
Browaroc'h people, 148
Brug-na-Boyne mound, 94,
    95
Brunhilda, 78
Buddhism, 228, 236
bull symbolism, 100, 102, 131

Caesar, Julius
  as authority/resource, 4–5,
    209
  on druids, 17–20, 32–33, 50
  on Gallo-Roman gods,
    60–61
  as politician, 25
  victory over Celts, vii, 3
Caesar's Commentaries
  (Hirtius), 8
cainte, 10
Calatin, 50–51, 134, 184
calendars
  Celtic lunar, 78, 164
  Christianized, 168
  Coligny Calendar, 164
Camulogenos, 82
Camulos/Cumal, 81, 82, 84
Caractacos, 118
Caradawc/Caradoc, 118
Carnac megalith, 76
Carnival, and fire, 153, 157
Carnutes, sanctuary, 17, 19
Carpe, poet, 172
Castor cult, 150
Cathbad, druid, 18–19, 33, 210

Catholicism. *see* Roman
  Catholicism
The Cattle Raid of Cualngé, 32
Cauldron of Ceridwen, 92
Cauldron of Resurrection, 71,
    92, 94, 118, 145, 155
cauldrons, 54, 71–72, 92, 101,
    231
Celtic language
  archaic, 33, 35
  etymology, 11–13
  as mother tongue, 45
Celtic legend, categories of,
    113
Celtic mythology, 208
  conflated with history,
    33–35, 53
  druid-king pair, 26, 27–28,
    88, 195
  extensions of, 84
  maternal goddesses,
    140–41, 167–68
  sacred objects, 54, 67
  sun symbolism, 78, 80, 99,
    131
  trebling/number three, 67,
    109, 151–52, 218
Celtic Restored Church, 200
Celtic societies
  agriculture, 2, 3, 77, 116, 137
  archdruid election, 17
  art, 217, 218
  destiny of, 19
  and God, 210–12, 220, 225,
    236, 237
  inseparability of druidism,
    ix, 3, 24, 50, 55, 201
  kingship, 24–26, 35–36
  livestock breeding, 3, 113,
    161
  nocturnal customs, 90
  oral tradition, 32–33, 35,
    169, 188, 215
  origin of, 3–4, 30, 54–55,
    146, 147
  pastoral/nomadic, 141
  predecessors of, 54–55
  sea, avoidance of, 146, 150
  totemism, remnants of,
    182–86
  warlike character, 30
Celts
  as Atlanteans, 150
  as "barbarians," 48, 205